D1334348

The Romance of
SCOTLAND'S
RAILWAYS

The Romance of SCOTLAND'S RAILWAYS

David St John Thomas & Patrick Whitehouse

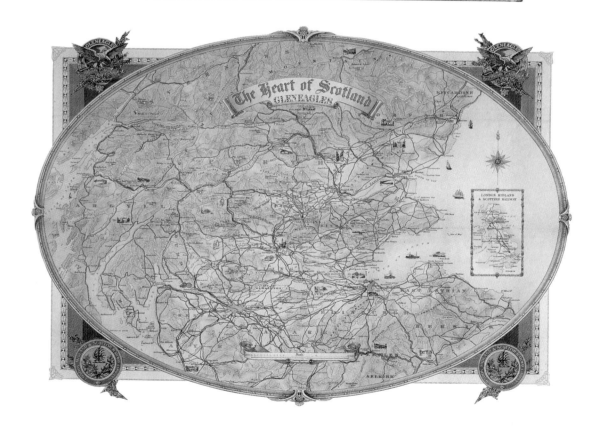

BCA

LONDON NEW YORK SYDNEY TORONTO

A once-familiar sight. North British Railway Glen Class 4–4–0s Nos 62496 Glen Loy *and 62471* Glen Falloch *both take water from the pair of water columns at Crianlarich in May 1959. The locomotives had been specially rostered to work the 5.45am from Glasgow Queen Street to Fort William for the BBC programme Railway Roundabout.*

First published by
David St John Thomas Publisher
an imprint of Thomas & Lochar

This edition published by
BCA by arrangement with
Thomas & Lochar

CN 5232

Printed in Great Britain

CONTENTS

In the colourful days of Scotland's railways most Sassenachs glimpsed their glories from the coloured postcards readily available from bookstalls, or even small town bookshops cum stationers. They were originally one old penny, going up between the wars to twopence each. Today, for good reason, they are collectors' pieces. These cards, published by the Locomotive Publishing Company, Raphael Tuck & Sons, Richard Tilling, E. Ponteau Valentine and J. Salmon had one thing in common: they showed off the railway liveries, locomotives and coaches, in their magnificent colours. They made stations like Carlisle and Perth veritable Aladdin's Caves. We were shown Caledonian blues (both shades) North British brown, Highland olive green and Glasgow and South Western dark green, much of this in superb scenery or recognisable railway surroundings. These cards, together with the oil paintings by the Locomotive Publishing Company's artists (under the corporate pseudonym, F. Moore), are treasures both in their own right and because there is little else surviving which shows these engines and their liveries as they really were.

A Locomotive Publishing Company card showing the Caledonian Railway's famous McIntosh-designed Cardean 4–6–0 with a train of West Coast Joint Stock which will have come through from Euston.

Another LPC card published originally pre World War I but reprinted between the wars as its caption states that this is an L&NER (North British Section) West Highland express in Glenfinnan station on the Mallaig Extension. The leading engine is a Reid K class 4–4–0 dating from 1910, No 865, whilst the assistant (coupled in behind the train engine to ensure that driver is in charge of the brake) is a Holmes class C 0–6–0, almost certainly based on Fort William shed.

Opposite below A Tuck 'Famous Expresses' series, The Grampian Express showing a McIntosh Dunalastair 4–4–0 No 780 of 1898. The front of the card ignores its rear caption and states that this is a 'Highland Express'! Note the Caledonian Railway route indicator at the base of the chimney proclaiming that it is a main line train, Carlisle to Glasgow via Motherwell.

Two Atlantic classes on a Locomotive Publishing Company card of pre World War I vintage as the inland stamp value is marked at ¹/₂d (a halfpenny). The background is deliberately wishy–washy but the two classes depict Edwardian (or early George V) engines from the North Eastern and North British railway companies representing the East Coast Route to Scotland.

A Richard Tilling card printed in the 1920s showing one of the large Glasgow & South Western Railway Baltic tanks No 545 (later LMS No 15405). This is one of the later LPC series as the engine did not come out of works until 1922.

An LPC West Coast Route shed scene balancing the top cards' East Coast origin. This shows Caledonian (918 class) and London & North Western (Experiment class) locomotives. The LNWR engine was used for trains north of Crewe on the main line to Carlisle though their reign was short, as they were unsuperheated. They were replaced by the Prince of Wales class and Claughton 4–6–0s.

1
INTRODUCTION

WHY, when we so enjoyed them did we not make more romantic dashes by train to and around Scotland? Was it that we so savoured the memory of the trips we had done, that magic of train and terrain everlastingly demanding our attention, that we were nervous to risk disappointment in returning...perhaps to discover that the grand continuity of yesteryear had finally crumbled? Or that we felt we had to follow the crowd to the sun? For many it was undoubtedly the arrival of children that made it impossibly complicated and expensive, necessary to use our own cars and only furtively follow the rails, making do with a snack at Crianlarich refreshment room between trains and a quick walk round Edinburgh Waverley or Perth General before bed.

How we regret our caution! For those rail-based holidays north of the border were always the best, ceaselessly opening new horizons. They had many ingredients but it was again the holistic relationship between train and landscape that was unforgettable. And indeed the rails *had* been placed there for our enjoyment of the mountain, loch and moor. As the two labouring locomotives of your West Highland train climbed a mountain ledge echoed through the empty land, you suddenly heard (and felt the coolness of) the water cascading down to track level, passing underneath and plunging again to the bottom. It was hard to keep your seat for long; but then you discovered that fellow travellers, even Scotland's own, were not indifferent to God's beauty either. Often they would alert you to the gorge coming up on the other side or some especially fine vista.

The people were indeed an important ingredient, as different as the countryside, and Scotland's own Lowlanders just as excited exploring the more romantic parts of their country...always warm, communicative, as interested in you as telling you about themselves. And you wondered at how predictably those prim and proper elder women got talking about that taboo English subject of money. The people of course included the railwaymen who, as is recorded in later pages, often went to great lengths to ensure your perfect enjoyment...though it has to be said they were increasingly bitter about what their bosses were doing to them. You now have to be pretty old to recall the days when railwaymen thought their lot was improving, though always new services were enthusiastically welcomed.

But, again as is told in detail later, well into BR days you found that the locomotives (many surprisingly clean) and rolling stock were often very different from those south of the border, much pre-1923 stock surviving the entire Grouping period. And into the sixties, even if you reached the junction by a diesel-hauled train of relatively modern though usually of

varied vintage stock, you might find that across the platform was a tender locomotive (sometimes quite new, more likely exceedingly old) at the head of a branch train in which you were almost certain to have your own compartment.

Another ingredient was of course (and still is) the magnificence of the great stations and bridges. Who did not feel himself excited having explored Waverley to take a seat in a tea car for the passage over the Forth Bridge (whose everlasting painting cycle was taught at school) and the Tay Bridge (alongside the cut-down piers of the first one that tumbled with a train in its high girders on that famous stormy, winter's night we had so often been told about)? Who could not marvel at the East Coast main line's daring cliff-top route north of Berwick and before Aberdeen, or the Highland's romantic passes protected by snow fences?

The railway simultaneously epitomised man's triumph (with hiccups) over the elements and unique relation of past and present in the Scottish landscape. Until the 1950s, for example, you could see the rotting

Scottish Pacific ex-LMS Princess Coronation class No 46223 Princess Alice *of Polmadie (66A) makes a superb sight climbing Beattock early one morning in the summer of 1960 with the 12.20am London (Euston) to Glasgow (Central). The fifteen coach train including sleeping cars and a restaurant car from Carlisle for breakfast, being banked by an ex-Caley 0–4–4T from Beattock, is seen at this impressive location near Greskine, where the low sunlight highlights the detail of the carriages and locomotive. Nothing could surely beat this as an introduction to Scotland.*

9

THE HIGHLAND RAILWAY
PASSENGER TRAIN, INVERNESS AND PERTH.

A Tuck 'Oilette' card in their 'Scotch Expresses' series showing one of Peter Drummond's Highland Railway Castle class 4–6–0s No 144 Blair Castle (later LMS No 14679) on the 8.40am train from Inverness to Perth supposedly near County March (Drumochter) summit 1,484ft above sea level. Connection at Perth provided a day service to the Metropolis.

Another 'Oilette Scotch Expresses' series with a then new North British Atlantic on an Edinburgh to Aberdeen express via the Forth Bridge.

A third 'Oilette Scotch Expresses' card showing a Glasgow & South Western railway train from Glasgow (St Enoch) to Carlisle with coaches for St Pancras via the Midland Railway's Settle & Carlisle route. The engine, No 385, is one of Manson's 4–6–0s built for this service in 1903.

N.B.R. Edinburgh Express.

CORRIDOR EXPRESS
(G.&S.W.R.)

London Midland & Scottish
Perth-Inverness Express on the Highland div.

TAY BRIDGE, DUNDEE.

An artist's impression of the new LMS days in Scotland in the 1920s. A later Tuck 'Oilette' series 'Famous Expresses' showing a train in colours of one of the then new Big Four, LMS red. This is a Perth to Inverness train on the Highland division and the engine, ex-Highland Railway, Clan Fraser as LMS No 14753. Note the Midland railway's influence not only in the colour scheme but also in the large numerals on the tender – ideal for reporting purposes.

A fascinating Valentine card from a watercolour by G.W. Blow. The date appears to be around 1935–39 from the cars and the fact that the P2 leaving the Tay Bridge is in green and the coaches LNER teak.

A Salmon card of the 1930s showing the then much publicised new 2–8–2 Cock O' The North built specially for the hilly Edinburgh to Aberdeen service.

An Austrian Goods at St Enoch carrying express passenger headlamps, ex-G&SW 51 class 2–6–0 No 17828 brings a passenger train into the Glasgow terminus in the early 1930s. Built by North British in 1915 to Drummond's design and superheated, the improvement in performance as compared with the 71s was, says David L. Smith, truly remarkable. The last survivor was not withdrawn until 1947.

remains of parts of the great Caledonian forest (sacrificed when sheep became supreme at the time of the Highland Clearances) from the Further North line, and there were everlasting castles, battlefields, harbours, canal swing bridges and other places of interest such as Gretna (railwaywise more notorious for Britain's worst-ever railway accident at nearby Quintinshill than its amorous blacksmith who once attracted many lovers by train). Even with its accidents, Scotland's railways did things the grand way.

But there was another ingredient of the romance, slightly more subtle but equally important: the organisation of the train services. Because of the distances and paucity of population, on most routes they were sparse, yet nobody could deny the importance of each of the trains. The West Highland, for example, might only have a daily pair, but neither was the least bit like an English branch line train. Each was a fully-fledged express, sporting express headlamps, double headed with restaurant car (and sleepers on the first down and last up). The ramifications of such trains were enormous, economic loads of passengers being brought together by miracles of timetable planning that had evolved over the years. So in this case there were scruffy islanders and mainland Highlanders returning home, nearly always a kilt to be seen in first class, while visitors ranged from rich English folk to the early continental adventurers on a hiking and climbing trip – and then there would be shoppers and others taking a short ride to the next station.

The timetable of many routes had to respect that Edinburgh, smaller

but grander, provided roughly the same amount of traffic as Glasgow – but English traffic might come through neither. In addition to a multitude of train connections, several starting before the engine and other crew would have gone to bed the previous night, ships and buses were often involved...and the entire distribution of mail, newspapers and perishables including on the West Highland even the daily bread depended on the guard's van.

The daily ritual varied in intensity according to the season, especially on the Highland route to Inverness where the contrast between February and August passenger loads could scarcely have been sharper, but always called for precision working. Something that always impressed visitors was the smartness with which trains ran into platforms and halted precisely, sometimes right by the water-column – and how little time it took to cross two full-length services. The most devoted Great Western enthusiast admitted that Paddington could learn something here.

Congestion and weather, and of course late arrivals across the border (England and Scotland have always and still do point the finger at each other), leave alone poor steaming and those minor derailments of goods vehicles being shunted at steeply-graded yards, meant that punctuality was seldom guaranteed. On the West Highland's busiest days, lateness was such to earn the crews of connecting Macbrayne ships heavy over-time. But however adverse the circumstances a good fight was nearly always put up, often with remarkable locomotive work.

Because worthwhile loads of passengers were brought together even on

A Pumper at Ayr. Ex-G&SW 71 class 0–6–0 No 17756, a North British Locomotive Company product of 1915 to Peter Drummond's design, slogs through Ayr station with coal empties for the Waterside branch in the late 1920s. The steam-operated boiler feed pumps that gave these heavy but very sluggish engines their nickname had by this time been replaced by injectors. The 71s were never superheated, and were hungry for coal. Note the unusual double water column.

13

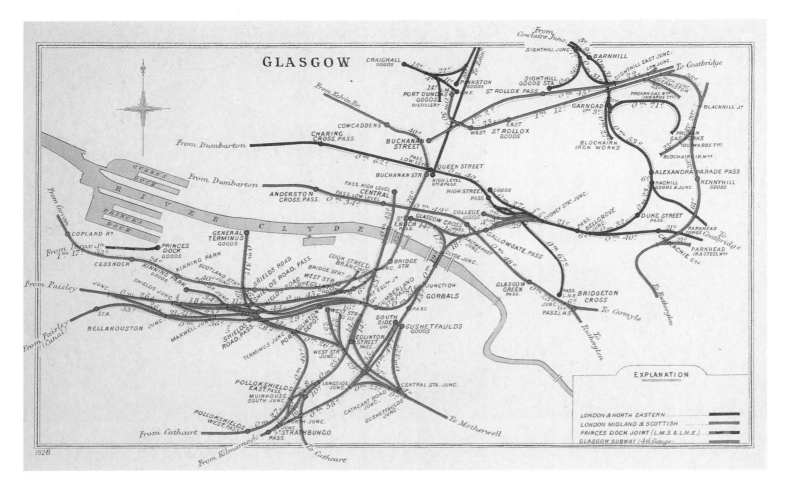

Railway Clearing House
Glasgow junction diagram 1928

All four main line termini were on the north side of the Clyde, three of them in the heart of the city with Buchanan Street on the fringe.

Glasgow enjoyed a heavy commuter traffic. On the north bank the ex-NBR and CR lines competed strongly from Dumbarton inwards (with stations close together) and also to some extent from Coatbridge/Airdrie to the east. The shorter distance traffic on branches serving inner suburbs such as Maryhill and Bridgeton was, however, increasingly lost to the trams. The underground sections and stations below the city centre were less than attractive with steam traction. There was a degree of rivalry between Queen St and Central for the Edinburgh traffic.

Central and St Enoch vied with one another for the heavy Clyde Coast flows to Greenock and Ardrossan, but in other areas each enjoyed a near monopoly. The Cathcart Circle, East Kilbride and Hamilton/Motherwell routes were almost unchallenged CR territory, while the G&SWR reigned supreme in Barrhead and almost the whole of Ayrshire.

A feature was the two CR/G&SWR joint lines, to Paisley and to Kilmarnock, resulting in complex junctions at Shields Road and Pollokshields respectively to give access from both

termini and various goods depots while minimising conflicting movements.

The principal goods depots were at Sighthill and High Street (NB), Buchanan Street and a clutch of smaller south side depots (CR), and College (G&SWR). The City of Glasgow Union Railway from Shields Road via Bellgrove to Springburn played an important role in giving access to College.

Two BR Standard 2–6–4Ts were specifically cleaned and decorated at Corkerhill (67A) shed prior to hauling a Princes Pier Boat Special seen here awaiting departure from Glasgow (St Enoch) on 9 May 1959. The leading engine No 80127 remained at Corkerhill until withdrawal in 1964, and two years later the station saw its last passenger train.

On 13 May 1961 ex-NBR Class N15/1 0–6–2T No 69163 banks the up Queen of Scots Pullman train out of Glasgow Queen Street station. The train engine was A4 Class No 60031 Golden Plover. In the adjacent platform one of the recently introduced express DMU sets waits its next turn on the Glasgow to Edinburgh (Waverley) service.

Kilmarnock, on the former Glasgow & South Western Railway c 1949. No 45589 Gwalior *of Holbeck (20A) leaves with the 10.25am express from Leeds to Glasgow, St Enoch. The locomotive has recently been repainted in BR lined green livery with a small totem on the Fowler tender and a new smokebox door numberplate with a particularly clear type face. The LMS Class 2P No 40688 has also been repainted but* Scottish Style *with large cab side numerals, full lining and a red background to the smokebox numberplate. The shed plate (30B) is the LMS code for Hurlford and would have been changed some time after 1949 when the new Scottish Region codes were introduced. Two of the loco crew visible are still wearing LMS cab badges.*

minor routes, restaurant cars ran over an amazing proportion of the system, on three routes north from Carlisle (each also having sleepers), to Crail on the Fife Coast Express, on all routes out of Inverness including Aberdeen, to Oban, and of course on the best trains on the competing routes between Edinburgh and Glasgow. Restaurant cars were a Scottish way of life. You went to them fully to savour the countryside and its culture (there was always someone to give advice and a very Scottish conversation, again often involving money, taking place at another table) and to fuel and water yourself. Not, alas, for luxury food. Years ago it was said that some of Britain's best meals were to be had on Scottish trains, the timetables boasting of Pullman cars and often specifically 'Pullman Breakfast and Lunch Car'. But that had ceased to be the case by the war. Thereafter even breakfasts were less generous than those served on English cars, while high tea was usually an indifferent substitute for dinner. It was strange this, for until their privatisation decades after nationalisation, the railway hotels upheld the very best of the Scottish catering tradition. Like everything else, the hotels were naturally on the grand scale: three of them in Glasgow, the competitive joys of three different companies who sent committees exploring Europe's most famous hotels to bring back the best ideas, two in Edinburgh including the North British towering over Princes Street, and country and seaside

institutions like Gleneagles and Turnberry. It comes as no surprise to learn that when Henry Hall, the chief LMS bandleader based at Gleneagles in the summer and the Central in Glasgow in the winter, was wooed by the BBC he took a fifty percent cut in salary.

The mention of competition is a reminder of that other Scottish railway characteristic: to beat thy neighbour. 'Scottish railways deprived of the opportunity of fighting would scarcely know themselves again,' wrote W.M. Acworth, the Victorian railway expert, in 1890. Though three fifths the size of England, even at its peak Scotland's railway mileage was little more than a fifth. When the timetable of *Bradshaw* occupied nearly 900 pages at the height of the railway's grandeur just before Grouping, less than one hundred were needed for Scotland. Yet there was hardly a traffic for which there had not been attempted if not successful competition, and even the most bitter of English battles between companies seem insignificant compared with those that raged between the Scottish ones. And this competition of course still colours the character of the system today; you can cut rival routes out, but never pretend they did not exist or do not continue to influence things.

Hottest on the heels of its competitors was the Caledonian, one of Britain's few truly great railways, still revered by many, and not just for its

A lengthy train of empty coal wagons is hauled past Annbank by ex-LMS Crab 2–6–0 No 42912 of Ayr shed on 22 June 1962. The signalman can clearly be seen in his box watching over the progress of the train and that of the oncoming one so clearly signalled by the tall ex-G&SWR home. The lineside gradient post indicates that the going will be easier towards Belston Junction and Cumnock.

17

By the mid 1950s it was rare to see an old North British Railway Glen class 4–4–0 on the West Highland Line – the coming of the LMS Black Five and the introduction of the LNER K1s had seen to that. This picture is historic in that No 62482 Glen Mamie of Eastfield shed (65A) had arrived at Fort William on the previous Saturday, replacing a failed ex-LMS class 5, staying on shed over the weekend to return on the 9.31am to Glasgow Queen Street. It was the pilot engine on the way home and as usual practice on the West Highland, it was coupled next to the train with the K1's driver on the front in charge of the brake. No 62482 is picking up the through coaches from the Mallaig train.

Also of historic interest is the Fort William station and the layout for in 1975 all this disappeared and a new station built some distance north of the original site. Everything bar the coaches is NB.

The 2.56pm express from Fort William to Glasgow Queen Street with through sleepers for King's Cross heads south across Rannoch Moor in March 1960. The locomotives are both class 5 4–6–0s, the train engine a BR standard and the pilot (coupled inside on this route) an LMS Stanier design. The coach in whose window the locomotives are reflected is of ex-LNER Gresley

excellent red brown with white upper panels coaches and locomotives in their splendid blue livery. It was a businessman's railway, very profitable but also consistent, providing an excellent continuation of the West Coast route to Glasgow and from Motherwell to Perth, that to Glasgow opening in early 1848, the line from Carlisle up Annandale completed by taking over rival Lanarkshire railways.

This is a celebration of Scottish railways rather than another recital of detailed history, but it is always worth noting that the difficulties of financing routes through long, empty landscapes, yet the desire to give the nation the best and competitive services, demonstrated themselves early in history. Believing there was justification for only one trunk route from England, a Royal Commission in 1841 backed what became the LMS trunk line north of Carlisle, the Annandale route, to serve Edinburgh as well as Glasgow. And – how familiar – when hoped-for government aid was not forthcoming even that made slow progress. Not until July 1845 did the Caledonian get its Act of incorporation. The Caledonian concentrated all its traffic including that from south of the border at Buchanan Street, makeshift and inconvenient terminals south of the Clyde later

There were two stations in Elgin, a Great North of Scotland and a Highland, although by BR days they were under the control of a single stationmaster. The present station is on the site of the Highland one although much rebuilt. In 1954 a former Caledonian Railway Pickersgill 4–4–0 BR No 54482, stands at the head of an Inverness to Keith local train at platform 5 in the Highland station which by then had its platforms numbered after those in the GNSR station.

Waverley Sojourn

For those from the south, one of the key pleasurable ingredients of a Scottish holiday was the arrival... alighting at the curved platform at Inverness a few minutes after enjoying the panorama of the Moray Firth becoming the Beauly firth as the train descended through Culloden Moor, taking in the panorama of the Clyde before stepping onto Glasgow Central in rush hour where passengers from south of the border were always in a minority, seeing the Castle at the top of the Royal Mile before plunging into the tunnel at the approach to Edinburgh Waverley.

The arrival at Waverley on an overnight train from England was always special, for it usually meant a break of a couple of hours, a very civilised breakfast and a sampling of the pleasures of Princes Street before continuing the journey *Continued opposite*

serving ever expanding residential and country services until the opening of Glasgow Central in 1879. Much of Scotland's later commercial history has been based on Central and its adjoining hotel; the terminus remains Britain's busiest in terms of train movements.

The Caledonian was pre-eminent in many ways, those who served it sounding like a roll-call of British railway history, but it was never content to rest in what might have been regarded as its natural territory, and ever pushed, pushed, so that it was important in Edinburgh, Perth, Aberdeen, on the West Coast at Oban (through the Callander & Oban) and down the Ayrshire Coast to Ardrossan. 'What will the Caledonian do?' was something everyone wondered when initiative was taken elsewhere. You get the picture when it is once more retold that when a Glasgow & South Western driver of a train on a joint single line saw a Caledonian goods heading toward him, he lifted the staff (his authority to be in that section) onto his shoulder to show he was in the right when the Caley man was found trying to take it from him to pervert the evidence. True or not, it summed up the feeling that the Caley never lost a trick.

This bred deep suspicion in the minds of Sou'Western men, and just about everything the Caley did the GSWR did differently. In practical terms an extension of the Midland from St Pancras via the Settle & Carlisle, though run as a very Scottish and profitable business, paying good dividends, the GSWR opened its St Enoch terminal well ahead of Central and certainly gave the Caley intense competition where their spheres of influences joined and overlapped west and south of Glasgow. But the North British, which began as a local concern from Edinburgh to the border at Berwick-on-Tweed (where for some years passengers had to transfer to stage coaches for their journey on through northern England) also became a powerful competitor in Glasgow. It indeed ran the major part of the city's awful underground services. These, of course, remained steam hauled well into nationalisation; the word acrid has no meaning if you did not experience Queen Street Low Level. The North British was also a keen third competitor for the Clyde, running as is told in later pages excellent trains and ships.

Nowhere else in the world, certainly in Britain, was there anything like such keen competition, resulting in lavish services and low fares, as to and on the Clyde. Well might Scots yearn for the good old days when a daily ticket was so cheap that there was no point in buying a season, the best trains had two minute connections to luxury ships, and still other routes dangled incentives for you to switch loyalty. Overprovision there might have been, but competition undoubtedly did stir trade and helped cement Glasgow's role as Britain's second city, commercially leaving Edinburgh in the shade. That Edinburgh's suburban services were never so well developed was in large measure because the North British had something like a monopoly there.

The North British scarcely got on better with the Caley than did the Sou'Western, and the Waverley route from Carlisle was developed specifically to enable it to trade with the London & North Western and Midland without Caley interruption. What days they were when trains for the industrial belt and further north set out from Carlisle by three different routes, each with prestige named services and the latest rolling stock and locomotives, while the fourth trunk route from England, the East Coast, boasted of the fastest and most famous like the Flying Scotsman. Not surprisingly many Scots developed idiosyncratic favourites. Some Glasgow businessmen would travel to Edinburgh because of the alleged better cleanliness of East Coast Joint Stock sleepers, while those who felt smoothness was all important regarded St Pancras as the only London gateway even if they travelled to Perth or beyond. But, then, sons followed fathers not only into their Glasgow businesses but inevitably made the

continued

north or west. All the overnight trains from King's Cross arrived well before breakfast, most indeed around 7.00am, the Night Scotsman usually being last, while even the slower St Pancras service with passengers from the West of England and all parts of the Midland was in before eight.

Business was brisk at the left luggage office, for those in the know forsook the station and its admittedly excellent dining room for the gastronomic pleasures of the North British Hotel, that monolithic monument to Scottish commercial enterprise towering above Princes Street where they charged their porridge and Loch Fyne kippers to their dressing
continued overleaf

Over the Ness Viaduct (which was washed away by flood debris in February 1989 and replaced by a new concrete structure fifteen months later) 0–4–0ST No 56011 (ex-CR No 270) trundles wagons from Muirtown Basin, at the entrance to the Caledonian Canal, to Inverness yard on 22 July 1952. This delightful little Drummond Pug, of which there were 39, was built in 1885 at St Rollox Works for £720!

continued

room. You could in fact wheel your luggage through a labyrinth of underground passages, lifts at either end, to the hotel, but the fashionable thing to do was to go up the lifts for your pre-breakfast shower and return down windswept Waverley Steps after visiting Jenners department store and venturing slightly into Princes Street Gardens wondering how it was that the city fathers of generations ago agreed to let the railway have the prime inner-city site.

For many years you returned to the platform to see the Queen of Scots arrive from Glasgow Queen Street on its journey south, followed by the departure of the Flying Scotsman at 10.00am just as the Aberdeen and Glasgow trains departed, racing each other to Haymarket. The Dumfermline and Perth express with through carriages for Inverness followed a few minutes later, allowing you to enjoy the whole play. Waverley was always such a convenient changing point, in contrast to Glasgow Central where the transfer to Queen Street or Buchanan Street was fraught with anxiety. Generally speaking it was Glasgow for Glasgow, Britain's thrusting second city, but Edinburgh for the northern world beyond.

Opposite, below *The LMS inherited a heterogeneous collection of locomotives from the three Scottish companies which came into its fold; they were soon renumbered into one series and repainted in LMS livery, the passenger engines in Midland style which looked most attractive. LMS No 14284, a former Highland Railway Skye Bogie in this livery is seen at Dingwall in 1925. The extraordinary vehicle behind the engine is a Highland Railway goods brake van totally enclosed against the weather and with a raised lookout for the guard.*

same choice of suburban train: fares, frequency, convenience of station, cleanliness or the lack of it, might have weighed in the decision, but so did history and sheer family prejudice.

Competition appeared in many forms. Most vital was that for freight. Only the brave survived as canvassers for the Caley. Incredible routes would be agreed to, and shunting movements made, to extend that company's sphere of influence.

Yet in one way competition was stifled: the notorious agreement that persisted well into the Grouping years not to accelerate between London and Scotland, which made nonsense of the Flying Scotsman running non-stop to Edinburgh since it had to dawdle all the more. The famous words of Patrick Stirling, the Great Northern's locomotive superintendent at Doncaster, on hearing that the LNWR planned to reach Aberdeen first – 'This of course we cannot permit' – may have promoted the most colourful railway racing Britain has ever experienced, in the mid-1890s, but while it showed what *could* be achieved it did not benefit ordinary travellers. Very much the reverse, though some would argue that the emphasis on comfort rather than speed was not a bad thing. It certainly coloured the great days of train travel from London to the North, enabling the Midland that could not possibly have won on speed to hold its distinctive own.

But that assumes the great days were immediately before and after World War I. But were they not later, perhaps in the twenties or after the 1932 abolition of the restrictive speed covenant? Or the end of the depressed thirties when spirits were raised by both LMS and LNER producing show streamlined trains? Or even after nationalisation when Gresley's streamlined Pacifics had their heyday racing a new series of lightweight expresses carrying the new businessmen between the Scottish and English capitals? Or even today when you hardly need consult the timetable since for hours on end King's Cross sees departures for Edinburgh at hourly intervals?

There has, of course, been romance in all eras, but if we could chose we would surely go back to the days when there was greater choice of route, if not train, when indeed you had to be privileged to travel between the two capitals at all. It cannot be emphasised too strongly how recently long-distance travel has been available for most people. In the great and colourful days, it was just not economically possible even for, say, schoolmasters and bank managers. Thus between the wars the LMS ran only two daytime all-the-year-round services from Glasgow to Euston at ordinary fares. The vast majority of Scots making their first trip to London did so on football and other excursions at a fraction of ordinary fares (and comfort) or when called up.

But then much of the romance lies in the fact that the railway opened up new opportunities, indeed opened up much of Scotland to tourists, pioneering services that at first were relevant to only a small minority, but steadily exploited their advantages...improvements ever being made. For example, the LNER introduced the Queen of Scots in 1925, gave it new sets of steel-framed coaches in 1928. The same year third class sleepers were introduced, and next year made the King's Cross–Fort William sleeper a nightly rather than a weekend event.

Left *The 10.00 Inverness–Keith Junction pulls out of Nairn and over the River Nairn bridge probably in the late 1920s, behind ex-HR Castle class 4–6–0 No 14690* Dalcross Castle. *The train connected at Elgin with an LNER service to Aberdeen via Craigellachie.*

Above *The Highland Railway 'Small Ben' 4–4–0s were pretty little engines even when carrying Caley boilers, from quite early LMS days. Most were fitted with tablet catchers for use originally over the Highland main line as seen on the cabside of No 14404 Ben Clebrig built by Dübs & Co in 1899 and withdrawn in October 1950. Under LMS and BR auspices they were classified as 2P. It was thought that No 54398 (HR No 2) would be preserved and for some time after withdrawal in 1953 it was hidden away in Boat of Garten shed. Sadly this was not to be as the purists decided against an engine not in original condition and in 1964 it was sent for scrap.*

The LNER, impoverished though it was, is looked back upon nostalgically – for improvements like these, and also for the greater continuity it allowed. Two of Scotland's five pre-1923 companies came its way: the North British, not in the top league like the Caledonian or its southern East coast partner the North Eastern, but still running many fine trains, and the Great North of Scotland which had begun as a truly shocking railway but turned itself (after excessive competition against the Highland) into an admirable enterprise. The LNER's secret was delegation. There was a strong central commercial lead, but much of the North British and GNSR management (and locomotive works) were left little disturbed.

The Grouping years were less kind on the LMS side with Euston's emphasis on standardisation and reorganisation. Caley, Sou'Western and Highland men all felt they had lost out, and individuality such as in the old favourite liveries was missed especially because there did not seem balancing benefits...though ultimately more powerful motive power enabled many expresses to become heavier as well as faster.

Both companies economised, though nobody would have dreamt of changing what seemed natural traffic flows on all four of the trunk routes to England. Some local competition was stemmed. Many more branches and stations lost at least their passenger trains than along similar mileage south of the border. But much Scottish individuality persisted. As elsewhere on the LMS, poor morale no doubt contributed to the decline into squalor of many urban and suburban stations, yet the Caley's tradition of enterprising station gardens at places where the public would be likely to appreciate them continued unabated, and even today station gardens and floral decorations are an attractive Scottish feature.

That hopeless frustration of the world no longer apparently caring for them only really hit Scottish railwaymen well after nationalisation. Then it was not just the railways but much local industry, notably shipbuilding and then coal and steel, that the steam locomotive had helped foster in its formative days that were under threat. Huge areas of once-intense industrial activity became derelict including Springburn's locomotive works that once built steam engines for the world. Scotland had ever been in the forefront of steam locomotive development but lost out in the diesel age.

Once it looked inevitable that there would be far greater route cuts than has turned out to be the case. It is hard to suggest there is romance in two-car Sprinters, yet even though most of them are Sprinters there is definitely joy that say Inverness not only retains its station of such romantic yesterdays but is served by far more daily (not to mention Sunday) trains than ever in steam days. The magic of those ribbons of steel winding and climbing through the Highlands is as strong as ever, and even if the trains are glorified buses they are fast and well used. The story of the railways even in the further north is not yet over.

Nationalisation brought the political triumph but little practical benefit of a Scottish Region. The tone alas was set by the first general manager living in an ex-LNER hotel in Edinburgh and commuting *by car* to the HQ on former LMS territory in Glasgow. In practical terms all important decisions were London-dependent and local enterprise could only go so

Man and Machine

Even more than their English counterparts, Scottish enginemen took great pride in their locomotive, and many a tale has been told about fine tuning made possible by a thorough understanding of a single machine's whims.

One driver, writing under the name of Toram Beg, told readers of the *Locomotive Express* how over a period of weeks he tamed *Hyperion*, a Gresley non-streamlined Pacific, the runt of its class, unloved by everyone and no better after a major overhaul then before. He 'listened' to her, and gradually discovered where knocks were coming from, how the springing needed adjusting, where the blind spot was in steam distribution until she was fit to haul the Royal train. 'The regular men can follow up and get things remedied,' he explained.

It was the LMS that first introduced common usage to push up the weekly mileage, and much pride not to say shine quickly disappeared. A keen sense of ownership has always been an important ingredient in the Scottish character. Much of the best postwar running on the crack expresses, especially on the East Coast, was achieved through allocating a locomotive to only two regular crews in an age where common usage was general.

Opposite, below *An unknown small Ben carrying ordinary passenger headlamp and with a heterogeneous collection of stock (including some six wheelers and a Midland clerestory) makes heavy weather of it near Achnashellach in the early 1930s. This is an unusual picture as the small Bens were seldom seen on the Kyle line. This one has been drawing air into the smokebox which is badly burnt possibly from a heavy accumulation of ash. Note the wooden post Highland Railway signals.*

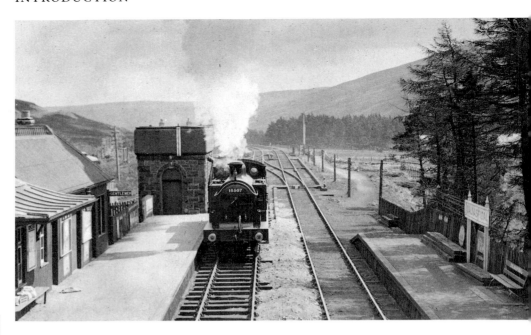

The Highland Railway purchased eight 0–6–4Ts from the North British Locomotive Company (four in 1909 and four in 1911) specifically for assisting trains over the more severe gradients. The majority of the class was always stationed at Blair Atholl for banking to Dalnaspidal. LMS No 15307 is seen at Dalnaspidal on 15 May 1928 waiting to return, bunker first, to Blair Atholl. Rebuilt in 1931 with an ex-Caledonian Railway boiler withdrawal soon followed in 1934. Ironically the first member of the class HR No 39 became the last, lasting from 1909 until December 1936.

Not Love at First Sight

In August 1931 fifteen new class 2P 4–4–0s came to Scotland and Corkerhill shed received Nos 636–640.

There was still a fair amount of 'one-man-one engine', and Bob Balmer got No 638. Balmer was always funny about a transfer to another engine. The engine he had previously was endowed with all possible virtue. His fresh acquisition was condemned utterly. Balmer had been running No 14673 (ex-512 ex-128), the Manson superheater 4-6-0, and had been doing good work. Now he was given this unknown, No 638. One day at Corkerhill he was standing at the front of No 638 when the foreman passed by. Balmer called him over. He pointed to the front buffer. 'Dae ye see that buffer?' asked Balmer. 'Aye', replied the foreman, a bit mystified. 'Come on then', said Balmer, and he walked the foreman down to the rear of the tender. 'Dae ye see *that* buffer?' 'Aye'. 'Then', said Balmer, 'between the twae o' them there's nothing but a damt heap o' scrap!' A fortnight later he was boasting of the prowess of No 638, and was ready to back her against all comers! – David L. Smith.

far...if only because those promoting it were themselves frequently promoted south. What nationalisation did bring was, again, more power: steam, diesel and electric, effectively moving London closer to home, giving Glasgow Britain's best transport system, and of course dramatically increasing the contrast between the fast main and slow secondary routes. And an unprecedented number of visitors coming up from the south and the first generation of Scots abandoning traditional close-to-home holiday playgrounds for those further away. Romance indeed there was at Central as railwaymen battled to handle the peak crowds at the beginning and end of Glasgow Fair holiday at the end of the 1950s and into the early 1960s. Newquay, Paignton, Bournemouth were added to Blackpool, Morecambe and Scarborough as resorts that any working class family might go to without being thought uppish. The Starlight Specials were a world to themselves; always full not only of passengers but convivial behaviour. The English increasingly came by Motorail, day and night services to Edinburgh, Stirling, Perth, Inverness (when the A9 was being rebuilt even a local Stirling–Inverness service) with their own distinctive culture aboard, passengers making the most of the dining facilities and three breakfast sittings not being unusual.

What a panorama of trains there have been over the years, on most main lines but perhaps particularly the Caledonian's from Carlisle: the best expresses of their day, perhaps anywhere in the world, the pioneering Corridor, the Special TPO that Auden made immortal in verse, the football, holiday and other excursions of peace and troop specials including those taking Americans off the Queens on the Clyde in World War II, the products of specialised manufactures the railways made possible as also the fresh meat, vegetables and milk that no longer needed to be produced in or around centres of population, people going to and from Northern Ireland and the Hebrides, on business, culture, fishing, visiting relatives. And coal, coal and more coal. Over Beattock summit they came, the freights and some of the passengers banked, day by day, year by year, the railway reflecting the economy it largely determined until recent times. You only needed to consult one figure to know how Scotland was faring: the Caley's freight traffic receipts.

Even the Caledonian's locals, though hardly comfortable and it is said often with inches of flies swilling in tossing water in the ceiling lamps, had a certain dignity, while the twelve-wheeled bogies on the first all-within Scottish corridor express, the Grampian from Glasgow to Aberdeen, made most English stock look positively cheap. But it was the trains from England, those summer monster ones for the Highlands, the Perths and the Glasgows and Edinburghs from south of the border (Birmingham, Manchester and Liverpool, and through carriages from Bristol and Plymouth that often had a two-hour layover in Crewe, sometimes on a platformless middle road) that gave the line real character.

Hamilton Ellis introduced many to the different flavours of the Scottish companies. The Caledonian, he said, was recognisable in the dark: 'Going north by the West Coast route at night, you could not

The highest point on any main line in Great Britain, Drumochter summit 1484ft above sea level, just in Perthshire. The 6.25am Perth to Inverness is breasting the summit hauled by two LMS class 5 4–6–0s. The leading van is a Highland Railway Travelling Post Office which carried mails from England off the West Coast Postal, 8.30pm from Euston the previous night.

suddenly wake up in a close-curtained sleeper and mistake Carlisle for Wigan. Up at the front you heard the voice of the new engine which had just come on, so different from the eldritch North Western shriek, a deep hoot as of a loud bassoon. England knows it now, for years after the passing of the Caley, the LMS revived something like that admirable whistle. It was more of the influential Dugald Drummond's work, modelled by him on the whistles of the Clyde steamers. John McIntosh's great 4–6–0 engine *Cardean*, which for long invariably took over the 2.00pm Scotch express from Euston at Carlisle, had, however, a particular whistle, modelled more on that of a Cunard liner. You could recognise *Cardean* miles away down the valley of Annan. At both Carlisle and Glasgow Central, she had her regular fans who gathered to see her off again and again... Many of the best trains were usually hauled by big 4–4–0 engines, the third enlargement of McIntosh's famous Dunalastair of 1896.' Excellent though they were, they were outshone by the Midland's less hungry Compounds and therefore did not develop into an LMS staple.

If the Caledonian's main line passed through the countryside, the GSWR's was a very part of it. The beautiful main line happily still survives

The Edinburgh connection. The 12.08 Perth – Edinburgh Waverley has collected passengers from the Inverness and Aberdeen lines before setting off behind class A4 No 60009 Union of South Africa, a sparkling Haymarket engine on 24 June 1954. The ex-LNER teak coaches, now in crimson and cream livery, lack the same enthusiasm for cleaning. Off to the left is the motive power depot, represented only by the ex-Caledonian 0–4–4 tank No 55213 doing some shunting.

Black 5 No 44796 of Perth (63A) shed takes a thirty nine wagon fully fitted freight out of Perth and heads towards Stanley Junction on an August evening in 1954.

BR Standard class 5 4–6–0
No 73007 passes St Leonards Bridge
on the approach to Perth station with
the down Granite City (10.00am
Glasgow Buchanan St – Aberdeen)
in May 1952. Moncrieff Tunnel is in
the distance and the extensive Perth
motive power depot is hidden behind
the train, a heavy 11-coach formation.

Kittybrewster shed got its wagon-
hoist coaling plant in 1932, but had
to wait another sixteen years before it
received an allocation of ex-LMS
class 2P 4–4–0s. They worked
passenger and some freight trains,
particularly on the Buchan section,
in the GNSR tradition. Here No
40663, probably recently back in
service after a general repair, calls at
the plant for a fill-up in the early
1950s. It still carries its original short
Fowler chimney to suit the Scottish
loading gauge.

though in very secondary status from Carlisle to Glasgow, through a once railway-dominated Kilmarnock with its station full of local and branch trains as well as the occasional dignified expresses, marshalling yards and locomotive works. The latter's traditions were founded by one of those Scottish giants of steam, Patrick Stirling, succeeded by his brother James when he went to the Great Northern. Proper cabs for engine crews and safety valves encased in what O.S. Nock describes as 'a tall brass column beautifully shaped and burnished to the last degree' (and soon a feature of the GN), and tall domeless engines in blue-green including the famous seven-foot singles...the Sou'Western had a fascinating locomotive as well as other history. It was however the individuality of the trains and their traffics, and above all the men who worked them over the hard gradients (especially by both roads to Stranraer), that gave the company its very special character, so splendidly captured in the works of the late David L. Smith. (We include several snippets in other pages.) Anyone who has read his anecdotes about trains and their drivers, many with nicknames like The Calculator and The Mool, will know just how much the Sou'Western coloured the territory it served. It was formed by a 1850 merger of the Glasgow, Paisley, Kilmarnock & Ayr and the Glasgow, Dumfries & Carlisle. Older readers will recall its excellent hotels including that you could rest in at St Enoch before catching your day or night express to

The south end of platform 6 of Aberdeen sees the smoky departure of the 9.35am Saint Mungo for Glasgow Buchanan Street on 7 May 1957 with Stanier class 5 No 45119 facing the 1 in 96 climb up to Ferryhill Junction. Note the ornate double lamp standard. The starting signal brackets are modern but the succession of signal gantries are of Caledonian Railway origin, albeit re-equipped with upper quadrant arms.

England, express for the coast or Irish ferry or wide range of well-patronised suburban and residential (an important social distinction here) trains.

While you might have to make a point of partaking of the pleasures of the Sou'Western and even of the North British's superbly scenic Waverley route, you could not possibly explore Scotland without intimate involvement with the NB's East Coast main line. It had that splendid gateway at Berwick (where later the LNER company obligingly told passengers by a massive lineside notice that they were now entering a different country), the route along the cliffs (travel that way a hundred times and you still find excitement in new detail that day's sky lights up), the romantic approach to Edinburgh (you have to be careless not to catch a glimpse of Holyrood House before plunging into the city), Waverley's unique blend of past and present, noise and quiet that characterise the capital's conveniently-situated lavish main station, and then the great Forth and Tay Bridges and more cliff-top hopping before the Granite City. Add to that the name of the Flying Scotsman and the North British could not fail to be among the world's best known.

The NB turned up in many unexpected places from Hexham to Mallaig. It carried vast quantities of coal. It almost shovelled up its equally large quantity of daily commuters, most making modest journeys of a few stations in dismal trains but with the grander (such as legal) men toing and froing between Edinburgh and Glasgow in great style. That it never ranked in the top dozen British companies along with the Caley was perhaps due to the bitty nature of its history. The collapse of the first Tay Bridge did not help. Even bitter was the variety of its locomotives, a ragbag of early one-off and small lots, some of which survived along with the fine big Reid Atlantics with commanding names like *Cock o'the North* into the modern age. The NB was a frugal railway, even No 224, one of the first standard gauge inside-framed, inside-cylinder express engines which went down with the crash of the Tay Bridge was fished up and lasted until after World War I (though it was said never to have crossed the Tay again). You did not expect the same level of luxurious comfort or food from its coaches, restaurant cars or even hotels as those that entered the LMS fold. Part of its charm was its matter-of-factness, competent ordinariness with touches of glamour. It was everlastingly dirty, fumy, a tradition the LNER exploited with aplomb. It was the *smell* of Waverley and Queen Street over at Glasgow that first impressed itself on English visitors.

Hamilton Ellis tells of the daily work of one of the NB's ill-assorted engines, No 38, built in 1863 out of scrap and odd parts, reboilered in 1893. She ran one of the fast business trains from Balloch over the joint CR and NB. Each company nominally started at the same time. There being only one pair of rails the arrangement was that they alternated weeks for first departure:

'At Dumbarton, their lines separated, running roughly parallel along the banks of the Clyde and crossing at different levels. The Caledonian train made an additional stop at Dumbarton East for Denny's shipyards, and on the days it started first, this enabled the North British train to

The sound of struggle floats over Aberdeen on a summer evening in the 1950s as Peppercorn class A2 Pacific No 60531 Bahram, *steam sanders working, gets to grips with the gradient up to Ferryhill Junction on the 7.15pm to King's Cross. This train conveyed a pair of sleeping cars, mainly to cater for passengers to and from intermediate stations.*

Magic Moment

We all recall magic moments in our travels. An especially memorable one was coming off the Crieff branch after an interesting saunter through the Perthshire countryside on a four-wheeled railbus, alas devoid of other passengers though luggage loaded at Crieff (where we occupied perhaps one fiftieth of the platform length) spilled from the 'van' into much of the seating.

Just as we came round the curve, with a prolonged view at a changing angle, an A4 dashed toward Glasgow with one of the three-hour Aberdeen expresses, complete with restaurant car, a busy one at that. But it was the head-on and then steadily angled view of the A4's streamlining enhanced by a compressed chime from the whistle of the racing locomotive that made this a moment that could simply never be forgotten.

Mind you, it was distressing that the branch train *could* have been provided with a well-timed connection for Glasgow. This was not the only Scottish junction one arrived at by branch line to see an express dash through...and had to wait an hour or more for a slower train for the continuing journey.

An unusual view of the Forth Bridge looking down from the top of the south stone tower as class D49 4-4-0 No 62704 Stirlingshire *heads on to the bridge with a local train from Edinburgh (Waverley) to the Fife Coast in the early 1950s. Dalmeny station can just be seen in the distance behind the train.*

catch it up, after which there was a glorious race from Dumbarton to Clydebank, with a final crossing near Partick. For much of the way the trains were in sight of one another and the sporting feelings of the two sets of passengers ran high. If you were betting against the North British, and No 38 was on the train, you could write that off, for she was inevitably away down the course by the time the Caledonian reached Bowling.'

Seeing other trains from your own remains a daily occurrence to many commuters. The section between Haymarket and Waverley is always busy (taking some services that used to run into the Caledonian/LMS Princes Street, of course) and often half a dozen trains are in motion over the Clyde at the throat of Glasgow Central. But another racing ground of former days, the quadrupled route from Glasgow to Paisley, has been rationalised to double line and, though still busy, utterly lacks the variety it once carried...including until the 1960s sleepers via the GSWR serving Paisley itself.

And so one could go on. Several excellent books have been written on

During September 1959 a number of special excursions were operated to Kelvin Hall station on the Glasgow Central Low Level line to convey visitors to the Scottish Industries Exhibition. On 10 September 1959, two beautifully restored engines, Caledonian Railway 4–2–2 No 123 and Great North of Scotland Railway No 49 Gordon Highlander hauled such a special comprising 6 ex-LMS coaches in BR maroon livery from Edinburgh (Princes Street). It is seen shortly after arrival at Kelvin Hall at 11.10am. The return working from Glasgow Central (Low Level) was at 9.35pm and was hauled by No 49 and North British Railway No 256 Glen Douglas which had, earlier in the day, headed another excursion from Wishaw Central together with Highland Railway No 103. Kelvin Hall is now the home of the Glasgow Museum of Transport where all four locomotives are normally kept.

many lines, such as the Great North of Scotland, with its own colourful tale and individuality that persisted well beyond nationalisation since Inverurie works on an LNER enclave beyond the LMS maintained an extremely independent view of life. Scotland's GN had many peculiarities such as never having either a single wheeler in its early days or any six coupled tender engine even for heavier work in the later ones. But inevitably one comes back to the Highland, neither larger nor better run than the GNSR, but far more stretched out, with some of the highest summits in the land, and used by the hunting, fishing and shooting aristocracy and the more adventurous wishing to explore the limits of our own country.

Add to that the fact that traffic came in tidal waves (3,500 military specials in 1918 carrying one and a third million tons of coal hints at World War I pressures) and you set the scene for grand drama. Miracles were performed on the lengthy single lines with their remote crossing stations, empty stock working often prolonging the activity once revenue-earning had quietened down. Even so at the beginning of the grouse season, every inch of siding at Inverness was full of coaches, sleeping cars, horse boxes, saloons, of every livery seen on English main lines. Some thought that the Jones and Drummond engines taken over by the LMS were the most suited to their work (if not positively the best) of all Scottish locomotives at the start of the Grouping years. Named after Bens, Lochs, Castles, Straths, they added more than their own touch to the romantic scene. Carriages were unusual but mainly austere. Though restaurant cars later became such a Highland feature, for many years people were all too pleased to stretch their legs at the refreshment stops at Aviemore, Achnasheen and Bonar Bridge, where we are told 'an insistent electric bell, in conjunction with an instrument that indicated "Train going

The ten BR Standard class 6 Pacifics were all allocated to either Polmadie or Kingmoor being utilised for similar work to that undertaken by ex-LMS Jubilee class 4–6–0s. In the late 1950s. No 72009 Clan Stewart starts away from Beattock after having obtained banking assistance, with a Manchester to Glasgow train.

North" and "Train going South", agitated anxious passengers as they milled alongside the bar.'

The first Scottish holiday was naturally the most memorable. Euston by the 1.30pm to Glasgow, a truly exhilarating journey; around Glasgow by tram; lunch time from Buchanan Street to Oban; then behind a diminutive tank through to Ballachuilish, reminiscent of Blaenau Festiniog with its slate mountain, and by bus with a tantalising glimpse of the catenary of the aluminium works line at Kinlochleven; next morning up to Crianlarich with a memorable crossing of a late down London sleeper at Rannoch with the Post Office on the island platform between two long strings of teak carriages each double headed; the longest of waits at Crianlarich and back again crossing the up train at Loch Awe to Oban, and high tea on a steamer to Fort William; next morning enthralled by that panorama of fresh and salt water lochs, islets and full-scale islands the Mallaig Extension commands and on the train's own steamer extension

THE ONLY TUNNEL.

The overnight rain has all but dried away as Stanier class 5 4–6–0 No 45179 prepares to leave Kyle of Lochalsh with the early morning train for Inverness. Two other forms of transport are represented by the MacBrayne motor vessel Loch Seaforth *on the Mallaig sailing and a motor coach apparently on tour – a rake of seven wooden bodied high sided wagons represents the freight business.*

Opposite *By 1960 BR's Scottish Region had restored four historic engines to their pre-grouping livery and to full working order earning their keep on special trains and, very occasionally, in regular service.*

continued opposite

along with the daily bread and livestock to Portree; by bus to Kyle of Lochalsh for the night, breakfast on the station, a leisurely shunt with the up passenger picking the restaurant car off the down train while up and down goods were also crossed at Achnasheen, and backward into Inverness for the convenience of those going south; next day up the Highland to Perth, back for the night by Aberdeen (a circuit you can still do and which nobody should miss); and next morning on the same train but in a quite different light highlighting different detail to Perth and on to Edinburgh marvelling at the Forth Bridge; another tram tour and finally next morning by Flying Scotsman south. All second class but (except on the Flying Scotsman) all with two window seats in considerable comfort for less than £20.

Later trips brought those intractable problems that faced many Scots as well as the English trying to cover the new system: how to enjoy the Stranraer roads in daylight, get to Peterhead and St Combs as well as Fraserburgh without devoting too much time to Buchan, take all three routes from Cairnie Junction to Elgin and change at picturesque Craigellachie for Speyside on one of them, at Tillynaught for Banff on another, and – most difficult of all – fit a trip in from the junction at The Mound for Dornoch while still achieving Thurso and Wick in a reasonable time span.

As you pored over the timetables and ruled out successive options, you realised that Scotland was really a series of nations. For example, even if you were prepared to rise in the wee hours journeys from east to west of Inverness could entail hours of delay. Patronage of some branches went up in their final years in the car-owning age since most regulars had long deserted them and now enthusiasts could make the short train ride with a much reduced time commitment. Complicated itineraries might involve parking one friend's car at one station, yours at another and still taking a taxi, say between the two stations in Grantown-on-Spey. They were great days for enthusiasts for the diesel multiple units opened up the view of the track ahead and the scenery was as delightful as ever, if not for the minor lines themselves (like that to Lossiemouth that had once carried the prime minister, Ramsey Macdonald, home to his constituency in a through sleeper from King's Cross) that had clearly finished their usefulness.

But if one had to content oneself with a single memory, it would surely be an early morning arrival off the sleeper at Waverley having already breathed the fresh Scottish air through the top light before the smelly arrival in a totally different world – assured of a kaleidoscope of fascinating trains and some of Europe's finest scenery in the days ahead. it was of course better when the railway was steam powered, common carrier, vitally needed, but do not underestimate the attractions now. Enjoy them while you can!

continued

One of them, No 103 – the Jones Goods 4–6–0 – the first class of this wheel arrangement to run in the UK, had been preserved for over 25 years being kept, 'Mirabile dictu' by the LMS. The drive behind this new preservation movement came from Scottish Region general manager, James Ness who readily acquiesced to the BBC Railway Roundabout TV programme's request for it to head the scheduled mixed from Kyle of Lochalsh on Monday 22 June 1960. Even in midsummer the 6.15am mixed from Kyle to Dingwall was too early a start for the slow cine film of the 1960s so the first few miles had to be 'mocked up' on the Sunday. No 103 runs towards Strome Ferry for the cameras thus placing on a moving record the running of one of Great Britain's last mixed trains. The filming proper began at Achnasheen.

The Monkland Railways

You will look in vain on most maps of Scotland for Monklands. It is a little-trodden area except by those who live there. The only sizeable towns are Coatbridge and Airdrie at its western extremity and Bathgate beyond its eastern end. The M8 motorway between Edinburgh and Glasgow skirts its southerly fringe. It is a plateau, mostly 600–800 feet up, which slopes off sharply to west, east and north. The River Avon rises on it and carves an eastward gash as it heads for the Firth of Forth by Grangemouth.

It was once a peaceful area of farms and peat hags. Then, at the beginning of the nineteenth century it was discovered that its fields concealed important deposits of coal (including cannel), black band iron ore, limestone and top quality fireclay – all the ingredients of an indigenous iron industry and coal to spare to supply the growing cities of Edinburgh and Glasgow. The Forth & Clyde canal was already open, with a connection from the Coatbridge/Airdrie area via the Monkland canal. An industrial revolution was soon under way on these windswept uplands, bringing a demand for railways to carry its resources and its products to market. Even as recently as the 1930s its coalmines, fireclay workings and iron works, and the villages that supported them, were tied together by an intricate tangle of mineral railways which carried the produce of Monklands to the metals of the

North British Railway 0–4–0 tender locomotive No 1011 was to become the last engine of this wheel arrangement to belong to any of the main line companies. Having a charmed life from 1868 to 1925 during which time essentials such as brakes were added, smaller driving wheels fitted and a new cab, the engine even had its own branch lines from Clarkston which from the NBR load book seemed specially reserved for it. The original cab, driving wheels and front bufferbeam are clearly visible when on shed at Eastfield in 1901. The rodding above the splashers and across the front footplating is for the front sandeis. The locomotive was driven from the right hand side.

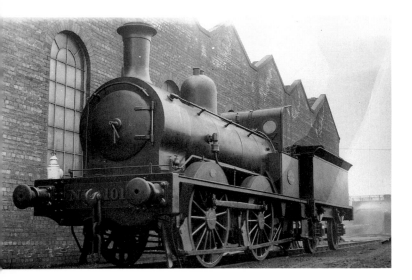

LNER, and to a lesser extent to those of the LMS, and thus all over Scotland.

Before the coming of the trunk railways to Scotland there was an established railway network in the area around Coatbridge and Airdrie. This, on a 'Scottish' gauge of 4ft 6in, grew up to serve the needs of the local industries, coal and ironmaking. The oldest of this group of railways, the Monkland & Kirkintilloch, opened in 1826, was the first to include the power to use locomotives in its Act and, when it came to buy locomotives, they were the first to be built in Scotland. The M&KR was soon extended eastwards by the Ballochney and Slamannan Railways and southwards by the Wishaw & Coltness, while the Garnkirk & Glasgow, the first to use locomotives, connected the Monklands to Glasgow. This came to form an important and successful group of companies with lines stretching from Glasgow to an eastern outlet on the Union Canal at Causewayend. For a brief spell before the opening of the Edinburgh & Glasgow Railway these lines together with the Union Canal even formed the fastest route between Scotland's two main cities.

The building of the West Coast Route to Scotland changed matters, for the new railway required access to Glasgow, which it obtained by making two of the older companies an offer they could hardly refuse; the remaining lines, the Monkland & Kirkintilloch, Ballochney and Slamannan, amalgamated in 1848 to form the Monkland Railways. The arrival of the other railways in the area prompted all the lines to change their gauge to the standard one, eliminating the awkwardness which was already evident in the break of gauge where the earlier lines met the Edinburgh & Glasgow Railway, preventing through carriages being run to Glasgow by that route. The change was made in 1847.

With its solid traffic base, the Monkland Railways continued to expand and develop its network from the original Kirkintilloch–Coatbridge–Causewayend axis to include lines to a harbour on the Forth at Bo'ness, two separate routes to Bathgate, one to Shotts and a large number of shorter spurs and branches to tap the mineral traffic available. The Monkland Railways was primarily a freight concern and the motivation for most of the lines was either coal or iron, the iron works at Kinneil (near Bo'ness) and at Shotts being the target of two lines.

Outside the Coatbridge area, and despite the MR territory's bleak nature, it nevertheless offered a passenger service – as a sideline. Indeed, for many years the MR only owned three passenger coaches, used for the Airdrie–Linlithgow service. When the company decided to divert this service to run to Bo'ness instead it was only after it had opened the line to Bo'ness that the railway discovered that it now needed permission from the Board of Trade for this, so the line was hastily closed again until these formalities had been attended to, a matter of some months, for the Board of Trade was none too impressed by what it saw. A full chronology of the MR's passenger services would be very complicated!

Larger scale railway politics dictated changes and, as

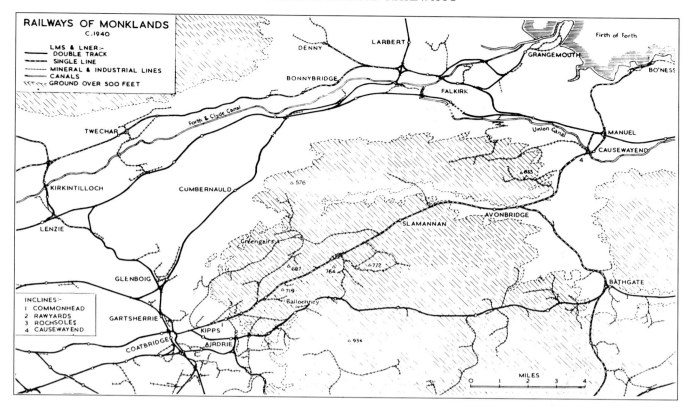

RAILWAYS OF MONKLANDS
C.1940

LMS & LNER:-
—— DOUBLE TRACK
----- SINGLE LINE
····· MINERAL & INDUSTRIAL LINES
═══ CANALS
▨ GROUND OVER 500 FEET

INCLINES:-
1 COMMONHEAD
2 RAWYARDS
3 ROCHSOLES
4 CAUSEWAYEND

part of the great process of amalgamations in central Scotland, the Monkland and the Edinburgh & Glasgow Railways were swallowed up by the North British Railway in 1865. The Monkland Railways had been a progressive and prosperous company, not notable attributes of the NBR at the time, so the shareholders were offered a generous settlement. After the amalgamation, things continued much as before, for the MR system formed a coherent unit within the larger company, the Monkland District, which in time came to embrace new lines and services. The Coatbridge–Bathgate line became a secondary route between Edinburgh and Glasgow, while the mineral branches altered fairly rapidly as coal mines were opened or became worked-out.

One of the features of railways, however, is the way they betray vestiges of events long since forgotten, and the Monkland lines are no exception. The earliest lines incorporated very steep rope-worked inclined planes, the Coatbridge–Bo'ness line having two sets of these, a consecutive self-acting pair at the western end, the Commonhead and Rawyards inclines, and a single one worked by stationary engine at the eastern end, where the line fell to its one-time terminus at Causewayend. In both cases the ruling gradient was 1 in 23; the self-acting inclines were, of course, double track but converging to single line at the bottom. Rope breakages were not rare, at least in early days, and mineral trains and empties – and on at least one occasion a passenger and a coal train – broke away to finish in a heap of wreckage at the foot. They caused many operating headaches for later generations of

railwaymen even after the traffic was worked by locomotives, and for many years passenger trains over the inclines had a locomotive at each end. In earlier times special rates were charged for traffic using these inclines so, despite their operational disadvantages, they began as good sources of revenue.

Locomotive activity centred on Kipps, between Coatbridge and Airdrie. The Monkland & Kirkintilloch introduced locomotive haulage in 1831, and after some internal arrangements for their repair, opened a new workshop at Moss Side, Kipps in 1838 which serviced the three constituent lines of the Monkland Railways. The works even built a few new locomotives in its first years, but thereafter concentrated on repairs. With the takeover by the North British it became a wagon repair shop which survived until the mid-1960s. Adjacent to it was Kipps engine shed, a depot which served the whole Monklands area and which at Nationalisation had an allocation of over fifty engines. It tended to be a home for vintage machines; the last 0-4-0 tender engine in Britain, North British Railway No 1011, was withdrawn from there in 1925.

The mineral traffic made extensive use of private-owner wagons, a constant source of trouble if the owners did not keep them in suitable repair. The Monkland Railways even found that couplings from its own wagons were being removed and used on private-owner vehicles, and had to police this carefully. The railway also permitted local firms to use their own locomotives and, although this was not encouraged, it turned out to linger longer in this area than elsewhere. The notable iron and steel making firm of

One of the 1892 Sharp Stewart built, North British Railway, Holmes class C, LNER class J36 engines hauls a lengthy goods train on the former Monkland & Kirkintilloch 'main line' at Muckroft level crossing near Lenzie on 27 April 1960. Twenty five of these locomotives saw service in France during World War I and the sole survivor out of the class of 168, NBR No 673 Maude, *is one of those veterans.*

W. Baird & Co, of Gartsherrie, continued to run its own locomotives and trains, with its own crews, over main line tracks until 1958, by which time there was only one route, from Gartsherrie over the bulk of the original Monkland & Kirkintilloch Railway and on to Twechar. This was probably the last example of a private-owner steam locomotive in long-distance commercial service on British Railways' tracks.

The railways of the Monklands had been built by and for the local industry, and were both well financed and bold enough to try new ideas. One example of this was in the working of the single lines, where the Monkland Railways introduced block working in 1863, a move well up to the best practice of the time. This not only improved the safety but greatly facilitated the traffic and was sufficiently successful for the system to be extended after the North British takeover. As the NBR at the time had a rather poor record for adopting such measures, this again distinguished the Monkland lines from elsewhere, although the system did eventually penetrate more widely. The Monkland method of working, with Tyer's Single Line Block as it came to be known, without the aid of staff and

ticket or tablet working, lasted on the goods line to Shotts until the 1960s.

The furthest extension of the territory of the Monkland Railways itself was to Bo'ness. Here there lay the Kinneil Iron Works, operated by a firm based in the Monklands, but much was expected of the harbour at Bo'ness. This had once been the main port in the upper part of the Forth, but its fortunes had been eclipsed by the newer harbour at Grangemouth, the eastern end of the Forth & Clyde Canal. Bo'ness caused problems for the railway from the start. The harbour itself was a running sore, for the town did not have the resources to invest in it to make it competitive, and there were interminable wranglings between successive railways and the harbour authorities. In the late nineteenth century the railway obtained powers to lend money to the harbour for improvements and eventually bought it outright. This did not happen without a curious intervention by the arch-competitor, the Caledonian Railway, which was wooed by the town authorities and obtained powers to run its own trains to Bo'ness. The Caledonian service to Bo'ness lasted for exactly five months in 1899. It was withdrawn after the two companies realised that they were wasting money in aggressive competition and came to a 'peace agreement'. In the end, however, Bo'ness never received enough investment to make it a serious competitor for Grangemouth, although it had a substantial trade in timber from the Baltic and in export coal. World War I hit the port, with its strong connections with the Baltic, very badly indeed and while some recovery was made afterwards the writing was on the wall, although the end did not come until the 1950s.

The railways of the Monklands were built to serve the local industry and as that changed so did they. The local ironstone was soon replaced by imported ore, while the coal mining shrank considerably after World War I, and with it the need for passenger services diminished at a time when bus services were being established. The one-time main line, from Coatbridge through Causewayend to the Edinburgh & Glasgow line at Manuel, closed to passengers in 1930 and the central portion around Slamannan was abandoned shortly afterwards, leaving two dead-end stubs. In 1956 the passenger services to Bathgate and Bo'ness ceased, and the remaining freight lines were all but elimi-

nated in the 1960s. Today the only ex-Monkland Railways lines with passenger services are the eastern end of the Glasgow Electric lines, from Coatbridge to Drumgelloch, and the preserved Bo'ness branch, although there is a short stretch of the West Coast Route north of Coatbridge, the 52 chains between Gartsherrie LNER Junction and Garnqueen South, which once belonged to the Monkland Railways and which sees occasional passenger trains. A few goods lines to the industrial heart of the Monklands, including a stretch of the original Monkland & Kirkintilloch, are the only other survivors. But as an example of local enterprise starting early in railway history and adapting to changing times the Monkland Railways have a tale that takes some beating.

CHRONOLOGY
Some significant dates in Scottish Railway history

27 May 1808	Kilmarnock & Troon Railway Act of Parliament passed. First railway in Scotland authorised by Act of Parliament.
6 July 1812	Kilmarnock & Troon Railway opened St. Marnock's depot Kilmarnock to Troon Harbour. 4ft gauge horse wagonway (leased to Glasgow Paisley Kilmarnock & Ayr Railway July 1846 and regauged).
1817	First steam locomotive in Scotland used on Kilmarnock & Troon.
Oct 1826	Monkland & Kirkintilloch Railway opened.
1 June 1831	Garnkirk & Glasgow Railway opened for passengers. (Ceremonial opening 27 September). First locomotive hauled passenger trains in Scotland.
10 May 1831	First steam locomotive built in Scotland by Murdoch & Aitken of Glasgow for Monkland and Kirkintilloch Railway.
16 Dec 1831	Dundee & Newtyle Railway opened.
21 Feb 1842	Edinburgh & Glasgow Railway opened (Haymarket to Queen Street).
22 June 1846	North British Railway opened (North Bridge, Edinburgh to Berwick-upon-Tweed and branch Longniddry-Haddington).
18 June 1846	Edinburgh Waverley station opened. (Suburban platforms Nos 20 & 21 opened 17 April 1898. Station rebuilding completed 1900.)
15 Feb 1848	Caledonian Railway main line opened throughout (Carlisle to Edinburgh and Carstairs to Glasgow).
29 Oct 1849	Edinburgh to Hawick open throughout.
28 Oct 1850	Glasgow & South Western main line (Glasgow - Carlisle, Gretna Junction) open throughout.
12 Sep 1854	Great North of Scotland Railway opened Kittybrewster - Huntly. Kittybrewster - Waterloo (Aberdeen), 24 Sep 1855; Huntly - Keith, 10 Oct 1856; Keith - Elgin via Dufftown throughout, 1 June 1862; Kittybrewster - Aberdeen Joint Station, 4 Nov 1867.
6 Nov 1855	Inverness & Nairn Railway opened.
1 July 1862	Hawick - Carlisle NBR opened (completing the Waverley Route).
9 Sep 1863	Highland main line opened throughout (Stanley Junction - Forres).
2 Mar 1868	Scotland Street tunnel closed.
31 July 1873	NBR introduced first Sleeping Car (first class only) alternate nights between Glasgow Queen Street and London King's Cross and vice versa.
1 May 1876	GSW Glasgow St Enoch station brought into use (not completed until 1879 and extended in 1901).
1 July 1876	GSW & MR Pullman Cars introduced between St Enoch and St Pancras. Drawing Room cars on day service and Sleeping cars on night trains.
1 Jan 1878	NBR First Tay Bridge opened (destroyed in gale 28 Dec 1879).
1879	GSW Glasgow St Enoch station was the first public building in Scotland to be lit by electricity.
1 Aug 1879	Glasgow Central opened. Enlargement completed 1906.
Sep 1880	Highland Railway steamship *Ferret* 'hijacked' by captain. Eventually turned up in Australia in 1881. Sold in 1883 to Adelaide Steamship Co. for £8,000. Wrecked in November 1920.
1 July 1885	CR and LNW West Coast Postal introduced between Aberdeen and Euston exclusively for mails (no passengers carried).

11 July 1887 NB Second Tay bridge opened.

1888 RACE to EDINBURGH:
13 August 10.00 ex Euston arrived Edinburgh Princes Street in 426 mins; 31 August 10.00 ex King's Cross arrived Edinburgh Waverley in 408 mins.

4 Mar 1890 Forth Bridge opened

1893 CR and LNW 1.30pm Glasgow & Edinburgh to Euston formed of corridor stock throughout. Nicknamed 'The Corridor' which name lasted well into LMS days.

3 July 1893 GSW and MR jointly owned dining cars introduced between St Enoch and St Pancras.

7 Aug 1894 West Highland Railway (NB) opened Craigendoran - Fort William.

Sep 1894 Highland Railway No 103, the first 4-6-0 built in Britain.

1895 RACE to ABERDEEN:
21 August 8.00pm ex King's Cross arrived Aberdeen 4.40am; 22 August 8.00 pm ex Euston arrived Aberdeen 4.32am.

14 Dec 1896 Glasgow underground opened, cable operated.
Converted to electric. Inner circle (anti-clockwise) 31 March 1935. Outer circle (clockwise) 5 December 1935. Re-equipped, closed 21 May 1977. Re-opened 1 January 1980.

1 Aug 1900 East Coast companies (NB, NE and GN) dining cars introduced on 10.00 King's Cross - Edinburgh and vice versa. 20 minute luncheon stop at York abolished.

21 Aug 1903 Connel Ferry bridge opened (road and rail) Ballachulish branch (Railway closed 28 March 1966. Creagan bridge not converted for road entailing an extra 5 miles).

2 May 1904 GNS motor bus service introduced between Ballater and Braemar.

1912 CR Pullman cars introduced including Observation car *Maid of Morven* between Glasgow Buchanan Street and Oban.

1922 CR last of 4-wheel locomotive hauled coaches introduced for Balerno branch.

1 May 1928 LNER non stop Flying Scotsman between Edinburgh and King's Cross. (LMS had run the Royal Scot in two portions both non stop between Euston and Glasgow and Euston and Edinburgh on 30 April. This was not repeated in regular service.)

10 Jan 1930 Burst tube on LMS ultra high pressure locomotive No 6399 *Fury* killing North British Locomotive Company's inspector.

20 Aug 1934 Railway Air Services flights Glasgow - Belfast - Manchester - Birmingham - London and vice versa commenced. One flight each way on weekdays. (Inaugural flight terminated at Manchester due to gale force winds damaging aircraft.) Full service 21 August
(Fare £10 return Glasgow - London.
Dep Central station by car 8.45 am,
Renfrew Airport dep 9.15 am
Croydon arr 1.35pm
Victoria arr by car 2.20pm.)

5 July 1937 LMS Coronation Scot introduced. 6½ hour schedule between Glasgow and London. LNER Coronation introduced 6 hour schedule between Edinburgh and London.

Nov 1939 Ex NBR 4-4-2 LNER No 9875 *Midlothian* withdrawn although proposed for preservation (NBR 875 built North British Locomotive Company Aug 1906.)

12/13 Mar 1947 LMS 5.10 pm Glasgow St Enoch - Stranraer stuck in snow drift ½ mile south of Glenwhilly. Passengers rescued on foot and train finally released on 20 March.

12/13 Aug 1948 **Floods in Border Counties**
Damage
East Coast main line, seven bridges destroyed between Grantshouse and Reston.
Waverley route – landslide at Tynehead.
Trains diverted via Newcastle and Carlisle or Settle - Carlisle routes, then via Caledonian 13-15 August.
Commencing 16 August via Tweedmouth - Kelso - St Boswells and Waverley route.
East Coast Main line re-opened: Freight 25 October 1948; Passengers 1 Nov 1948
Branches
Eyemouth - bridge over Eye Water destroyed. Re-opened 29 June 1949.
Reston - St Boswells blocked between Greenlaw and Duns.
Through passenger service withdrawn 13 August 1948.
Worked as two separate branches, freight only St Boswells - Greenlaw. Reston - Duns passenger service withdrawn 10 September 1951.
Lauder branch (freight only) closed 13 August 1948 reopen 2 Nov 1950.

31 Jan 1953 Great storm around all coasts of Great Britain and much flooding. M.V. *Princess Victoria* sunk en route from Stranraer to Larne.

10 Apr 1953 Starlight Specials (cheap overnight travel between Glasgow St Enoch and London St Pancras, and Edinburgh Waverley and London Marylebone) commenced. Passengers could return 8 or 15 days later. Fare £3.10.0 return. These ran every year from April to September although by 1959 they ran only at Easter then late May to early September.

15 June 1953 First DMU service in Scotland. ACV 3-coach 4-wheel experimental set tried on Dalmellington branch and certain trains Ayr - Kilmarnock for two weeks.

15 June 1955 First car carrying train, 'Car Sleeper Ltd' commenced. Ran Tuesdays and Saturdays 8.00pm Perth - King's Cross and Wednesdays and Sundays 7.45pm King's Cross - Perth. (Fare £15, vehicle and driver, additional passengers £4.10.0.)

7 Jan 1957 First regular DMU service in Scotland between Glasgow Queen Street and Edinburgh.

25 Mar 1958 Experimental battery electric railcar introduced between Aberdeen and Ballater.

5 Oct 1960 Glasgow electrification (north Clydeside services) commenced. First main line electrification in Scotland.

19 Dec 1960 Steam services reinstated due to electrical defects. Full electric service reinstated September 1961.

18 June 1962 Ex LNER class A4 4-6-2s introduced on Glasgow - Aberdeen service. (Replaced by diesel locomotives on 15 September 1966.)

13 June 1965 Stranraer - Euston service diverted via Ayr and Kilmarnock due to closure of Portpatrick and Wigtownshire line. (Stranraer Harbour station opened 1862. First through carriages to Euston 1 Nov 1885).

6 Sept 1965 Edinburgh Princes Street station closed.

27 June 1966 Glasgow St Enoch Station closed.

7 Nov 1966 Glasgow Buchanan Street Station closed.

1967 Ex Highland 4-4-0 BR No 54398 cut up after being in store for possible preservation since Feb 1953. (HR No 2 built Dübs July 1898.)

31 Dec 1967 With closure of Carlisle Kingmoor depot last regular steam locomotive workings in Scotland ceased.

3 May 1971 'Push & Pull' diesel service commenced between Edinburgh and Glasgow with a locomotive at each end of train.

17 Mar 1979 Penmanshiel Tunnel collapsed whilst being enlarged to take 'European Gauge' containers. Two contractors men killed. Line diverted around tunnel and reopened 20 August 1979.

Walking the Forth Bridge The familiar girders of the Forth Bridge encase a local train in charge of ex-NBR class D30 No 62427 Dumbiedykes *during August 1953. The walkways can be clearly seen either side of the running lines.*

Walking the Forth Bridge

Walking the Forth Bridge (thanks to a Scottish Region temporary walking permit with the usual caveats and disclaimers) was exciting. Even early on a Sunday morning trains rolled in close proximity. When the cantilever section was reached the walkway was found to be spotted with pennies flung out of passing trains whose passengers hoped to obtain good luck – if their coins hit the water! Automatically these were picked up – almost a hundred were collected – over seven shillings and sixpence in old money, enough for five or six pints of good ale. At the other end, a relaxed track gang were passed setting off for the bridge. Only when the car was safely on the move was it realised that *their* purpose was to get their Sunday drinking money!

Many railways adopted the 'open' station principle with tickets being checked at special ticket platforms just outside the passenger station. The last of these, Perth North, is seen here in the late 1920s or early 1930s with a down Highland train passing hauled by HR Castle class 4–6–0 Gordon Castle No 14678 and an unidentified Clan class 4–6–0. The platform finally closed in BR days.

2
SOME SCOTTISH STATIONS

PERTH GENERAL. To most people it might suggest a central Post Office but to the traveller, the engineman, the *Bradshaw* aficionado and the reader of railway lore, it conjures up a station of stations. The stopping place for the down Special TPO, the night expresses from London, connection *par excellence* with the Highland line, a rich variety of livery, locomotives and rolling stock: Perth General has had more than its moments. In days gone by it had its regular State occasions for Queen Victoria used to breakfast there in the Scottish North Eastern Board Room, holding a sort of levee of prominent railway officers. G.P. Neele, the LNWR's superintendent of the line, has much to say of these occasions in his readable and authoritative *Railway Reminiscences* wincing as he wrote at the unlovely appearance and unquenchable affability of 'Kippen Davie', Mr Stirling, chairman of the North British.

Others have memories of the midnight travelling from Edinburgh to Sutherland or Caithness being dumped out of the warm (but sometimes smelly) North British train about 11.00pm and waiting until sometime around 1.00am. Perth, like many junction stations, had periods of intense activity followed by spells of somnolent peace. Up there in the Highland bay the coaches of the northbound train would be waiting chilly but homely with murmurous conversations in English, Scots and Gaelic whilst the intermittent rumble of trolleys reverberated from the platform outside. Sooner or later the lights came on revealing the haggard faces of coming bedfellows and it became a relief to get out for a while to walk a mile or two up and down the long long platform. Midnight saw the arrival of the express from Glasgow with at least one sleeper and through coaches for the north; after that Perth General became a place of roaring safety valves and strange shunting movements. In pre-Grouping days this involved elderly tank engines from three different companies.

In those far off days, round about 12 August, there was the celebrated Harlequin Train – a motley collection of vehicles from all over the country, of all conceivable shapes, sizes and colour which went clattering off into the mountains through the morning mists. Even in later times Southern and Great Western coaches could be seen on this train but in pre-Grouping times as many as 36 vehicles from nine different companies were not uncommon, needing two engines from Perth and three from Blair Atholl.

Over the mountains, there were two fascinating triangular junctions, one at Forres on the old line via Dava, the other at Inverness, jumping off place for the Further North trains. Forres was the only actual triangular *station* and, for many years, the home of elderly 4–4–0s, in the latter days

Route Indicators
Such was the intensity of services at Glasgow Central, and the variety of routes served, that locomotives displayed an indicator on the lamp stud at the centre of the buffer beam or, in the case of light engines, in front of the chimney (or at the rear of the tender if travelling tender first). 'Engines that have arrived at Central and do not require to leave before departing with their next train, must carry the indicator on the stud it has arrived on, with the arms in position for its next train, when following the carriages out of the dock, until it is shunted into the dock it is to start from.' Fixing the indicators was the fireman's job, though the driver had to check. One wonders how often mistakes were made and with what consequences.

Opposite *Perth station was extremely interesting to the railway observer especially in pre-grouping days, being served by three out of the five main railways, the Caledonian, North British and Highland. Even in BR times it was still very busy. At the south end on 22 July 1952 the 9.35am Aberdeen – Glasgow, The St Mungo, is headed by a new BR class 5 4–6–0 No 73009, while in the bay is the 12.08 departure for Edinburgh with class A3 4–6–2 No 60099 Call Boy. The driver is sitting on the locomotive running plate relaxing prior to departure. Under the station roof there is an LMS class 5, No doubt with a train off the Highland line, whilst an LNER B1 can be seen passing the station on the left hand side.*

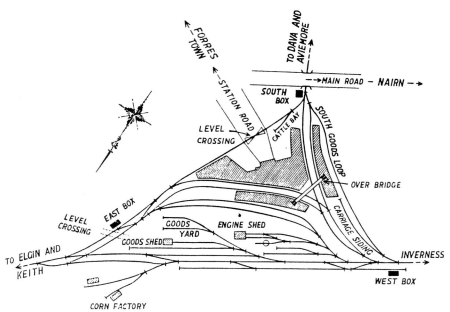

Diagram of the layout of Forres station and yard

The layout of Inverness station is curious as the lines from the south and north abut at the apex of a triangle. By running past the station on the Rose Street curve and backing the train in it was possible to make cross platform interchanges. This train, however, has arrived from the south and run directly into platform 2. The locomotives are two class 24 diesels and the date is probably the early 1970s, BR's blue period.

small Bens and Lochs; the last ever, *Ben Alder*, albeit with an ugly squat Caley boiler, lived on Forres shed. Inverness was (and still is) another matter altogether.

The old headquarters of the Highland Railway, Inverness is a remarkable station. Its eccentric track plan is well known to many who have never seen the actual layout. The station's barn-like halls and the short overall roof from which extend long curving and extremely narrow island platforms give it a very special character, as of course does the traffic it handles.

The buffers are at the southern apex of the triangle formed by the lines from the south and north, the northern base consisting of a through avoiding loop known as the Rose Street Curve. Today the curve sees little regular activity though specials such as cruise trains take it, but for generations most trains from south and north went round it and then backed in – alongside the connecting series for the continuing journey. The station and the former railway hotel outside provide great historical continuity. For example, a wall of the station concourse proclaims (emblazoned in full colour) the arms of the Highland Railway's oldest constituent, the Inverness & Nairn. The HR's Lochgorm locomotive works once stood sturdily within the triangle of rails where today's trains are still serviced in a depot that because of its isolation is still remarkably self reliant. Another link with the past is the water tank adjacent to the locomotive shed

Strathpeffer originally spurned the railway which it later regretted. The branch was eventually opened in 1885 but closed in 1946. The trains ran to and from Dingwall and were for a time worked by a Sentinel steam railcar. The train seen here is a mixed with two Highland Railway coaches hauled by 4–4–0T No 15014, one of five originally ordered from Dübs & Company by the Uruguay Eastern Railway. As they were unable to raise the necessary finance the five were purchased by the Highland in 1893. For a time, as Highland Railway No 102, it carried the name Munlochy. *The photograph was probably taken in the early 1930s as the locomotive is in black livery.*

49

Innovative

Deep in the countryside, rail-waymen were often the best paid people and led the way to a more luxurious life. For example, in one settlement on the GNSR the stationmaster caused a real stir (and was thought a bit 'uppish') when he ordered the daily delivery – of course by train – of a news-paper other than the area's obliga-tory *Press & Journal* from Aberdeen.

Railwaymen were often the first to shop by post, signalmen no doubt having ample time to study the new catalogues, and it was often railway gardeners who won the most prizes at local horti-cultural shows having brought in new varieties or strains of plants and seeds. The fact that they were in communication with others around the countryside spread ideas and habits. If anyone broke ranks by ordering something other than the traditional dram at the local pub it would most likely be a railway employee.

But what consternation when a porter who felt especially pleased with himself having earned a handsome tip handling an excess of baggage travelling with the nobs from the 'big house' asked the guard to pop into an Aberdeen grocer in his lunch time to buy one of those new-fangled tins of sardines for his tea. And fresh fish passing by the trainload!

The Great North of Scotland station at Elgin in the 1930s with a departing local train comprising 6-wheeled stock, probably for Lossiemouth, hauled by GSNR class D40 4–4–0 No 6852 Glen Grant. Under the LNER re-numbering scheme of 1946 the engine became No 2279 and finally under BR, 62279 before being withdrawn in December 1948. It is interesting to recall that five similar locomotives were delivered to the South Eastern & Chatham Railway in 1899 from the builders, Neilson Reid, at a premium of about 10 per cent.

concealed in a sort of triumphal arch: it was built at the height of the Victorian craze for disguising things.

That excellent author of railway lore, C. Hamilton Ellis, tells the story of a day in the August rush when, at the height of things and with the first of a succession of tourist expresses already on its way down from Culloden Moor, *Ben Loyal* inconveniently left the road right on the western point of the triangle making a merry morning of it for all concerned. The last he saw of the proceedings was the unfortunate *Ben* being backed, partly on the sleepers and partly on the rails, whilst the stymied express whistled repeatedly and lugubriously afar off. It took about an hour to get the outlying parts of *Ben Loyal's* anatomy off the fairway.

Inverness station, alas threatened by a redevelopment scheme, natu-rally has lengthy lulls between activity and the arrival of the sleeper from London (there is no lengthier or heavier passenger train on BR), echoes of those August caravans of yesteryear, and the departure of the summer tourist trains to Kyle of Lochalsh always attracts an audience.

The Highland (and this still applies to BR) had great variety in its stations; Strome Ferry where once there was a riot over Sunday trains; Lairg, the station for Durness 56 miles away, its name once appearing on the hotel notepaper as if it was just down the road; Forsinard, a flower tree screened oasis in a land of no trees where once the crews of two snowed-up trains were on continuous overtime for a week while enjoying the hospitality of the inn; and similarly Georgemas Junction, a sort of Scottish Dovey Junction. But the prettiest of all stations lie on the old Callander & Oban line (even though the section from Dunblane to Crianlarich has long been swept away) and on the West Highland, the latter complete with wooden shingles. The real charm lies in their small size, their neat-ness and their gardens as well as in their superb situations. The Oban line's stations sported such charming adornments as leaden storks supporting fountain nozzles.

CENTRAL STATION HOTEL, GLASGOW.
CALEDONIAN RAILWAY.

C. LORD
Manager

A Caledonian Railway advertisement for the Central Station Hotel, Glasgow, probably produced either for or soon after its opening in 1885. There is some artist's licence invoked as the closeness of adjacent buildings would have restricted vision. The seven arches on the left form the main entrance to Central station and are now masked by an overall awning.

Glasgow Central after the 1905 enlargement is a well laid out terminus with 13 platforms, now electrified, for both main line and Clyde coast services. In the late 1950s BR class 4 2–6–4T No 80001 stands in platform 8 with a Caledonian main line local train as signified by the semaphore route indicator in the middle of the buffer beam. The Caledonian electro-pneumatic semaphore signalling was replaced in 1960 by colour light signals controlled from a new power box.

Too Much

David L. Smith loved to relate how Stranraer men had some heavy work during World War II. The 5.10pm from Glasgow would load to 14 coaches, often full and standing.

Four coaches came off at Ayr and two more at Girvan, but the engine still had to tackle Glendoune (3¾ miles mainly at 1 in 54) with eight. But the engines were good – usually a Class 5X from Kingmoor or Crewe North.

When Sandy McKnight and Harry Anderson were on that job, they used to carry an extra shovel, then when it came to a bit of heavy work, it was one on each side of the firebox to shovel in coal. One night they were on the first portion of the London Paddy (10.00pm ex Stranraer Harbour). They had a Crewe Class 5X, a good one, and a load of 305 tons, just nice for the Port Road, with its ruling grade of 1 in 80. Just before the start came word of a derailment at Southwick and everything to be diverted via Girvan, Ayr and Mauchline.

This was quite a different problem, for with their 305 tons they had to tackle New Luce bank, with its three miles of 1 in 57. 'Oh Sanny, we canna gie ye a pilot! There's no' an engine aboot the place. Ye'll just hae tae gae on an' dae the best ye can.' They did even that; they went through New Luce full tilt and up the bank as best they could; but she just went up to about a mile from the top and came to a stand in full forward gear and full regulator! They were 57 minutes on The Neck dividing the train, and it was 4.00am before they got to Carlisle. Likewise it was midday before they got back, as passengers, to Stranraer.

Crianlarich (once Crianlarich Upper) is now the junction for the Oban line with trains running up over the mountainous West Highlands. It has always been an important place for passengers on the Fort William line for here, like Swindon in the old days, there was the lunch stop, used regularly for both up and down trains which did not carry restaurant cars. Even in the days of World War II when restaurant services were severely curtailed and meat on ration, there was a large notice on the station 'Lunch, Dinners, Teas – Time Allowed by Trains'. The down non-restaurant car train waited for 23 minutes for lunch and the up 11 minutes for tea. Even if these trains were running late, no encroachment was allowed on the passengers refreshment prerogatives. Furthermore, Crianlarich refreshment room had no rival for its wartime fare of meat, cheese, jam, sandwiches, buttered Scotch scones and pancakes and other delicacies. At the end of the mealtime allowance the station master rounded up his flock and returned them, well satisfied, to the train. The privately-run refreshment room on the now otherwise unstaffed typical West Highland island platform still attracts those who come to see the trains as well as catch them.

Only a generation ago Glasgow's multi-coloured trams would take you to the one-time gateway to the north: Buchanan Street station where sleek green ex-LNER A4 Pacifics worked out their last days on the expresses to Aberdeen: *Union of South Africa*, *Bittern*, *Kingfisher*, each saw out its time way north of designer's intentions. But in the times of the old companies the station was at its best, a place full of tongues where the green coaches and teak-brown sleeping cars of the old Highland Railway met the glory of the Caledonian's *Maid of Morven* Pullman car, the envy of its competitors. Even in LMS days one world moved to another especially around ten o'clock at night. Then the dusk to dawn caravan began its long slow pilgrimage to Inverness when anyone with an ear for intonations could pick up not only the different branches of English and Scots but several varieties of Gaelic too.

While Buchanan Street sat against the grey face of Cowcaddens, Queen Street was even worse, scarcely an ornament to the city or to the LNER either. In the beginning it had a unique characteristic, its rope worked incline up to Cowlairs; long ago an enthusiastic reporter called it a 'fairy palace'. The west side office building was once a church, hence the North British phraseology 'gang tae the kirk' meant being had up on the carpet. Beneath lies the Low Level, now efficiently electric. In steam days during the rush hours it resembled a brimstone factory; at other times it was a place of chilly cavernous emptiness. In its later days, the West Highland trains were worked in tandem (unless there was a K4 about) usually with an adapted and named K2 plus a NB Glen, the pilot being put in behind to give the train engine driver charge of the brake. It was always worth seeing the morning diner for there would be three engines involved with a shunt before departure. The train was brought in by the usual N14 class 0–6–2 tank but the train engines remained on the opposite platform face with two further coaches until just prior to departure. The reason was that with this loading the pilot would have been well out of the station and fouling at least three roads. But it was always a good noisy send-off.

The only good thing about Buchanan Street was its atmosphere. The individual components were awful. The LMS's other two Glasgow termini were altogether grander. Indeed both Central and the late St Enoch were fine spacious stations, both firmly planted in the centre of the city and each with a good hotel.

Central is a Scottish institution. Thousands of couples first met there! Just everything happens in the miniature world that is BR's station with the greatest number of daily trains. Until the end of steam it was a stronghold of Caledonian parentage with Caley locomotives (especially such numerous things as McIntosh goods and tank engines) defying extermination over many years and eclipsing their pre-Grouping sisters.

In a sense Central is like some of the Southern's termini just north of the Thames, the bridge over the Clyde forming a similar bottleneck. Stand at the end of one of the platforms projecting out over the river and the sound of metal wheels on metal rails and of changing points hardly ever dies away. And in rush hours there is a continuous throng of hurrying passengers sweeping across the broad and slightly sloping concourse, in the corner the entrance to the Central Hotel, the Caledonian's pride and

Glasgow Central station on 6 May 1957. Polmadie Stanier Pacific No 46221 Queen Elizabeth *sets off for Carlisle with the Royal Scot for London (Euston). At Carlisle another Princess Coronation would be provided for the remainder of the journey. The two Fairburn 2–6–4Ts Nos 42056 and 42275 wait for their next turn of duty on the ex-Caledonian local services.*

The Glasgow & South Western's terminus in Glasgow was St Enoch, originally opened in 1876 with echoes of St Pancras and extended in 1901. By 28 August 1965 when the photograph was taken, the station was in its last year and very much run down. The original roof is that in the centre with the newer extension to the left.

Painful End

The most romantic gateway to Scotland was by the 5,590 ft single line viaduct over the Solway Firth, opened in August 1870. In its first year 44,700 tons of iron ore crossed it, but cheaper ore then imported ones quickly ruined the Cumberland trade and thereafter there was little traffic... but many problems. Ice flows brought down 45 of the 193 piers in 1881 and reopening was not until over three years later. Scouring tides racing at up to 12 knots were a constant problem. Closure in 1921 was due to the need for £70,000 repairs... so the LMS inherited a moribund international branch. Dismantling was finished by December 1935... but that was not the end.

Thousands of tons of stones deposited over the years formed a dangerous reef for shipping, no longer warned by the presence of the viaduct itself. The Board of Trade insisted on the stones' removal... and the drawing out of the piers which occasionally appeared like gaunt teeth. The only solution was removal by hand, stone by stone, there being one workable hour per day at low tide for three days a month, and even then a gale blowing in, or rivers being in spate, could mean that the gang of up to forty men would be sent home without achieving anything.

joy. (It was the first building in these parts to be electrically lit following the company's Hotel Committee's tour of the grand hotels of Europe.) Yet there have always been very distinctive Scottish features... and more than the fact that until very recent times Christmas Day here was just like any other. Trains to and from England use one extreme, usually indeed platform 1 itself, and there have always been so few of them that their arrival and departure has always been an event of note; at the opposite end, and where steam stayed alive longest, the boat trains to Gourock have also always had special character. In between are a dozen platforms that have for generations accommodated a pair of trains each at busy times. Even in electric days this calls for precision working, for the first train in is obviously the last out yet stationary 15 minutes at most at busy periods. In steam days the number of light engine movements made the Great Eastern's Liverpool Street seem child's play.

But perhaps the single most colourful feature about Central until quite recently was its great departure board display. Well after other termini had adopted some form of electronic information panel, Glasgow Central had a long display of boards in the windows of the first floor offices, changed manually. One board per train, hundreds of them, displayed with precision timing, read by millions in the course of a year, with far greater efficiency than the now-standard electronic information (often belatedly updated) provides. Cathcart Circle, London Euston, Gourock and the list of steamship connections, front train, rear train... it was endlessly fascinating and many people indeed felt it should have been preserved as a national monument.

St Enoch was very different. This was not only a terminus of the Glasgow & South Western whose locomotives, the ruling powers that were (Caledonian men to their toenails) saw off as quickly as they could, it was also the terminus for trains coming up over the last trunk route built from England, the Midland's Settle & Carlisle.

Some have said that St Enoch's atmosphere declined with the annihilation of the G&SW engines – from domeless 4–4–0 veterans to the huge 4–6–4 tanks, but that is far from so. The beautiful sweep of the roofs survived, and certain Midland associations even intensified until the coming of the Stanier engines. Class 2Ps and compounds and even LNWR Claughtons came up once displaced from the West Coast main line. Even with the Jubilees on the Stranraer trains the whole scene stayed more old worldly and very Scots; the lowland murmur more soothing to the English ear than uninterpretable Gaelic. Memorable times included the superb Sunday excursions to places like Keswick often behind a Claughton to Carlisle, borrowed for the day from Corkerhill shed and maybe a Jumbo 2–4–0 and a Cauliflower 0–6–0 onwards. The joy of course was the restaurant car which needed no drinks licence for those were the days when alcohol could only be sold on Sundays in Scotland to bona fide travellers. And outside was the unique tower-like station (it alone survives, the grand hotel also having been felled) of the Clockwork Orange, Glasgow's unique single circle tube with its short platforms all on a hump, descents on either side.

Maybe it was the climate, maybe the Scottish character, nearly all stations were good of their type, solid stone structures and wooden overall roofs being much more common than in England. Many excellent modest stations survive either in use or preservation such as the GSNR's 'Queen's Own' at Ballater for Balmoral, of course less grand than Aberdeen's joint effort at the other end of the Deeside line but every bit as suitable and civilised for its purpose.

A WEST HIGHLAND STATION (ARROCHAR AND TARBET).

On the evening of 10 September 1959, St Enoch station presented its usual line up of steam traction with, left to right; ex-LMS Jubilee class 4–6–0 No 45621 Northern Rhodesia, BR Standard Class 4 2–6–0 No 76092, BR Standard class 5 4–6–0 No 73171, Fairburn 2–6–4Ts Nos 42190 and 42272 and ex-LMS class 5 No 45466. The Jubilee has just arrived to work to Stranraer while on the far platform the class 5 prepares to leave for Carlisle. Other departures are for Greenock Princes Pier, Kilmarnock and Largs.

The Elizabethan awaiting departure from platform 10 at Waverley for its non-stop run to King's Cross in 1953. The locomotive is class A4 No 60011 Empire of India. Platforms 10 and 11 still form one long track with a scissors crossover in the centre so that two trains can arrive or depart independently.

But what of Scotland's most famous station? Waverley, in steam days, was a place of stone, iron, smoky glass and crowds, filled by the harsh song of Westinghouse pumps and right in Edinburgh's midst. As you emerged you were at once in the brilliant length of Princes Street, its rather vulgar Victorianism gentled by the evening light which likewise made the Scott monument soar into a new and august dignity. Opposite the old town glowed and smoked and sprawled up to the Castle Rock whilst between the two the railway glimmered below the darkening gardens before plunging through the classically adorned Mound. In the dark its brilliant signal lamps and mounting smoke clouds flaunted it all.

To arrive at Waverley on a train originating in England whether over the East Coast main line or the Midland via the Waverley route itself was always an experience to remember, the engine's whistle shrilling as the train skirted the misty bulk of the Salisbury Crags and taking the final plunge into Calton Hill tunnel. Not here the outskirts of suburbia or the

56

slums approaching King's Cross or St Pancras but entry to the very heart of Edinburgh. If it was evening even the old Calton Gaol took on something of the savage grandeur of a Doré drawing and to many this was scarcely spoilt by the rising smoke coming from LNER engines in the ravine. Indeed the gaol was often mistaken for the Castle by innumerable tourists. No Scots station could ask for a better front door.

Great was the opposition to giving the railway the very heart of Edinburgh, allowing it to fill the entire valley and pour out soot and smoke fouling the air of the Scottish capital. To this day many visitors taking in Princes Street and the gardens wonder how it happened. Yet the station served the city well...and still does. Where else in Britain is so busy a station so central, so accessible even by private car with its separate down and up slopes? Suburban services declined here early, but people have always commuted long distances to Edinburgh and crowds of serious-faced passengers determinedly climb the steps first up to the

Edinburgh Waverley is a vast station of 21 platforms in the valley between the old and new towns, but it suffers with a low roof with a maximum height of 42ft, due to the Scottish law of Servitudes or the equivalent English version Ancient Lights. An up express, probably The Elizabethan for King's Cross is loading at platforms 10 and 11 in the early 1960s.

Opposite, above *The Caledonian Railway's station in the capital, Princes Street, was a fine structure after the 1894 rebuilding and completion of the hotel in 1903. The train services were never very prolific, main line to Carstairs for England, Leith locals and one of sorts to Glasgow via Shotts. Ex-Caledonian Railway class 3F 0–6–0 No 57550 is leaving the station on a local train, probably for Leith North, c 1955.*

Waverley west end bays on 6 May 1957. Gresley designed class V3 2–6–2T No 67620 rests between empty stock duties as Thompson post war mixed traffic 4–6–0 class B1 built by the North British Locomotive Company in May 1947 waits with the 10.40am to Dundee. The B1 clearly shows the Scottish Region practice of using both the LMS type smokebox door shed code plate and the ex-LNER practice of painting the class code and shed name on the front buffer. The electric lights were rarely relied upon and a locomotive headlamp is in use rather than the intended white disc.

station bridge reminiscent of Liverpool Street's before its rebuilding and then the notoriously windy Waverley Steps.

Many a Sassenach has feared that those steps will cause his death as he has lugged luggage up them against the stiff easterly downdraft. Today even those wishing to transfer from station to hotel (alas, no longer the North British but renamed the Balmoral, though as dominating in its sheer bulk as ever) have to use the steps, since the labyrinthine underground passage route involving two separate lifts has been closed for our inconvenience. It is especially hard on those decamped from their sleepers at platforms 20 and 21, beyond the main station, built for extra suburban traffic and now seldom used by daytime trains. London departures have always been more frequent here than at Glasgow Central, though only since the closure of the Caledonian/LMS far less grand Princes Street (at the street's other end) have services arrived from Euston as well as King's Cross. Those from St Pancras are but a distant memory.

Yet in a sense no memory is distant at Edinburgh Waverley. The station epitomises the link between past and present. Choose any vantage point and you quickly recall the various steam ages, events of great importance, war and peace, and realise that here is one of the world's greatest stages where the performance ever changes.

Left *Princes Street station Edinburgh with a Caledonian Railway Pickersgill 4–4–0 No 54503 at the head of a semi-fast to Glasgow over the Caley route. The engine carries class A headlamps but the stock is still wooden bodied non-corridor coaches, the whole scene bar the BR livery reminiscent of the 1930s. The backs of the houses are scarcely representative of the normally acknowledged Princes Street panorama. Note the fine ex-Caledonian bracket signal with its lattice posts now fitted with upper quadrant arms and safety hoop at the top of the ladder. A very economical piece of infrastructure.*

Diary of a Fifties Spotter

Many English enthusiasts were given walking and other permits to record the early days of BR steam when traffic and speeds were back to something like prewar normality but there was still huge variety of rolling stock as well as motive power. Here are extracts from one diary which will bring back happy memories to many who experienced such pleasures themselves and make others envious. The year is 1951.

Arrived in Edinburgh in luxury by the Pullman Queen of Scots, via Leeds City, Harrogate and Ripon...very enjoyable, but (a hint of things to come) no drop lights to poke one's head out to survey the railway scene. To Princes Street Gardens next morning, and photographed B1 No 61102 on 8.47 Inverkeithing–Waverley, D11 No 62678 *Luckie Mucklebackit* on down Inverkeithing, A2/1 No 60509 *Waverley* on 6.05 from Aberdeen, ex-LMS Black Five No 45011 on the up Perth via Forth Bridge, and then the simultaneous 10.00am Waverley departures, neck and neck, blue-liveried A4 No 60011 *Empire of India* for Aberdeen and A3 No 60054 *Princes of Wales* with the Glasgow Queen Street express. Next was another Black

Gresley class K4 No 61995 Cameron of Lochiel *is in appropriate clan territory as it approaches the Banavie swing bridge over the Caledonian Canal with the 4.50pm Fort William–Mallaig passenger on 16 June 1951. The engine still wears its LNER apple green livery. Ben Nevis, still bearing snow in the corries, dominates the scene.*

Five on the 10.10 to Perth with Inverness carriages, No 45488.

Then to Dalmeny, with good luck via a diversionary route, the single track spur via Ratho and Kirkliston. Rejoined the Forth Bridge main line at Dalmeny South Junction and to stop at the station once we had passed the North Junction where the line from Glasgow via Polmont trails in. Then down to South Queensferry, taking several shots (including two with a pair of freight trains) of the Forth Bridge from the ferry *Mary Queen of Scots*.

The first train seen after climbing to North Queensferry station was D30 4–4–0 No 62429 *The Abbot* with the 3.43 Waverley–Ladybank. Welcomed into Forth Bridge North Signal Box, and through its south window caught class J38 No 65929 on the northern viaduct. This Gresley 0–6–0 was in charge of a Niddrie Yard to Perth 'D' express one-third fitted. Managed to get one of the ferries below in the picture, too.

Five minutes later, on the down platform, D11 4–4–0 No 62687 *Lord James of Douglas* left the North Queensferry tunnel and passed through on the 2.30 Crail–Glasgow Queen Street, which runs via Thornton Junction and the bridge. And in two minutes B1 No 61403 emerged from the tunnel with a Naval leave special at a good 30mph.

Nobody objected to use of the railwayman's footpath spotted running along the top of the tunnel, so to the north portal and down to the outside curve of the North Queensferry bank, where the first train was a green-liveried

A2 4–6–2, No 60527 *Sun Chariot* climbing briskly with a Class C fully-fitted express fish train from Aberdeen. V3 2–6–2T No 67606 passed on an up express and Gresley J38 0–6–0 No 65919 headed a down coal train from the bridge viaduct. What variety!

Time to return to Waverley, but with windows that opened caught within the steel network of the Forth Bridge a class J37 Reid ex-North British 0–6–0, No 64551 headcoded as a class H through freight but only comprising engine and brake van. At Haymarket passed blue-liveried A3 No 60037 *Hyperion* paired with a GN tender returning light to its Haymarket home shed (64B).

Next morning at 9.21 saw A4 No 60023 *Golden Eagle*, in blue livery, bring the empty stock of the up Flying Scotsman into Waverley and at 11.33 (at Haymarket) *Hyperion* again carrying the Queen of Scots headboard running light engine. At 11.45 the Pullman from Glasgow Queen Street ran through Haymarket at about 30mph headed by that morning's third blue-liveried Pacific, A3 No 60098 *Spion Kop*.

Then by a crowded 1.00 Waverley to Glasgow Queen Street, full of workers returning home at Saturday lunch time, headed by Peppercorn Class A2 4–6–2 No 60529 *Pearl Diver*, one of five locos of the class modified with double blast pipe and multiple valve regulator. It backed out of Queen Street with its empty stock sharply after our arrival down Cowlairs incline.

Then the trip of a lifetime on the West Highland, starting unpromisingly through Glasgow's suburbs but soon opening up what must be some of the world's best views from a train window, albeit slightly restricted at times by the steam and exhaust of the two locomotives working hard on

The fireman of Stanier class 5 No 45138 trails the single line token for the Rose Street signalman in June 1951 as the 10.45am from Kyle of Lochalsh takes the Inverness avoiding line. The train will set back into one of the southbound platforms to make simple connections for Perth and Aberdeen. The leading vehicle is an ex-LNWR Wolverton built 12-wheel Restaurant Car which has been transferred from the Kyle bound train at Achnasheen.

a summer Saturday train crowded to the gills. We had K2/2 side-window cab 2–6–0s No 61764 *Loch Arkaig* piloting No 61770, one of the un-named few of that series. What an exit we made up Cowlairs bank. And what a welcome by pipes at Fort William as the train perhaps bringing the week's largest single contingent of tourists arrived beside the loch.

On Sunday of course not a wheel turned, but on Monday, the Contessa Nettel Press camera was used to good avail. Mallaig Junction was starting point where K2/2 2–6–0 61791 soon came by towing a brake van; in the sidings was a 17-ton bulk alumina hopper wagon (E52957) of the open-door mineral conversions, with wooden body on a steel underframe; and also an ex-LMS express fish van (M40476) and a LNER 6-wheeled end door CCT(D) car carrier still in brown livery on a steel channel underframe. Soon one of those reasons for the West Highland's existence came into sound and sight – and smell – a fish special for London, 8.45 from Mallaig, hauled by 2–6–0 61774 *Loch Garry*. It ran smartly through to allow a K2/2 No 61764 (Saturday's pilot from Glasgow) to back onto what was now the up end, the brake van switched ends, and off the load went no doubt to be sold at Billingsgate first thing next morning.

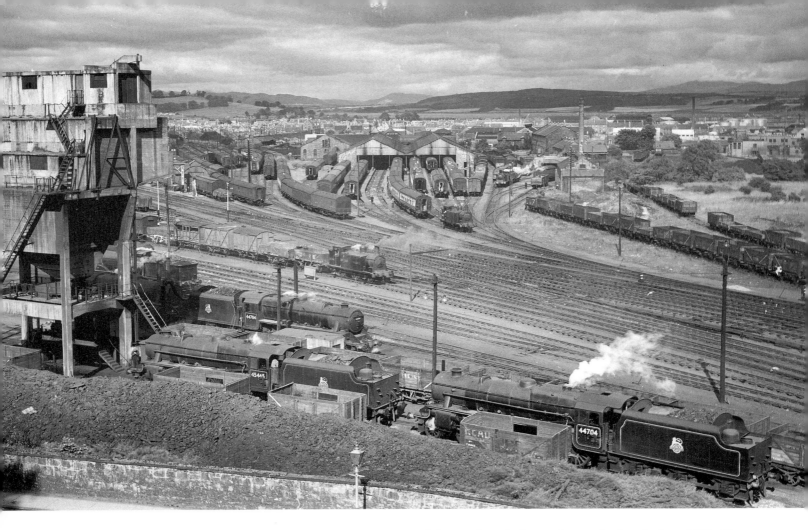

Part of the Inverness shed yard and the carriage shed, on 28 July 1952. Three Stanier class 5 4–6–0s Nos 44784, 45465 and 44704 commendably clean, cluster round the concrete coaling plant (installed in 1935). Ex-CR 0–6–0T No 56341 gets on with some shunting beyond, while two sister engines are active in the distance.

Surprise, surprise, rain interrupted play, and only one more photograph could be taken – and that in poor light – of the West Highland, at Inverlochy Bridge where No 61789 *Loch Laidon* piloting 61790 *Loch Lomond* on the 1.5 express from Mallaig made a stirring sight. It was next Saturday before weather and personal arrangements made it possible to be seriously interested again… and what a day. At 10.2 the early morning express from Glasgow appeared under the bridge near the connection to the aluminium works at Inverlochy, headed by Thompson class B1 4–6–0 61334 piloting class K2/2 2–6–0 61781 *Loch Morar*. At 10.50 No 61786 came up the 1 in 59 with an up Saturday empty coaching stock working, under class F instead of the usual C class; F denoted express freight or ballast train not fitted, and one wondered whether the stock had suffered a brake failure. At 11.10 61993 *Loch Long* headed an up non-fitted express goods.

Then a gap until 12.25 when K4, No 61998, *MacLeod of MacLeod* came through with a down goods.

Then to Inverlochy viaduct and a locally-based K4, No 61995, *Cameron of Lochiel*, ran past with the 1.05 from Mallaig paired with the usual high-sided LNER tender (whereas the K2/2s were paired with Great Northern ones). No 61789 *Loch Laidon* was on the 3.00 express up fish, and 100 minutes later returned on a train of down empty fish vans. This was photographed just short of Banavie swing bridge as the locomotive was about to pass the ladderless lattice girder Banavie up home, with Ben Nevis still with some snow in the background. Then it was the turn of 61995 *Cameron of Lochiel*, still in LNER apple green and bearing the company's initials on the tender, to reappear – on the 4.50 Fort William to Mallaig, a four-coach mixture of Gresley and BR mark 1 stock in carmine and cream. The day was nearly all LNER including sleeping and restaurant cars, though one Black Five appeared on an express to Glasgow. While there were long gaps in movements even on a summer Saturday, the fact that there was an extra passenger to and from the south, and the fish and freights ran as on any other weekday, and that the disposal of a long train arriving at Fort William and the making up of an express south with through carriages (but not all) from Mallaig with the addition of extra coaches and restaurant car (and sleepers) inevitably involved several movements, there was a great deal of interest. It was almost as though the terminus served two different routes. By the day's end the sidings were full, as indeed was the locomotive depot, so chock-a-block that you could not sensibly photograph a single engine. The day's last memory is of sitting on the lochside seeing the final train set out for Mallaig, its plume of steam leaving a great arc as it headed first east, then north and finally west into the slowly setting sunlight.

Incidentally at this time over a hundred railwaymen were employed at Fort William, where the aluminium works received 1,800 tons of alumina a week from Burntisland plus a large tonnage of pitch and coke for making carbons for the electric furnaces. Up to 800 tons of aluminium ingots left weekly.

Then from LNER country to LMS one at Inverness where nationalisation had yet seemed to make little difference. The first train seen was hauled by McIntosh ex-Caledonian 3F 0–6–0 tank, built in St Rollox works in 1905...a shunting movement of course, of which there seemed many at the V-shaped station with the Rose Street curve completing a triangle, and a splendid display of upper quadrants. Many trains were hauled by Black Fives, such as No 45479 heading the afternoon express to Glasgow Buchanan Street, and No 45365 arriving from Wick, taking the curve and backing into the station's southern arm. Points of interest included the famous

Highland Railway TPO Sc 30321, built at Inverness in 1918; it still ran to Dingwall on the morning departure for Wick and was stabled in the bay platform, postman still busy sorting, till continuing its journey to Kyle of Lochalsh.

Another Black Five, 45090, came onto the Rose Street curve past Rose Street box with a class K stopping goods. The fireman was at his cab with the token for though most Highland routes had long been equipped with automatic token exchange, the curve was not. An LMS tubular post signal at the platform end beside two Highland lattice ones, one bearing a pressed steel arm and the other a short shunt signal arm (also upper quadrant) completed a nostalgic scene. A few minutes later another Black Five, 45123, swung round Rose Street curve with a northbound class H through freight, and then Pickersgill ex-Caledonian 72 (3P) 4–4–0 No 54487 added the delight

Saughton Junction, Edinburgh controlled the parting of the ways for the Glasgow and Aberdeen routes. Class D49/1 4–4–0 No 62713 Aberdeenshire *with Walschaerts valve gear, has charge of a surprisingly lengthy stopping train, the 3.43pm Edinburgh Waverley–Thornton Junction, on 3 July 1954. The Aberdeen and Glasgow routes were linked by crossovers in each direction.*

taking the curve with a Tain–Inverness semi-fast that backed into the station's southern arm. Next it was another Black Five 45138 in BR lined 'blackberry black' on the 10.45 from Kyle of Lochalsh, the first vehicle being then restaurant car that had swopped from down to up train at Achnasheen, a twelve-wheel job of LNWR vintage that must have given its customers a smooth ride. Again the signalman picked up the token loop from the fireman and the train backed into the station's southern arm, for

Seen from a southbound train, ex-NBR Reid class J37 0–6–0 No 64551, a Polmont engine, picks its way through the Forth Bridge girders on 8 June 1951 with nothing more than a brake van in tow, despite the 'through freight' headlamps.

the convenience of passengers continuing south.

It was only five minutes later that another Pickersgill rounded Rose Street curve from the south under clear signals. This was No 54470 of a different sub-class to the one 'bagged' earlier, this being of the earlier 1916 build and designated class 113 and 928 by the Caledonian. It was in charge of a local from Keith which backed into platform 5 on the station's northern arm. Finally before time for refreshment at 2.35 the 8.35 from Wick came in under lowly B headcode but with a staffed Travelling Post Office of Highland Railway origin as its first vehicle behind yet another Black Five, No 45365, its coaches a mixture of LMS red and carmine and cream (or blood and custard) and almost full, most passengers indeed making an across-platform change at the station's southern arm for their continuing journey south. To allow this to happen, the previous arrivals had been disposed of rapidly.

Stirling provided a lot less variety, indeed of the first nine trains recorded eight had the ubiquitous Black Fire workhorse of the Highland and Callander & Oban lines, whether it be the St Mungo for Aberdeen, an express to Inverness, oil trains with their obligatory two 'barrier' wagons, or locals...but fine work they seemed to be making, with smart get aways whatever the load. The one exception was a Thompson B1 61341 with a parcel train for Aberdeen, leaving one wondering whether it would travel via Dundee or take the road for Stanley Junction and Forfar.

Sure enough another Black Five turned up, on the Special TPO, 3.30pm from Aberdeen, (consisting of two TPOs, two TPO stowage vans) all in LMS livery with side corridors and with marker lights on the TPO sides fitted with picking up nets and dropping gear, plus a full brake van for the guard in carmine and cream, which left smartly to head down the main line through Motherwell. A double-headed Black Five had a contrast of 44955 in grubby condition, 'British Railways' just showing through the grime on the tender, piloted by a smart 45464 nicely polished and with the Mark 1 'totem' on the tender. They were on an Aberdeen–Glasgow express, blowing off steam heartily before a rapid departure.

Three years later on, and little has changed, the variety if possible greater in the Edinburgh area. Back to North Queensferry station and along the footpath over the tunnel to the rails at the other end, and first on the scene was a V1 2–6–2T No 67610 rounding the curve near the tunnel mouth with an up local from Dunfermline, followed by V2 2–6–2 60838 on the 9.43am from Dundee, and then a Robinson 1920 design D11/2 4–4–0 No 62681 *Captain Craigengelt* with the 10.56 Thornton Junction to Waverley. The last two had burnt smokebox doors.

Through the cutting close to the viaduct at the end of the 'inner bay' near Inverkeithing on which there were shipbreaking yards, a Riddles ex-WD Austerity class 8F 2–8–0 No 90513 came into view with an up H class fitted freight of 38 mixed wooden and steel-bodied trucks plus van, the ensemble banked by ex-NBR Reid (1908 design) J35/4 0–6–0 No 64513. The banker did not seem to be

helping much and the train was struggling at no more than 15mph, but another freight came through more rapidly with a Reid as train engine and banker. Next in this varied procession was a D49/1 Shire 4–4–0 No 62713 *Aberdeenshire* with an ex-GC tender, on a Thornton Junction–Waverley stopper. Then an A2 No 60534 *Irish Elegance* romped up the bank with the morning Aberdeen–Edinburgh express, the Haymarket locomotive beautifully polished.

Then at the south end of the cutting an A3 No 60041 *Salmon Trout*, followed on a Perth–Waverley express, and another Austerity based at Thornton MPD (62A) with an E express freight rattling over the catch points a few yards from the tunnel mouth.

Now a turn to the south of Edinburgh, catching a local to Joppa shortly after the Queen of Scots Pullman had left. The local ran via the Abbeyhill station loop, and then it was a walk to Monktonhall, down in a deep cutting with a nice overbridge when the Heart of Midlothian raced by with a highly polished A2 No 60529 *Pearl Diver*. Down to Monktonhall Junction and a class C express freight for

With a white feather at the safety valves, Gresley class V1 2–6–2T No 67610 fights her way up the 1 in 70 from Inverkeithing to North Queensferry tunnel and the Forth Bridge with the 10.51am Dunfermline Upper–Edinburgh local on 29 June 1954. In the background are the installations of Rosyth naval dockyard. The short track alongside the engine is linked to the catchpoints which derailed a sleeping car train three months earlier when it ran back after the engine slipped to a standstill in the tunnel; the object behind the bufferstops is part of a coach bogie from that accident.

Niddrie yard about three miles further north was in the charge of V2 2–6–2 No 60927, and another V2, this time 60818, headed a down class C freight from Maiden Lane yard at King's Cross. A highlight of the day was the passing of the down 9.30am King's Cross Elizabethan with A4 No 60009 *Union of South Africa* in gleaming BR lined green and carrying a sort of 'Springbok' emblem on the third cladding sheet of the boiler. The fireman was shovelling coal, possibly for this journey's last time.

Failure on Drumochter

Locomotive failures on trains have always been rareties but these shots of an ailing Black Five show that they do sometimes occur. Importantly to the passenger matters should be dealt with as swiftly as practically possible, in this case little time was lost over and above the struggle up the hill at a snails pace. As soon as the passing loop at Dalnaspidal was reached the ex Caledonian 4–4–0 was switched to the front of the train for the short sharp climb to the summit at Drumochter and the run down to Aviemore giving first aid in a minimum time and the photographer an unusual set of pictures.

A Glasgow and Edinburgh to Inverness train nears Drumochter summit in August 1953 hauled by an ailing LMS class 5 No 45496 of the 1943/4 Derby built batch, and banked by Caledonian Railway Pickersgill 72 class 4–4–0 No 54494 (CR No 90) built at St Rollox in 1920. The second coach appears to be a former Great North of Scotland Railway corridor brake composite.

The rear of the same train showing the bank engine which was doing most of the work.

By the time the photographer had run back to the 'old' A9 road and driven to Dalnaspidal the bank engine had transferred to the front of the train to assist the cripple either to Aviemore or possibly through to Inverness.

3
THE CALEY'S BREAD AND BUTTER

Unloved But Cared For

Think of Scotland's least-loved locomotive type and you will probably settle for the NB type 2 diesels. Their reliability record was rock bottom, and when those stationed in England were moved across the border 'to be closer' to their builders, nobody was at all happy. Indeed, that the streamlined Pacifics had their Indian Summer on the Glasgow–Aberdeen expresses was largely due to the type 2s having so frequent breakdowns when they were tried on that prestige service. The Pacifics were almost literally rescued from the scrap heap.

Yet every cloud has a silver lining, and this was the fine work done on the class by Inverurie works. The former GNSR section had an allocation of twenty, and only those who experienced the inadequacies of the class can relish the full pride behind the claim by the works manager that he once had all twenty simultaneously at work for an entire twenty four hours.

Eventually all 58 were entrusted to Inverurie. There was great joy when it was announced that some were to have Paxman engines. Even Caley adherents admitted that the former GSNR works did a much better job than St Rollox, though that is where they (the re-engined ones not that much more reliable than the rest) ended up.

THE Caledonian Railway was universally referred to with affection as The Caley. Even thirty years into BR days the public address system at Glasgow Central Low Level station, just after its re-opening, was wont to announce trains for Motherwell which would be calling at Bridgeton Caley, rather than its correct title of Bridgeton Cross.

The classic romantic view of the Caley was the straight section on the main line at Rockcliffe, a few miles short of Carlisle, well known as the location of photographs of such prestige trains as The Corridor, the afternoon service from Glasgow Central to London Euston. Shining blue locomotives with passenger stock conjured up a romantic view of railways, the romance of long distance travel.

This was the Caley's shop window, but it was not what buttered the parsnips. That was the incessant but unromantic stream of coal trains that came out of the Lanarkshire coalfield branches to feed the steel works, factories and homes of the Central Lowlands.

Towards the end of last century there were some 250 pits in Lanarkshire and they poured out seventeen million tons of coal per annum on to the railway system. The vast majority of this, some twelve million tons, was carried by the Caley. Processions of coal trains and vast sidings with row after row of coal wagons were a regular feature of the Lanarkshire landscape. Ross Yard, in the Clyde valley at Ferniegair handled 4,000 loaded wagons each day on round-the-clock shifts; working timetables from the turn of the century show a continuous flow of coal traffic, many signal boxes being open continuously.

Picture the scene at Hamilton Central as late as the 1950s, even though the coalfield was now in almost terminal decline. It was still a busy station then, with two platform lines and two centre through roads, and there was always something moving, if only the 0–6–0T station pilot. There were the passenger trains to and from Glasgow, with the occasional service for Strathaven and Coalburn. But what imprinted itself on the memory was the sound and fury of the coal trains from Ross Yard, charging through the centre road to get a good run at the 1 in 76 grade up to Hamilton West, a Caley Jumbo 0–6–0 leading, sparks flying from its chimney, the crew lit by the glow from the open firebox door as the fireman shovelled for all his worth. The click click of the wheels of the loose coupled wagons on the rail joints and the clatter of fallen brake handles gave way to the roar of another Jumbo banking at the rear, live coals streaming from its chimney. The clunk of the signal arm dropping back was almost drowned by the sound of the train on the grade, only gradually fading into the distance.

Sometimes the coal train was held on the centre road to allow a

Glasgow bound passenger service to precede it, inevitably a rake of grubby non-corridors headed by a Fairburn 2–6–4T. After the passenger train was on its way there would be a clang of bells from the signal box, the crash of levers, the exchange of whistles between the train engine and the banker, the sound of the couplings taking the strain and the bark of the locomotives as they attacked the grade.

Coal helped make the Caley the great company that it was. Although only a small part of the total system, the lines serving the Lanarkshire coalfields enjoyed a runaway prosperity in the latter part of last century and the early part of this, their traffic contributing to the massive revenues that made the Caley rich. The coal traffic from the Lanarkshire lines was the Caley's bread and butter – the passenger traffic was just the icing on the cake! The opposite of BR today.

As early as 1853, a group of local businessmen had formed the Lesmahagow Railway Company and obtained an Act of Parliament to

Conversation piece 20 May 1947. Against a background of McIntosh 812 class 0–6–0 No 17568 (ex-CR No 830) outside Motherwell shed, the preparing driver pauses from his oiling, feeder and cotton waste in hand, to discuss weighty matters with a colleague. The engine, a Neilson Reid product of 1899, has been fitted with vacuum brake – note the very long brake hose – and steam heating for passenger work. These engines regularly worked out of the nearby Ross Yard with colliery trips.

Walking Signalmen

The job of signalman conjures up a picture of a self-contained existence in a snug box, but for many Scottish bobbies it involved everlasting walking. Numerous crossing stations had separate cabins at either end of the loop, the block instrument usually being in or near the booking office: no wonder the signalman at each station tried to persuade the next one down the line that *it* would be more convenient for crossing extra or late-running trains.

One of the busiest walkers must have been the signalman at Slochd Crossing at the summit of the direct Aviemore–Inverness line, 1,315ft above sea level, approached by steep gradients on either side. Trains were piloted from Aviemore and Inverness, the pilots returning light engine to their starting point. Until 1944 the layout was controlled by cabins at each end...both worked by one man, based at the south cabin. It was hard to get him on the phone as he was always on his walk.

When a twelve hour day was abolished, five men were appointed between two signalboxes kept continuously open, the odd one spending four hours in each and being allowed two hours for the walk between. That usually meant a five mile or longer section between crossing stations – and rarely a suitable train for an unofficial lift.

When snow made bicycling impossible, many bobbies had to leave home earlier on foot, and there are indeed stories of those who only spent three or four hours at home between arriving home exhausted and setting out again, several days in a row.

build an 18 mile railway from Motherwell, via Larkhall and Auchenheath to Bankend to tap the 63 million tons of coal known to exist in the area. The first seven miles of the line would be on top of a continuous coalfield, with seams totalling up to 30 feet thick. The next three miles was on top of the prized cannel coal in the Auchenheath area and near the terminus at Bankend, the line would enter the unexploited Douglas coalfield. Opened in 1856, the line's purpose was to bring the coal from the pits to a railhead, where it could be distributed or sent onwards for export. Passenger traffic was not considered for another ten years.

As the nation's appetite for coal increased many more lines were built, some financed by the coalmasters themselves. Those built of single track were quickly doubled as traffic mushroomed, the culmination of development being the opening in 1904–5 of a series of lines in the Larkhall, Stonehouse, Strathaven and Lesmahagow area, most of which were dupli-

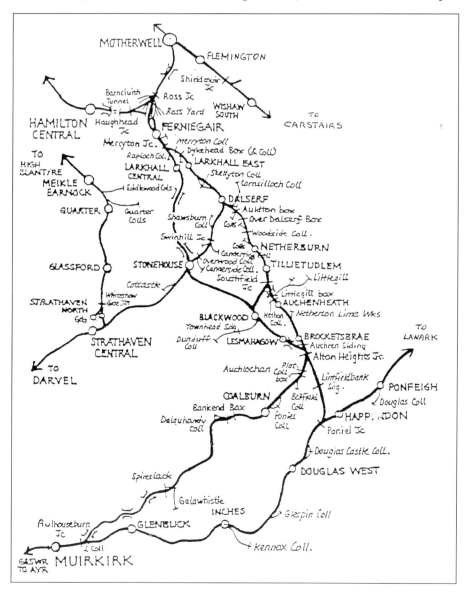

cations of existing Caley lines: an incredibly dense network, there not being a scrap of doubt that the coalfield depended totally on the railway for its very existence as the railway depended on coal.

With such an Eldorado, the Caley naturally fought with all its might to keep usurpers out. The North British had penetrated from Shettleston and Coatbridge to Bothwell and Hamilton, siphoning off a little coal, but that was all. The Glasgow & South Western, not satisfied with its exclusive hold on the Ayrshire coal, had ambitions to get its tentacles into the heart of Lanarkshire and the riches to be won there and was persistent. Muirkirk is now a quiet former iron making and mining town in north eastern Ayrshire, most signs of its industrial past having been landscaped into pleasant open areas, but in the early years of this century the town took on the role of a frontier between the Caley and the G&SW. Since 1873 the latter (from Auchinleck) and the Caley (from Lanark) had made an end-on junction there. Both companies saw Muirkirk as an entry point to their respective territories and both were hell-bent to ensure that the other kept to its own patch, even though relations at local level were amicable enough.

Meanwhile the Caley had extended westwards from the terminus of the Lesmahagow Railway at Bankend, and by 1888 had reached Spireslack, a mere four miles from Muirkirk.

All was not well, however, between the local coalmasters and the G&SW. The coalmasters were becoming disenchanted with the ever increasing rates for conveying their coal to Ayr, and in time decided that enough was enough; they would build their own line and carry their coal themselves. The Muirkirk, Mauchline, Dalmellington & Ayr Railway was promoted and received parliamentary approval in 1895, but a general

Another class 2F hauls a lengthy train out of the loop at Haugh Head Junction with a train from Motherwell towards Hamilton probably in early BR days. The condition of the smokebox and the quality of the exhaust partly masking the tall Caledonian signal reflects on the work performed by these locomotives – no doubt at minimal cost. This particular locomotive had now received vacuum brakes in replacement for the original Westinghouse, the air pump having been removed.

71

LMS 0–6–0 No 17401 (ex-CR 719 of 1896) passes Hamilton shed on 26 February 1949, with trip working No P18. The engine is equipped with Westinghouse air brakes and steam heating apparatus for the occasional passenger working. The cross wind has lifted the cab weather sheet clear of the crew and blown the excess steam from the safety valves sideways. Burnt smokebox doors from the ignited smokebox 'char' seem a common feature of this long lived class 2F.

Fingers Crossed

On the Kyle line, down trains were faced with a vicious four-mile climb from Fodderty Junction (where the Strathpeffer branch diverged) to Raven's Rock summit, at 1 in 50 except for a brief easement through Achterneed station and with much 20-chain curvature.

There was a prohibition on double headed trains in HR days, but some trains were banked to Raven's Rock summit from Dingwall. ...These bankers (pilots in the rear, in HR terminology) detached in section and returned to Achterneed, with no discernable form of protection. In 1921 the whole business was regularised and a banking key was installed at Achterneed, this key being carried by the banker as authority to be in section, the train engine carrying the tablet in the usual way. Before another tablet could be obtained for the section, both the train and the banking key had to be returned to their instruments. – *Highland Railway Journal.*

election was called, Parliament dissolved and the Act fell before it could receive Royal assent. When the bill was re-presented to the new Parliament it had two important amendments, both of which made the G&SW see red (or blue?). Firstly the line was to be worked by the Caley and secondly it had to have a four mile extension from Muirkirk into the hills to connect with the Caley at Spireslack, with a spur from the extension to connect with the Caley's Lanark line. The new amendments would allow the Caley to penetrate deep into traditional G&SW, but the Act reached the statute book in 1896. However, before construction work on the line began, the G&SW reduced their rates and managed to persuade the coalmasters to abandon the bill and all appeared well again in Muirkirk.

But they were not! Like a bad dream, the Muirkirk to Spireslack line would not go away and continued to haunt the G&SW. It appeared again the same year in the Caley's Mid-Lanark Lines Act of 1896, this time as part of a through line from Muirkirk to Darvel via Coalburn, Blackwood and Strathaven, a mixture of existing lines and new construction. To disarm G&SW opposition the Caley included a clause granting them running powers over the lines in the Act *when they were completed.*

The G&SW Board must have thought Christmas has come early! The Caley had a near monopoly of the lucrative Lanarkshire coal traffic, yet were going to allow them access at least some way into their traditional territory! They should have smelt something fishy.

The other lines authorised by the 1896 Act were opened in 1905, but the section from Auldhouseburn Junction, just east of Muirkirk, to Spireslack, an expensive line to build over difficult country, mainly on a 1 in 50 grade and with three large viaducts, although completed in every respect, was never submitted for inspection to the Board of Trade and was abandoned by Act of Parliament in 1910. The popular story is that the

Caley, to protect its monopoly position, never *intended* to use the Muirkirk to Spireslack line, but built it at considerable cost, then intentionally abandoned it, so preventing the G&SW from exercising its running powers. Romantic as the story may be, a much more plausible explanation is that there was a geological fault in the Spireslack area which caused any attempted sinking of mine workings to flood; the Caley would have used the line had mining proved feasible. This is perhaps supported by recent history, in that the last traces of the route are being swept away by a vast opencast coal development at Dalquhandy, stretching from just outside Muirkirk, right over the hills to Coalburn.

The Muirkirk to Spireslack line was not the Caley's ace card for keeping the G&SW out of their territory. They had other plans which would have been much more cost effective. The real dirty trick was in fact carried out at Stonehouse, where a short spur, one side of a triangle that would have allowed through running from Blackwood to Strathaven, was only partially completed. Points were not put in at the Strathaven end and the spur was used only as a double track siding with access from the Blackwood end. Thus were the G&SW's expectations of running powers into the coalfield thwarted while the Caley achieved the end result that it wanted, but not quite in the way it had planned.

The coal traffic peaked during World War I, then began to recede fast. Built on the prosperity of coal, the Lanarkshire lines also quickly faded into oblivion. Some of the pits in the Quarter area were worked out as early as 1910, all of the pits in Hamilton had gone by the mid 1930s. Then only the dwindling passenger traffic, never heavy at the best of times, was

Beattock station in the 1950s was a hive of activity round the clock. Here one of Motherwell's WD 2–10–0s pulls out of the down sidings with a through freight for Mossend banked in the rear by a 2–6–4 tank to Beattock Summit. Twenty-five of these locomotives were retained by BR and all were allocated to the Scottish Region mainly working over the ex-Caledonian lines. Many interesting features have been captured in this scene. The neat four-wheeled coach in the siding to the left, the low sided wagon being pushed by manpower near the Moffat bay platform and a wheel and axle set in the second wagon of the freight train. Behind the ex-Caledonian North box, Beattock shed is the smoky home for the small group of engines spending their lives pushing on the ten mile climb to the summit and returning light engine.

Mountain Railway

Despite plans for one up Ben Nevis, Scotland is usually presumed to have lacked a mountain railway. But there was in fact one: from the Dalmunzie Hotel at Spittal of Glenshee up Glen Lochsie, and was still carrying guests up and the beasts they shot back down the zig-zag route (no cog) until 1974, well after the Beeching closures. Two miles long, of 30in gauge, it had two petrol engines, appropriately called *Dalmunzie* and *Glenlochsie*. You can still see the railway's remnants including a carriage at the hotel. Closure came because the cost of safety work was prohibitive.

left. Stations were inconveniently sited and new bus services took away most of what business there was.

Between 1935 and 1968 the Lanarkshire lines were decimated. First to go was that between Dalserf and Stonehouse in 1935, followed by that between Strathaven and Darvel as a wartime economy measure in 1939. Blantyre to Strathaven via Quarter surprisingly survived the war, but closed immediately afterwards in 1945. Passenger services on the original Lesmahagow Railway to Brocketsbrae ceased in 1951, Lanark to Muirkirk closed in 1964 and the last passenger trains in the area ran in 1965 when those from Hamilton to Larkhall, Stonehouse, Strathaven, Lesmahagow and Coalburn were withdrawn.

The last pit in the area was Auchlochan Colliery at Coalburn which managed to survive until, on 12 July 1968, the last coal train left; that marked the end of an era that had spanned 112 years. All that is now left of that once vast network of lines is the six mile section between Blantyre and Motherwell via Hamilton. Its half-hourly electric trains funded by Strathclyde Transport are efficient, but they hardly conjure up the excitement of a pair of Jumbos noisily struggling to lift coal out of Ross Yard.

Neither LMS Nor LNER

You could fill several books with the detailed histories of Scottish industrial lines, many of which had no allegiance to a 'main' company. There were indeed some collieries that could send their coal out by different systems so as to avoid the risk of being at the end of monopoly treatment. This piece is more about the oddities, but in passing the extensive Monklands system to Scotland's own gauge of 4ft 6in (though it appeared elsewhere as on the Plymouth & Dartmoor Railway) is mentioned elsewhere in these pages.

There was also a 4ft 4in gauge system. The Fordell Railway in Fife ran from Alice Pit near Crossgates lying between Dumfermline and Cowdenbeath, via Fordell village to the small harbour of St Davids on the Firth of Forth, a distance of 5¾ miles. It served several collieries on the way, and crossed under the North British's main line between Inverkeithing and Aberdour.

Like several other such lines it was of early origin, dating back to the second half of the eighteenth century when it was a wooden waggonway. Wood was replaced by malleable iron rails in 1833, but locomotives had to wait until 1873 after the adoption of steel rails in 1868.

A new pit, the Alice, was sunk near the NBR's Dunfermline to Cowdenbeath line in 1880, giving a connection with the outside world by a siding of mixed gauge, only 4½ inches different. Waggons were similar to chauldrons used in England's North East, though they carried only 48cwt to the English 53½. The last shipment of coal from St Davids was on 10 August 1946, after which most of the line was taken up and remainder absorbed by the National Coal Board and converted to standard gauge,

finally closing in 1966. The NCB was of course a major railway operator. The story of many coal and iron railways (such as in the Dalmellington area) is as fascinating as it is complicated. A good example is the once-busy Wemyss Private Railway, linking several collieries on the Wemyss estate north of Kirkcaldy with the port of Methil on the north of the Firth of Forth. Coal was its sole traffic, hauled in sizeable trainloads by Austerity and other 0-6-0Ts.

More understandably romantic were waterworks railways, Scotland's most extensive being that built by Edinburgh's water department in the 1890s linking Broughton station on the Symington–Peebles branch with construction sites of new reservoirs in upper Tweeddale. It had a short life with only a single day of real passenger service since once the water works were completed and ceremoniously opened it was promptly dismantled. But it has left a legacy of earthworks and bridges which often mystify travellers on the A701 where there remains a 'dog leg' where it crossed the main line.

Shipbuilding yards also had their private systems. Picture a little green steeple-cab electric locomotive venturing out of the Fairfield shipyard gate and scampering along the tram tracks of Glasgow Corporation to Govan goods depot to bring back supplies of steel. This little gem is now in the keeping of the Scottish Railway Preservation Society at Bo'ness. There may have been a certain sameness about the railways that ended up as LMS or LNER, but among the railways that belonged to neither camp, variety was the name of the game.

Perhaps the best known oddity was the very Scottish 'Duke of Sutherland connection'. Successive Dukes had an agreement with the Highland Railway (which the family did much to promote) for the use of a train even for shop-

The classic shot of the *Campbeltown & Machrihanish Light Railway 0–6–2T* Atlantic *awaiting the arrival of steamer passengers at Campbeltown Harbour on 2 August 1930. The ship is an early Clyde puffer with open bridge.*

A very rare period piece, the Campbeltown & Machrihanish Light Railway's publicity postcard advertising the train service which connected with the Caledonian Steam Packet Co's steamer from Gourock.

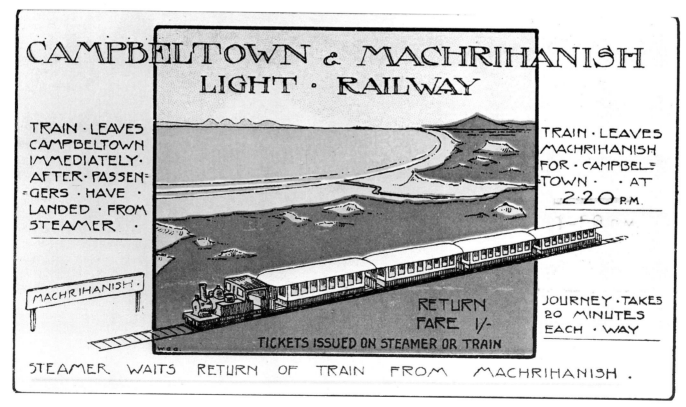

75

The Fordell Railway, unlike the Wemyss Private Railway, was taken over by the National Coal Board and locomotive No 4 (NCB No 37) built by Andrew Barclay & Company of Kilmarnock is seen at the tunnel mouth approaching St David's harbour in March 1949. The locomotive was of squat build to suit the low bridges on the line.

ping expeditions to Inverness. There were two engines, both named *Dunrobin* after the Ducal castle.

The first was a 2–4–0T built by Kitson & Co of Leeds in 1870 which was sold to the Highland in 1895 becoming HR No 118 *Gordon Castle* and withdrawn in August 1923 without entering LMS stock. The second Ducal locomotive *is* an 0–4–4T designed by David Jones of the Highland and built by Sharp Stewart & Co at Glasgow in 1895. This was kept in a small shed at Golspie and used, infrequently, to haul guests in one of two private saloons between Dunrobin (private station) and Inverness.

Dunrobin (II) was seconded on loan to the Highland Railway from 1916 to 1918–19 for shunting purposes probably at Invergordon and/or Alness. During World War II it entered temporary LMS service again shunting at Invergordon as well as Rosyth and Dalmuir. After some negotiation BR withdrew permission for the special working over its lines and *Dunrobin* together with the smaller of the private saloons was sold for preservation ending up at New Romney on the Romney Hythe & Dymchurch Railway in March 1950. There they stayed for 10 years before being sold to Canada.

The small four wheeled saloon No 58A was built at Lochgorm works in 1909 and was the one usually used between Dunrobin and Inverness. The eight wheel bogie saloon was a grand affair built at the LNWR works at Wolverton in 1899: this was allowed much further afield, regularly finding its way to Euston when the erstwhile Duke visited London. It was numbered 57A and was the prototype for the magnificent LNWR Royal saloons of 1902. A vehicle of some historic merit No 57A now resides in the National Railway Museum at York.

Scotland's only narrow gauge passenger line (until the current preservation scene) was the Campbeltown & Macrihanish Light Railway some six and a half miles long and far from any standard gauge railway; it was born in 1877. It began as a mineral line from a colliery at Kilkivan running to a depot in Campbeltown. By 1881 this pit had become exhausted and the 2ft 3in gauge tracks were extended to a new mine at Drumlemble to form the basis of the Campbeltown & Macrihanish. In reality the line began at Campbeltown pier where the Clyde steamers came in and crossed the narrow neck of Kintyre where the Atlantic rollers roared into Macrihanish Bay. Passenger services began in 1906 and ceased in November 1931 shortly after the pit's closure in 1929. Road competition and the scarcity of passenger traffic in later days, when tourists had swopped golf for motorcars, made this end inevitable.

The C&M passenger trains were worked by two handsome 0–6–2Ts built by Andrew Barclay in 1906 and 1907. Each carried a name – *Argyll* and *Atlantic*. They were painted olive green, lined out in yellow, black and vermilion. The olive green and cream coaches were bogie saloons with open end platforms, centre corridors and measured 43ft 6ins over headstocks. They were, perhaps, rather too long for the sharp curves.

Other true narrow gauge systems were those owned by the British Aluminium Co at its plants at Kinlochleven and Fort William. Both of these were 3ft 6ins. The shorter of the two connected the Kinlochleven factory with a wharf at the lochside and was worked by overhead wire electric locomotives using 500 volts dc. This closed in 1960.

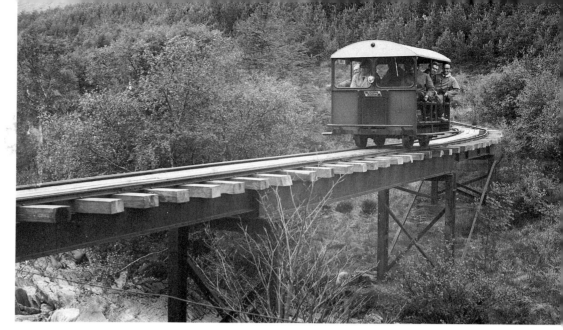

The British Aluminium Company's three foot gauge line climbed to a summit of 1120ft and crossed a number of valleys on trestle bridges. A Wickham trolley for a special party is crossing one of these trestles on 5 June 1971.

The terminus of the British Aluminium line at the north end of Loch Treig 825ft above sea level on 5 June 1971. The West Highland line runs along the east side of the Loch.

The Wemyss Private Railway relied on large 0–6–0Ts for its pseudo main line and No 18 built by Andrew Barclay & Company of Kilmarnock heads a coal train from Michael Colliery to Methil on 2 June 1966, consisting of NCB wagons.

There were a number of collieries in the Doon Valley between Ayr and Dalmellington and their sidings and lines were, until the 1960s, worked by steam locomotives. On 27 May 1963 0–6–0T No 17 built by Andrew Barclay & Co of Kilmarnock is seen hauling a loaded coal train at Craigmark en route to Waterside where the wagons were handed over to BR.

The Fort William line was built to assist with the construction of a dam at Loch Treig whence hydro electric pipe lines ran to the works which generated its own electricity. It was nineteen miles from dam to factory and twenty one to the pier on Loch Linnhe. Most of the railway was retained after the dam was completed carrying materials for maintenance purposes. The motive power was varied, steam, diesel and battery electric locomotives were used as well as Wickham petrol trolleys which comprised the 'passenger' trains. Final closure came in 1977 due to a changed freight flow (making the pier line redundant) and washouts on the upper section.

In the remote Orkneys there were two separate lines used by contractors engaged in raising sunken German ships from the bottom of Scapa Flow whilst towards the conclusion of World War I it was intended to construct an extensive harbour as well as a Royal Naval hospital at Lyness, a small village on the island of Hoy. Considerable blasting and excavation took place in connection with these works and lines were laid down to take away the spoil. Two locomotives are known to have been involved in these far north lines, a Hudswell Clarke & Co 0–4–0 saddle tank said to have been involved in the construction of the Aviemore line of the Highland Railway (fixing the date as 1861–63) though the only particulars visible on the locomotive during its time on Orkney were on a plate marked 'Rebuilt by A. Barclay & Co Ltd 1902'. The other was a Hunslet 0–6–0T built in 1892 for HM Government which was originally employed on the Peterhead Harbour line carrying granite and other materials needed for the building of the huge breakwater using convict labour from the nearby prison.

4
THE SCOTTISH
COUNTRY RAILWAY

LONG platforms and even longer loops, solid yet mellow stone buildings, well-kept signals and footbridges, often colourful gardens and arrays of posters, even more concentrated activity between longer lulls than was normal in England. The Scottish country station, built for posterity and managed as the most important trading post for miles around, has always been attractive. Many happily survive in good order still in business and others closed as interesting monuments of a different commercial age.

Like their southern counterparts, they reflected the character and trade of their patch, but the difference was of course in the size of that patch. While those congregating at most English stations came from a similar background, in remoter Scotland those from totally different geographies and ways of life jostled for the porter's attention or best seats. And with rapid changes in the terrain, often adjoining stations might as well have been hundreds of miles apart for all their appearance and traffic had in common.

Whatever their role in life, most stations fitted well into their individual environment. The use of local stone helped, but geography often dictated a picturesque position in the glens or beside lochs. On a long journey, especially if you had travelled from England overnight, just momentarily to step on the platform surrounded by heather-clad hills and breathe the fresh air was to experience Scotland.

Most of the country lines fell in two distinct categories: they were very long, with varied claims to main-line status and through traffic, or very short...like apple trees pruned the old-fashioned way with well-spaced (but occasionally overlapping) branches and short fruit-bearing spurs. The English naturally mainly experienced the first category and were struck by the sheer scale (311 rail miles from Stirling to Thurso) but sometimes had the doubtful pleasure of changing to a branch off the branch to reach places like Banff or Killin. Many junctions only existed as such, not serving worthwhile local communities; several such as Killin were indeed strictly changing places with no public access. You had to leave by train.

For most of the year, the Scottish country railway ticked over like clockwork, but unusual not to mention disastrous occasions upset the pattern all too soon: bad weather (much publicised but actually infrequent), Glasgow Fair and other holidays (very disruptive but lucrative), derailments and breakdowns far from help, and umpteen local events that just occasionally brought the whole world and his wife to nearly every station in turn. Relief shunters and porters moved on from one over-taxed station to another, the local men (especially the stationmaster) enjoying temporary importance but being pleased when normal routine returned.

Helping Hands

The Highland Railway's severe gradients brought a need for assisting engines, usually on the front of the train. The following extracts from an article by David Stirling in the *Highland Railway Journal* show that it was not always a straightforward operation.

When the pilot was detached before the summit the evidence is that the normal practice was to remove it without stopping the train, the pilot being uncoupled on the move and running smartly ahead of the train into the 'wrong' line at Dava, Dalwhinnie or Dalnaspidal, all of which were then crossing places on the single line. The road was reset for the pilot and changed again once it was inside. For a few years Dalnaspidal even had a special signal for the movement of northbound pilot engines into the wrong line. Of course, this seems outrageous to modern observers, but in earlier times it was by no means peculiar to the HR. It was certainly hazardous for the fireman who had to climb forward to uncouple the engines.

In the early years the HR was largely a railway of tender engines, which had to be turned to run chimney first on passenger trains. The main points where assisting engines were attached, Forres, Grantown, Newtonmore and Blair Atholl, all had turntables but it was another matter for locomotives detached in between. These had to return light engine, tender first, an unenviable task on a locomotive with a small tender in a

continued page 81

Yet most of the year the same trains approached either end of their appointed crossing loops within seconds of each other, the signalmen controlling the next loops seldom having to fling their levers and rush round with the tokens to save precious seconds. Many loops were rarely used, and when they were it was generally for extra livestock or fish traffic.

When timings went seriously wrong, everyone north of the border assumed it would be the reflection of problems imported over it, or because a ferry was running late. Until the quality of coal and locomotive declined temporarily in both Word Wars and permanently from the mid-1950s, locally-induced delays were genuinely unusual. The enginemen loved their jobs and worked themselves and machines hard when the need arose. Most station work was exemplary, and more than two minutes for crossing usually meant the other train was late or the engine was taking water.

Generous layouts helped; setting back into refuge sidings because the loops were not long enough hardly ever happened in Scotland as it did in parts of England, and the Scot who was delayed on the Cambrian because both trains at a crossing loop had to use the same single platform could hardly believe his eyes. In Scotland both platforms had proper protection from the weather, and fires would be lit in both waiting rooms even though it might be five hours before the next train. Some thought it was a pity there were not more island platforms as on the West Highland or more stations signalled to allow up and down trains to use the main platform when there was no crossing.

Just as stations serving wide areas brought together farmers, fishermen and others from totally different cultures, so many branch trains had passengers making the kind of assortment of journeys you expect to find on a modern air service. The range of opportunities provided by connecting services was incredible. Those aboard slower trains had ample time to satisfy curiosity about each other, and many a farmer improved his technique reviewing the passing crops with someone from another district or experience. Nosily looking round guard's vans or pieces of new-fangled equipment being unloaded from the station truck brought to a stop opposite the parcels office also resulted in the spread of new techniques.

The termini of short branches had their own distinctive culture. The actual despatch of a train seemed an anti-climax after passengers had chatted in the booking hall and the enginemen and guard had put the world right in the signalbox. Most termini were naturally designed for the exceptional rather than everyday traffic, and so much income came from special occasions that it would have been unthinkable to turn business away. But economical curiosities like engines changing ends by the train being allowed to pass by gravity were there for the finding...and extravagant oddities, too, like the mile from Killin to Loch Tay surviving decades after the pier was closed solely to allow the tank engine to reach its shed at the dead end without any siding or point. Wherever there was an engine there were onlookers and, like more conveniently but less splendidly situated sheds, this was a very social coaling and watering place.

But back to the traffic. No railways worked harder to raise it than the Scottish. Even after nationalisation you were made more aware that the

Gleneagles – 'Alight here for Gleneagles Hotel and Golf Course'. On 11 September 1965, BR Standard Pacific No 70003 John Bunyan arrives with the 9.25am from Crewe comprising six coaches and three full brakes for parcels and mail. The loop line tracks had recently been removed and the only service remaining was that on the main line to Perth. The station and gardens were maintained in excellent condition befitting its status as nearly all customers were for the then railway-owned hotel.

continued
winter blizzard. W. Duncan relates a tale he was told in the 1930s by J. Mackay, then near retirement, about returning from Dava to Forres with the old Jones engines; if there was a freezing north wind, the crew would start the engine out of Dava and retire to the comparative shelter of the front buffer beam, using a knife to ease off the front vacuum bag to apply the brake when required. They were a hardy breed in those days!

Thurso yard on 23 August 1960 with ex-Caledonian Railway 4–4–0 class 3P No 54482 leaving with an afternoon freight to Georgemas Junction. The cattle wagons alongside the island platform were representative of the variety of traffic lost by the railways in the 1960s. This typical Highland branch terminus was provided with a wooden overall roof to the station, substantial goods facilities and a small but well built engine shed. In a reversal of roles the passenger service to Georgemas Junction was worked by ex-Caley 3F 0–6–0 No 57587 and the return journey could be undertaken for 2/3d.

railway was a business. Scottish stationmasters did not need to look up their traffic figures. They knew them. This was perhaps especially true on the GNSR system which lacked substantial through traffic but made an honest living serving its proud territory through running few but well-timed passengers and only a single daily freight up many of the branches.

Its stations epitomised the best of the country railway. The staff were men of the countryside, used to working long hours who knew their traffics and their customers intimately. The seasonal rhythm was as strong at these stations as on the farms or at the fishing ports themselves. They ever had an eye on the weather and were indeed often expert forecasters, for tomorrow's workload would depend on what the elements brought. Cleanliness might have been second to godliness but punctuality was close behind. Fools were not suffered lightly, if they spoilt the immaculate cleanliness of waiting room or signalbox or delayed the evening train's departure.

Days of elation were when every point and siding, and that bay platform, thoroughly justified their existence and takings reached a new record. Stationmasters who saw the same empty seats go up and down several times daily waxed lyrical when there was an excess of humans. On many routes it was the decline in the market day crowd that first told of the effectiveness of bus competition. In addition to the seasonal cycle, there was of course the weekly one, Tuesdays to Fridays a market day somewhere, Wednesdays and Thursdays early closing somewhere else, Saturday football and of course the cinema. Edinburgh to Dunbar, North Berwick, the Waverley route, Aberdeen to Fraserburgh and Peterhead (non-stop to Maud), Leadburn to Dolphinton, Inverness to Tain (a full-length formation incredibly crowded so far as Invergordon during both World Wars), Ayr to Dalmellington, Mauchline to Catrine, once even

One of the most famous signalboxes in the world – certainly in relation to its size, because of its key role in the 1895 Races to Aberdeen – Kinnaber Junction is host to a Brechin–Montrose goods trip hauled by ex-NBR class J37 0–6–0 in 1964. Since there was no provision for running round the train at Kinnaber there was a standing authority to propel to Montrose North, despite the 1 in 88/90 falling grade.

Campbeltown to Machrihanish, the busiest trains were often the Saturday night ones after business had ceased other days.

Remember the sounds and smells of those boisterous Saturday night specials? Always a bit more boisterous north of the border, with the wee dram as opposed to beer normally mingling with fish and chips and cheap make-up and the normal local steam train to give an unmistakable whiff in the air. The guard always seemed a touch taller as he called out the stations for those whose alertness was not quite what it had been on the journey into town. The knots of alighting passengers proffering their tickets as though a church collection were being taken were proof that the railway served the community...a proof that the more conscientious and concerned members of staff increasingly looked for to assure themselves things were not so bad as they seemed most of the time. But on many, indeed most, routes they became steadily and then rapidly worse, till those (or their descendants) who had been at the heart of rural life found their jobs irrelevant. Emptying passenger trains and shortening freight ones spelt redundancy, the end of a way of life that in many cases had lasted three or four generations since opening time.

The wonder, as stated in the section on closures, is that so much survived. Modernisation (faster, shorter, more frequent, cleaner trains) as largely responsible for what has been saved, for at their lowest even country lines which vigorously survive today were carrying very reduced traffic.

Let us home in on the North East, a region that provides almost all the ingredients one could desire for a gourmet lunch or dinner. The very name conjures up thoughts of Scotch salmon, Aberdeen Angus beef and Scotch seed potatoes, Baxter's luxury tinned foods, shortbread. In days gone by all these travelled to market by rail, even if the salmon tended to travel singly, enfolded in a matting carrier, with the guard. It was white fish that provided the major flows; cod, haddock, hake and herring. Whereas meat and potatoes were freight-rated and journeyed largely in express goods trains, most fish was passenger-rated and moved faster than many passengers.

Fish from Aberdeen and the area beyond was once enormous business and even by the 1960s still big enough for railways – in contrast to other Scottish ports further south and in the west. But fortunes change, in fishing as in transport; a combination of overfishing in the North Sea, the Icelandic 'cod war', the decimation of the mighty herring and other factors have brought long rail-less Peterhead to the forefront as *the* white fish port, with a corresponding decline in the others.

Many ports are but a shadow of their former selves. The likes of Eyemouth, Pittenweem and Arbroath increasingly serve local and Scottish needs. Ullapool lives by the Russian and Polish factory ships. That has been bad news for railways, which thrived on the long and heavy trunk hauls rather than on the odd van swinging on the back of a passenger train. In 1964, with the aid of outside marketing experts backed by the first moves into traffic costing, BR declared the fish traffic uneconomic and it was abruptly terminated – to outraged howls from the fish merchants' associations.

John Thomas

The first full length manuscript of my publishing career was John Thomas's *The Springburn Story*. Like most English enthusiasts, I had made a couple of forays into Scotland, interrupting tea in the ex-Caledonian wooden-panelled converted Pullman when we crossed trains two days in a row at Loch Awe on route to Oban, wondering at the marvels of the West Highland, utterly unprepared for the Hell-hole of Glasgow Queen Street Low Level in steam days. But I knew nothing about the world John so lovingly portrayed as the world's locomotive capital.

The book, of a kind then almost unknown, was an immediate local best-seller, most copies going through the linen department of Springburn Co-operative Society since great though the industrial complex was it was without bookshop. And then began a unique relationship, John for example writing the Regional Railway History volume on *Scotland: The Lowlands and Borders* (and beginning the *North of Scotland* one before his untimely death) while I had started the series with the West Country one. Many thought we were one and the same person and we were for ever getting each other's mail.

By any standard, John was not only the doyen of Scottish railway historians but a major performer on the national British scene, few titles for example rivalling *The West Highland Railway* in its sheer narrative excitement, people and events ever bought to life by examples and short quotations. Living in one of Springburn's tower blocks (the address 240 Gourlay Street ever remembered by many of his friends) John was a door-to-door insurance salesman and must have cheered the lives of thousands of customers with his ready banter.

Persuading him to become a

continued overleaf

continued
full-time writer took courage but paid off handsomely, his work always being of the best possible quality, based on much original research. Scottish railway historians were lucky that their records were stored in Edinburgh, while wherever you lived in England you had expensively to go to London to consult yours. Without that John (and the world) would have lost a lot.

Quite a few of John's books are kept in print as a tribute to a great author and friend as well as for a genuine continuing demand from the younger generation. During his lifetime I paid a different kind of tribute: John was given a literary lunch on board a restaurant car shunted the length of Springburn's platform while we had our sherry. – D. St J.T.

REMNANT OF THE CALEDONIAN FOREST.

Yet even into the early 1960s Aberdeen was running one heavy fish train to London, the 13.43 SX, supplemented on bumper days by a 12.30, travelling at up to 75mph and Pacific-hauled. Latterly they were composed entirely of 'Blue Spot' fish vans with roller bearing axleboxes to avoid trouble en route, and these were loading up to eight tons apiece. There was a head of two or three similar vans from Fraserburgh – years ago of course one or more complete trains – arriving in Aberdeen on the passenger at about 13.10 and immediately transferred to Guild Street for the London train. It would pick up odd vans on its journey from Edinburgh and elsewhere, and the contents were on sale in Billingsgate market before 05.00.

If BR had a near-monopoly on London fish, it suffered fierce competition from road hauliers to other destinations. The heavy Manchester market flow was lost in the 1950s, leaving only the smaller consignments for towns in Lancashire and Yorkshire that the road people were not interested in. So the 14.15 West Coast fish train was a rag-bag of ex-LMS type six-wheeled vans, their loads divided into six or more separate stacks, often of less than a ton each, for the Blackburns, Burnleys and Skiptons of this world – probably to be unloaded by the sole night-shift porter during a stop in the wee small hours.

It had all been different in the days of the herring. Some surprisingly heavy flows – seasonal, of course – originated in the smaller east coast ports and in Mallaig as the shoals migrated. The picture postcard harbours in the East Neuk of Fife, Crail, Anstruther, St Monen's, Pittenweem, Elie and the rest could be bustling centres which came near to swamping the single line from St Andrews to Thornton Junction. Anything up to six trains a day had to be sent south where odd vans or open fish trucks usually sufficed. Empty vans had to be moved in and Thornton shed combed for power.

Meat provided a much steadier flow. Aberdeen and the Buchan area is a volume producer of high quality beef with a special emphasis on the London market and the south of England. It was carried, hanging, mainly as full sides weighing over 700lb dressed, though with some half sides, and it was fresh, not frozen, ideally kept at about 38°F.

To deal with this flow Aberdeen ran a fast daily meat train to King's Cross Goods at 10.05. It was a solid load of BM containers, loaded at abattoirs in the city and surrounding countryside, travelling on conflats. From midnight the containers were being craned onto lorries at King's Cross for the short haul to Smithfield market. Alas, from the fifties it was neither profitable nor did it give real customer satisfaction against burgeoning competition.

The BM container was too small at four tons capacity and was not particularly hygienic (though nor were some of the abattoirs!). Its only temperature control was by ventilation louvres. The ten-foot wheelbase conflats did not ride well at speed, and the oscillation tended to blacken the fat on the meat as the hung sides rubbed against the container sides and each other. Once or twice a week a conflat suffered a hot box in transit; few were fitted with roller bearings. If lucky this happened somewhere which allowed the container to be quickly transferred to another

wagon and picked up by the King's Cross fish train three hours later. In the early 1960s there was a single bogie conflat in this service, an adapted coach underframe still on its Gresley bogies, which gave the BMs a smooth ride. More of them would have been a godsend, but it remained a loner.

With the opening of the Aberdeen Freightliner terminal in 1969, giving an afternoon service daily to King's Cross, there was new hope for the London meat traffic, even though it spelt the death of the long-running 10.05. A major Aberdeen producer invested in new 20-foot and 30-foot insulated meat containers with automatic temperature control by liquid nitrogen for his beef, markedly raising standards. But Aberdeen proved a frail node for container traffic and road competition with ever larger lorries was intense; they loaded at the abattoir (more than one if necessary to make up a full load), and had mechanical cooling under the driver's supervision at all times. The lorries would load to capacity, then draw forward and stop suddenly; the carcasses closed up on the hanging rails and thus left space for another couple of sides to join them. Various moves to improve rail profitability led to train timings which were less than ideal for Smithfield's selling schedule. Rail transport of meat died before the Aberdeen terminal closed in 1987.

On 28 May 1958, Peppercorn class A2 Pacific No 60527 Sun Chariot *pounds up the 1 in 70 from Inverkeithing to the Forth Bridge with the 1.43pm Aberdeen–King's Cross fish after emerging from the 420 yard Inverkeithing Tunnel. Behind the engine is the shipbreaking yard which saw the end of many famous liners and warships, while the Rosyth dockyard branch is just out of sight below the main line.*

Class A1 No 60161 North British, a Haymarket Pacific, coasts past Burntisland links and slows for the 25mph restriction on the station curve with the 10.05am Aberdeen–King's Cross meat train on 29 May 1958. The load is light, only 12 BM containers and a Vanfit for offal. Unusually the fifth container is loaded in an open wagon instead of a conflat. The diverging tracks lead to Burntisland harbour, which handled imports of bauxite for the nearby British Aluminium Company works.

By comparison with fish and meat, seed potatoes might seem an inert and insensitive traffic: not so, for they needed watchful handling in transit. Produced mainly in Strathmore and the Mearns country, they were usually stored after harvesting on the farms in clamps of straw with earth covering until called for planting from November through the winter months, depending on the weather in eastern England. They were then lifted, bagged and brought by the farmer or agent to a range of country stations to be loaded into Vanfits. These were uplifted daily and conveyed by express freight services, many on to the GN/GE Joint line for distribution.

Great care was taken to protect the potatoes against frost, which would make them valueless as seed. The end ventilators of the vans were blocked with straw, the floor covered with scrap wagon sheets and straw and the sides and ends, especially round the doors, lined with protective straw.

Sheep, Sheep, Sheep

In winter there are now three daily two-car Sprinters each way; in summer four daily services, most of them four-car Sprinters, plus the occasional cruise train specials. In theory it is the best service Lairg in Sutherland has ever enjoyed, and undoubtedly the trains are faster than ever, but go to the station below the village whose shops serve an enormous area of straths and moors and the evidence is of busier bygone days.

Today there is no freight, yet the railway was deliberately swung deeply inland (greatly lengthening the route to Wick and Thurso) so that supplies could be unloaded here and sheep sent away – often by the trainload. O.S. Nock tells of 17 August 1949 when 26,000 Cheviot sheep and lambs left in a single day.

'The regular station staff of three clerks, three porter-signalmen and one porter, in addition of course to the stationmaster, was heavily reinforced for the occasion; an engineer's dormitory carriage provided sleeping accommodation for the extra staff, and loading began at noon. The work continued until dark, by which time four special trains had been despatched. The fifth and last followed early next morning.' The trains totalled 220 trucks, yet the loading bay accommodated only 24 at a time.

Today the station is of course staffless, signalling being by radio token. Seldom is there more than a taxi-full of passengers. Yet it is not so long since the regular staff were kept busy handling parcels, the station probably being railhead to the largest area in the entire country. Even Sunday brought a newspaper train, met by a score of road vehicles, some destined for the furthest north west.

On weekdays half a dozen buses met the morning passenger train. The whole area's oil and petrol
continued on p90

Long-stemmed wheat straw was the most stable, but was becoming unobtainable as farmers changed to short-straw varieties. Loading finished with a top blanket of more straw. Transits were normally within two days, and farmers were notified to collect on arrival.

But claims were frequent. Probably some potatoes were frosted once the clamps were opened and not spotted before loading. Some damage arose in transit if the straw lining collapsed. And it was by no means unusual for a wagon to arrive, say, on 23 December during a cold snap, the farmer too busy with his Christmas decorations to collect until after Boxing Day, and then claim for his potatoes which were frosted!

It is a safe bet that nowadays, when the articulated lorry arrives at his gate with twenty tons of seed, that same farmer does not tell the driver to come back in two days' time because he is busy!

Whatever the mystique about what makes a great whisky, for those in the world of transport what matters is getting the barley or malt into the distillery in good condition, carrying the finished product (in cask or in bottle) safely to its destination, and conveying the waste products to their purchasers. The pre-Grouping companies of course loved the traffic which remained largely faithful to rail until well into BR days.

The old BR Aberdeen District, bounded by Kinnaber Junction, Ballater, Cromdale, Elgin and Fraserburgh, served no less than 52 distilleries and several separate maltings. They were – and remain – mostly small units, few using more than 1,000 tons of malt a year, with a small staff of two dozen or less – and fiercely proud of the reputation of their own whisky.

There is a heavy concentration along the banks of the River Spey, but otherwise they sit, dotted across the countryside from Fettercairn to Glenlivet, the distinctive roof vents of their malthouses seen against a background of wooded valleys and rolling fields. A pleasant aroma wafts from their bonded warehouses. By contrast the grain distilleries, using mass-production patent stills, are usually found in main population centres close to the blending plants.

The malt distilleries, often on cramped sites where available storage area is devoted to the bonded stores in which the whisky is aged (for anything from five to twenty years) rather than the storage of ingredients, were seldom able to receive barley or malt in bulk. Not many distilleries were rail-connected. The Carron stationmaster on Speyside was unique in controlling two such, the Imperial and the better-known Dailuaine with its own 0–4–0 pug for shunting. So much of the barley and malt was brought, bagged, in vanfits from East Anglia and transferred to road motors based at Ballindalloch, Craigellachie, Aberlour and a host of other small stations for delivery. Dufftown, a centre of importance out of all proportion to its 1,500 inhabitants and host to four distilleries and two maltings, of which only one (Glenfiddich) had its own siding, kept three lorries occupied during the winter months and two in summer when the distilleries closed for six weeks or more.

Malt is sensitive to delay and damp in transit, and recipients complained vigorously if it became 'slack', affecting the sugar content of

Speyside in winter. In the early years of nationalisation a smart ex-GNSR class D41 4–4–0 No 62248, a Keith engine, leaves Craigellachie on the afternoon whisky pickup for Aviemore. The track in the foreground is a long headshunt, and the bridge carrying the Elgin line over the Spey can be glimpsed over the train. No 62243 was withdrawn in January 1951.

Grantown on Spey station loop in 1951 sees the crossing of the whisky train, in the hands of class D41 4–4–0 No 62255, and a local passenger train for Craigellachie behind another engine of the same class No 62241. It was almost the swansong of the D41s; within two years both these engines had been withdrawn.

continued
came in by train (that continued until the collapse of the bridge over the Ness at Inverness). Well might the stationmaster have viewed himself as an important functionary; certainly nobody else could better tell the fortunes of the sheep flocks, the crofters, and the fishermen in many a remote cove.

And when it was not Lairg's own turn to provide specials, they frequently came down from Helmsdale, Wick and Thurso, once eleven sheep specials from just Thurso in four days.

The 'Big House'

Often in rural areas a station would be dominated by the 'big house' – a country mansion or even a castle housing an important, occasionally a noble, family. The stationmaster himself was present to attend to their comings and goings, and obsequious porters opened and closed doors... Drymen on the Forth & Clyde had as its big house Buchanan Castle, seat of the Duke of Montrose.

'When there was a reception at the castle the duke sent his men down to the station to erect a canopy over the gate and part of the platform. The NB positioned a horsebox in an adjacent siding for the exclusive use of the duke; in those motorless days he took his coach and horses with him by rail when he travelled any distance. And there is an echo from another age in this instruction to the Drymen stationmaster: 'I am to inform you that the Duke and his suite are travelling to Edinburgh on the 21st inst., to attend the General Assembly of the Church of Scotland. It is desired that the travelling allowance of 100 pounds of luggage per person should be waived in this case.' – John Thomas

the mash fed to the stills. With the prospect of many distilleries becoming remote from a railhead after Dr Beeching had done his worst, Scottish Malt Distillers, a DCL subsidiary and the largest single company in the business, set up a centralised malting plant at Burghead on the Highland's Hopeman branch to produce economies of scale and carry out the process close to the users. In 1965 DCL ordered a fleet of bulk grain wagons of $22\frac{1}{2}$ tons capacity to carry barley to Burghead; these wagons aroused interest from the variety of brand advertising carried on their sides. They have been largely superseded by bogie Polybulk wagons.

The transport of mature whisky from the distillery bonds to the blending plants in Perth, Glasgow, Leith and Kilmarnock was traditionally in hogsheads, loaded on end in open wagons – remarkable, perhaps, for a commodity of such high value on which duty had been paid on leaving the bond. From Speyside it travelled on the much-photographed afternoon freight from Craigellachie to Aviemore behind a Great North of Scotland 4–4–0 or, later, a class 21 diesel. It was carefully supervised in transit, but inevitably there were occasions when not all that left the bond arrived at its destination., 'Incidents' included barrels being broached by a rough shunt – and invariably on dark nights a furtive figure with a large receptacle might be seen under a stationary wagon with an augur, boring through the floor *and* the barrel end to get at the nectar. Quick action was necessary if the loss were to be minimised, the culprit apprehended and the Revenue officer notified – in that order.

Of the by-products, the main one was spent grains from the mash, known as 'draff'. Not much of this travelled by rail, though there was a rail-connected by-products factory at Rothes. The normal transport for this wet, steamy stuff was by lorry or farm tractor-hauled bogie, either direct to farms or to a processing plant which dried, blended and bagged it for animal feed. Lucky cows! But Ballindalloch and Craigellachie had 'pot ale' gantries in the yard for pumping spent liquor into tank wagons. It certainly could not be discharged into such a salmon-fishing river as the Spey.

The railway's role in servicing the distilleries was of course catastrophically curtailed following Beeching. The Speyside line between Boat of Garten and Aberlour, and the route from Craigellachie to Elgin, both closed to freight traffic in 1968; the Dufftown–Aberlour section followed three years later. Even the Keith–Dufftown line went into decline, freight finally ceasing in 1985. At the time of writing, but perhaps for not much longer, barley still comes rather irregularly by rail into Burghead (via Inverness with reversal at Elgin) and some malt comes out, especially for export. Whisky itself was railed from Elgin (in freightliner containers) linking to the Aberdeen–London service, but that ceased in 1987. Until 1992 Keith served as the railhead for the last modest whisky flow still on rail.

The industry naturally developed with the railway's help and the virtual end of the partnership in this most Scottish of products is naturally regretted. At the time of writing plans are afoot to save and reopen the Keith–Dufftown line, used by occasional excursions bringing visitors to tour a distillery until 1991.

Ore For Ravenscraig

Motherwell is unashamedly a steel town, though recently its links with the industry have become tenuous. It has been a steel-making centre since the 1870s. It specialised – though not exclusively – in producing large plate to supply the Scottish shipyards and the railway locomotive and rolling stock manufacturers as well as a wide range of other engineering uses. The name of Colvilles and its Dalzell plate mill was writ large in railway circles; it supplied the frame and nickel steel boiler plates for Stanier's Duchesses, among many others, and its special 'Ducol' plate formed the steel fireboxes of Bulleid's Pacifics and many export locomotives.

With nationalisation of the steel industry in 1951 and an emerging Government policy of widening the Scottish industrial base, notably into car and truck manufacture, a new integrated Ravenscraig complex opened in 1956. Two new blastfurnaces enabled raw steel production to be stepped up well above a million tons a year. A new gas-holder dominated the town and proclaimed the identity of the works that surrounded it. A new hot coil plant supplied a modern cold-reduction strip mill at Gartcosh, seven miles away. The Dalzell plate mill was re-equipped.

It was almost certainly the wrong decision in practical and economic terms; the raw steel production at least should have been moved to the coast alongside deep water. But politics, the art of gaining short-term advantage, were the deciding factor, and railwaymen were grateful for it.

The industries consuming Ravenscraig steel blossomed briefly and then died. In the 1970s the shipyards were decimated by foreign competition, and the motor industry at Linwood and Bathgate never captured a worthwhile market share and closed. Rolling stock manufacture flourished briefly on the back of BR's Modernisation Plan and

then, starved of further orders, expired. General industry faltered in a recession. There was considerable over-capacity in the steel industry and Ravenscraig, now out on a limb and remote from consumers, paid the price. The strip mill at Gartcosh closed its doors in 1987, the Ravenscraig hot coil plant three years later, and steel making ceased in 1992. The Dalzell plate mill continues to roll slab brought in from England, but is scheduled to close in 1994–5. Finis.

Imported iron ore, generally of a higher iron content than home-produced ore, began to come into the Clyde in the 1870s, but for more than three decades the quantities were not thought sufficient to warrant special facilities and it was handled at various riverside quays until the new Rothesay Dock (on the north bank, just upstream from the famous John Brown shipyard at Clydebank, birthplace of the 'Queen' liners) opened in 1907. Here the ore was grabbed from ships' holds into general purpose wagons and trundled off to Motherwell and other steel plants, mainly by the Caledonian Railway.

The route was a hotchpotch of passenger and freight-only lines from Yoker to Partick, Possil, Balornock Junction, Coatbridge and Mossend. By the 1950s these trains were made up of 27-ton tippler wagons, and because of the severe gradients involved – there was a mile and a half of 1 in 77 and 1 in 89 either side of Possil – a pair of WD 2–8–0s from Dawsholm shed (65D) (with an occasional visiting Stanier 8F) struggled mightily at their head, depositing their hot cinders lavishly as they crossed high above the north end of Eastfield shed yard. Some of these trains went to Bairds' Gartsherrie ironworks, others took the Carmyle line at Coatbridge to serve the Clyde Iron works, but Motherwell got the lion's share.

The new Ravenscraig plant took in its ore at a new signal

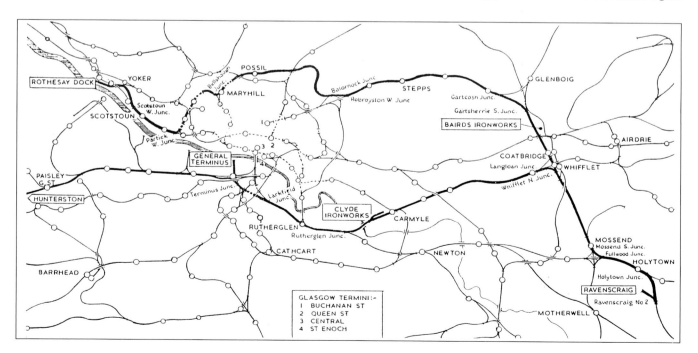

WD 2–8–0 Nos 90114 & 90193 on an ex-Caledonian Railway freight line near Springburn, Glasgow, with an iron ore train from Rothesay Dock, Clydebank, to Ravenscraig on 16 July 1960. Both engines were built at the nearby North British Locomotive works in 1943 and after their return from war service spent all their working life based in Scotland. No 90114 (WD77016) saw service in Belgium at Schaerbeek and No 90193 (WD77225) was for a time NS 4490 when working from Eindhoven.

box, Ravenscraig No 2, on the Holytown–Law Junction line. A new purpose-built ore terminal was opened up-river on the south bank at General Terminus at the beginning of 1958, and a fleet of 270 33-ton vacuum-braked hopper wagons was built to move the ore to Ravenscraig and Clyde Iron.

The ore was grabbed from bulk carriers by a pair of kangaroo cranes into pouch-like hoppers in front of the operators; from there it travelled by conveyor belts to a large overhead bunker, end-on to the river, whence it was pre-weighed into 33-ton batches and dropped into the wagons below. The cranes and bunker were clearly seen downriver from the platform ends at Glasgow Central, about half a mile away. It was not true 'merry-go-round' – the site did not permit it – but loading was rapid and the sections were quickly made up into trains of 28 hoppers and a brake grossing 1,280 tons, which ran as Class 6 fully-fitted freights on special timings.

Again it was a pair of WD 2–8–0s, now from Polmadie shed – or one engine might be one of the three Stanier 8Fs from that stable – that did the honours for the seventeen mile haul to Ravenscraig or the five mile hop to Clyde Iron, via West Street tunnel, Larkfield Junction, the Carmyle line, Whifflet, Mossend and Holytown Junction. The start from General Terminus was far from easy with such loads, and on a wet night much of the city heard when an ore train was leaving! The testing section, however, was the sharp curve on a 1 in 77 grade from Mossend to Fullwood Junction, where flanges squealed loudly, and the ensuing 1 in 86/93 past Holytown. A brace of 2–8–0s with a load like this on their tail were extremely vocal! The trains were then propelled into the ore sidings and positioned over the ore bunkers for discharge.

Steam haulage lasted until the summer of 1962, when the 2–8–0s went to their Valhalla and pairs of Class 20 diesels took their place, only to be replaced in turn by Class 37s in multiple. But events caught up with political expedience, as events will; General Terminus had insufficient depth of water to handle the new breed of bulk ore carriers, and it was necessary to move to deep water at Hunterston, on the Ayrshire coast alongside the Largs branch. This opened in June 1979 and General Terminus was first run down and then razed.

Hunterston was an all-singing, all-dancing sort of place. Set in splendid scenery in the lee of the Cumbraes, there was ample room for ore and coal buffer stockyards. There were also two ore preparation plants which pelletised the ore into an optimum form for the blast furnace burden. The separate rail loading bunkers, a 3,500 ton one for ore and a 2,500 ton one for coal, overlooked the installation and could load complete trains without splitting; trains were moved through by automatic 'mules'.

And what trains they were! Ore moved in 21-wagon sets of 100 ton gross bogie tippler wagons fitted with rotary couplers so that the train could be discharged without uncoupling; they had been introduced in the dying days of General Terminus. Three trains a day was the normal service. Coal initially moved in trains of 36 hoppers (those 1957 ore wagons were not quite life-expired) but these were soon replaced by merry-go-round hoppers (HAA) made up into 46-wagon trains – one or two a day – grossing nearly 2,100 tons. Both were originally hauled by a pair of Class 37s, but early in 1991 they were superseded by single Class 60s, the throbbing beat of whose engines was heard to advantage as they fought their way up the 1 in 116 to West Kilbride. Local residents were less enthusiastic and tried to take BR to court over it. The route to Ravenscraig, via Shields Junction, West Street, Larkfield and then as before took them through some heavy suburban traffic, available paths were few and progress was often slow. The decision to reduce the Glasgow & Paisley Joint line from four to two tracks at the time of electrification must often have been rued.

Ravenscraig, while it lived its full role, called for railway operation in the heroic mould. Nothing less would do. And now that Ravenscraig is little more than a name, we are not likely to see its like again in Scotland, but the memory and the record of the great days of trains conveying maximum loads serving a gigantic industry that at least temporarily put economic heart into the nation. There was real pride in the job.

5
RUNNING THE BON ACCORD

BIG Dougal Ross reaches up to put his oil feeder on the cab floor and climbs after it into the warmth. He is glad of it, for preparing an A4 in the open in a March gale blowing across Ferryhill shed yard is not much fun. He looks appreciatively round his workplace; Ian Ingram, his fireman, has put on a sizeable fire, swept the cab floor and washed it clean. His shovel sits on the tender shovelling plate, its blade deep in some decent-looking lump coal. The pressure gauge stands at 190, and there is half a glass of water.

Dougal has been up since just before five, and eaten his breakfast to the sound of rattling windows. Coming out of his back door looking down on Footdee, the wind hit him hard, but propelled him nicely on his bike towards the shed. 'Have to watch it above Cove Bay', he mused, knowing that with the wind from the east the rail can well be slippery with driven salt. His thoughts are also on the 'crack' in the bothy; the district super is getting flak from the Granite City's business men about the timekeeping of the three-hour trains, and has even been seen riding the engine *himself*. Word is that if the punctuality record of any of the three depots involved, Ferryhill, Perth and St Rollox, is lacking they could well lose the work.

He wriggles into his bucket seat and glances along 60009's shiny boiler casing towards the shed. Almost automatically he removes his greasetop cap, wipes the band and then the top, puts it back on his balding head and looks at his watch. 'Time we were not here', he calls to his mate, and then winds the reverser into back gear and drifts down to the outlet signal. Ian climbs down to the phone; 'Seven ten, Glasgow' he announces to the bobby in Ferryhill Junction box, and by the time he is back in the cab the signal is off. Dougal sounds a quick blast on the chime whistle and gives a tug on the regulator handle. *Union of South Africa* begins to move in a flurry of steam from open cylinder cocks and picks her way gently through the crossovers and under the signal gantries to the station. The stock for the 7.10, and the south end shunter, are waiting to receive them in platform 5.

While Dougal is casting an eye over the coupling procedure, Ian has the big firehole door open and is filling up the back corners before closing it and firing round the box below the flap. At a sign from Dougal he stops long enough to turn on the heat to the train. Whatever happens on the way the passengers will not lack for comfort, anyway. A voice from the platform interrupts a study of the Weekly Notice. 'Oh, it's you today, Dougie. You've seven for 256 tons. I'll do the brake test when I get back to the van. Right time in Perth?' 'Aye, if you leave your handbrake alone'. The guard walks back, chuckling.

Absent Directors
Many short Scottish lines were country businesses run by a handful of local directors and a manager. The Leven Railway's manager, a man called Wilkie, discovered that one of his main tasks was to persuade the directors to bother to turn up for meetings, often abandoned for want of a quorum. The directors should have been more attentive for the six mile line down the left bank of the River Leven from Thornton to Leven itself had plenty of problems. Its engineer was Thomas Bouch, who two decades before his infamous involvement with the Tay Bridge demonstrated his propensity to make mistakes, like ordering a locomotive for the line as originally planned but unable to go round the sharper curves actually built fast enough to keep to schedule. Local landowners were excessively awkward and greedy, the springs of the six ton wagons 'were so depressed that the buffers went under those of the neighbouring wagon' even when loaded with a single ton... and Bouch's own patent signals never worked and had to be replaced by conventional ones.

Working the Bon Accord express, 7.10am Aberdeen to Glasgow. A4 No 60009 Union of South Africa *is at grips with the 1 in 92/102 of Carmont bank on the fine morning of 20 March 1965 after the Stonehaven stop.*

Prompt at 7.10 Ian calls the rightaway from the platform and Dougal pulls gently at the regulator. It is a sharp pull up to Ferryhill, at 1 in 96, and then from Craiginches South you are on a steady pull past Cove Bay, part at 1 in 102, up to the summit before Portlethen, so to make the 16.1 miles to the Stonehaven stop in the 19 minutes allowed means no havering. The reverser comes quickly to 30 percent and Dougal tests how much regulator she will stand. By Craiginches yard it is fully open with 25 percent and 60009 is making 40mph when she hits the bank and starts into the long curve.

Now the blustery wind catches the train on the exposed embankment and stops its acceleration dead. They are on the cliff top now and the sea looks leaden and angry. Just before Cove Bay the engine goes into a heavy slip, as Dougal is expecting, and he slams the regulator shut, waits for the pandemonium to end, and opens it again. By the concrete ruins of the old works she slips again, and then again. He looks down to the sea boiling in the little cove under his window. Ian is working the sanding lever but probably the sand is being blown straight off the rail. There is only one thing to do – let her make her own pace until some better rail appears. As the line turns inland she soon settles down, but at the top they are only doing 42 instead of something nearer 55.

Dougal now hauls her up to 20 percent and lets her fly. By Muchalls the speedometer says 74, falls to 64 on the golf course hump and sweeps up to 77 before he shuts off on the left hand curve towards Glenury viaduct. Sharp braking brings the train into Stonehaven, but they have dropped almost two minutes.

An elderly passenger in a wheelchair, sheltering from the wind under the awning and needing help and the stepbox to get into the train, makes it three down when they get the green from the guard. Ian has been firing ready for the pull up to Carmont, five miles averaging about 1 in 100 with just a brief respite by the tiny Dunottar box, but Dougal warns him 'I'm going to give her some stick now. We've got a bad slack at Bridge of Dun'.

On the move, the reverser comes back to 30 percent and Dougal hauls the regulator up to the stop. Ian gets down to work. Now the A4 starts to talk in an almost even beat. By Dunottar she is doing 52, darts away to 58 on the easier stretch, and pounds up the winding glen holding that speed on the final grade to Carmont and its level crossing. Ian's skilful firing has kept the needle round the 240 mark, the exhaust injector singing away continuously. Now Dougal brings the reverser back by degrees to 18 percent, the regulator unaltered. He is an ex-LNER man and has been brought up that way. The engine gallops down into the Mearns country. By Fordoun they are doing 77, tear through Laurencekirk without falling below 75, and romp down to the North Esk viaduct at 82. At Craigo Dougal shuts off and starts a brake application soon after for the 60mph restriction on the curve past Kinnaber Junction. 23 minutes allowed, 21 taken.

In the dip beyond Dubton, on easy steam, they are up to 74 but then Dougal shoves the regulator shut again and starts braking. There is a bridge renewal job just beyond Bridge of Dun and the speed restriction is to 5mph; you cannot play ducks and drakes with that! A warning blast on the whistle and they crawl over the bridge with just a breath of steam on.

Now they are faced with Farnell Road bank, 3½ miles easing from 1 in 96 to 1 in 143, and Dougal sets 60009 hard at it, the regulator full open and 40 percent on the screw, easing to 35 percent and then to 30 percent as speed builds up. They hit the bank at 51, and by the crest that has improved to 54, with the *Union* very audible at the chimneys. Now it is back to 20 percent and they bowl round the curve to Guthrie at 65 and gradually accelerate against the grade until by the time the regulator is shut for the Forfar stop they are doing 73. The run-in is fairly cautious because of the 30mph curve at the platform, but even so they make it in 40 minutes and are back on time.

In spite of some difficulty in relaying the guard's green flag along the curved platform the train is away practically on time, and now Dougal winds her gradually back to 20 percent with the regulator where nature intended it. This is the racing stretch through Strathmore, more or less level until the final drop from Stanley into Perth, and with just 31 minutes

Perth water stop. The incoming crew have 'got the bag in' at No 4 platform as the new crew take over No 60024 Kingfisher *on an Aberdeen to Glasgow express – not one of the three hour trains, which were allowed only a 3–4 minutes stop and consistently overran their time taking water. The column is to a modern BR design with dipping arm and short rubber hose. On the right the Dundee platforms curve away.*

NEW FAST SERVICE —

3-HOURS

between

GLASGOW

and

ABERDEEN

TWO TRAINS
IN EACH DIRECTION
calling at
STIRLING,   PERTH
FORFAR and STONEHAVEN

DAILY (except Sundays)

18th June to 8th September, 1962

*for Speed and Comfort
travel by train*

BRITISH RAILWAYS

*See other side for
details of services*

for the 32½ miles. Even with only seven coaches you have to keep pushing along. The little dip beyond Glamis sees them up to 79 and then they hold this fairly closely, with a brief spurt to 84 at the Tay viaduct beyond Cargill. By Stanley Junction Dougal has the regulator almost closed, and they run down past the new Perth yard – who would have imagined that a few years later only Inverness trains would run this way into Perth – and into platform 4 to make a careful stop at the water column in just 30 minutes. It helps that the column is on the driver's side.

The relieving Perth fireman is up on the tender back before Ingram is in the six-foot to swing the column arm to him and turn on. Meanwhile Dougal is handing over to the Perth driver, Alastair Dewar. 'Seven on, and she's a good 'un.' The fireman, Willie McKay, is back in the cab, big fire-door open, aiming his shovel to inspect the fire. He starts to feed the back corners and puts some under the door and down the sides, with the odd shovelful to one or two thinner patches. Then he shuts the door and sets the flap. It is against the collar to Dunning and then climbing hard to the over-bridge beyond Gleneagles, and he expects his mate not to stand around.

'OK, Willie, we've got enough water now', trying the gauge pipe. 'We're only going 63 miles, not to Crewe'. He watches the gauge needle

September 1966 saw the end of rostered steam working on the Glasgow to Aberdeen services and the handful of A4 survivors were then withdrawn. With only a month of life remaining, No 60034 Lord Faringdon *bursts out of the 620 yard Kippenross tunnel south of Dunblane with the 13.30 Aberdeen to Glasgow express.*

A push-and-pull fitted ex-NBR Class C15 No 67460 runs into Garelochhead with the Craigendoran two coach auto set. This service ran from Arrochar & Tarbet to connect with the Clyde coast Helensburgh to Glasgow service at Craigendoran.

Scottish Standard. Only 20 Class 3 2–6–0 standard locomotives were constructed, half of them allocated to the Scottish region. No 77015 of Hurlford Shed 67B heads a Muirkirk local across Glenbuck Loch causeway during March 1961.

Andrew Barclay 0–4–0 ST, Dailuaine *rests outside the exquisite distillery engine shed near Carron station on the Speyside branch. Fortunately preserved, the locomotive now can be found on the Strathspey Railway.*

The last Great North of Scotland locomotive in service, Class D40 4–4–0 No 62277 Gordon Highlander *at Banff with ex-LMS compartment stock during July 1957. Twelve months later on a visit to Inverurie Works, Gordon Highlander was overhauled and repainted in a GNSR green livery as No 49 before joining the other restored engines at Dawsholm shed, Glasgow.*

continued opposite

Long Delay

David L. Smith told how several of the Stranraer line signal boxes had lady 'signalmen' during the war:

The classic story of the signal-women time is that which is related of Glenwhilly. The train was the 4.20pm from Stranraer, and just as it got dark it was running into the down platform at Glenwhilly. Usually the girl would be standing on the platform with the tablet, but that evening she was a bit late; as they ran in, she came down the stairs on to the up platform. To save her crossing over, the fireman threw his tablet to her, and she threw hers to him, but he missed his catch and it fell into the six-foot. As soon as they stopped he got down and went back to retrieve it. The hoop was retrieved at once, but alas the pouch had burst open and the tablet gone. The fireman went back for a lamp, and made a long search, but in vain. There was nothing for it but to inform Control.

Control would arrange for Barrhill (8½ miles away) to provide a pilotman. They telephoned Barrhill. 'Pilotman!' cried the solitary porter. 'What d'you think I am? It's Saturday afternoon an' I'm here by masel'. I can dae nithing for ye'. Too bad, so they then called Pinwherry (12½ miles), the staff were no more numerous there, but the station-master (off duty) was in his house adjacent; he said that he would officiate and called up a taxi. It was going to be a long, cold wait, so the fireman went up into the signalbox, and the girl made him a cup of tea.

Now the fireman was a voracious reader, and he found the signalbox a perfect treasure-house. Old McGibney had been a bit of a magpie – his cupboards were crammed with books and magazines and papers dating back to the erection of that box in 1907.

as he blows the brake off and it creeps up to 21 inches. Dewar is an ex-LMS man, brought up on Black Fives, but relishes the power of the Gresley Pacifics on the Glasgow–Aberdeen road even if the vertical reverser brings out the very worst in him. If there had been time he would have put it in mid-gear and then looked where the radius rod was in the link from the ground. That soon told you whether the cutoff indicator on the backhead was telling lies!

Overtime taking water puts them a minute down getting away, and Dewar goes for it. By Moncrieff Tunnel he has pulled 60009 up to 25 percent, with the regulator virtually full open, and Willie is busy with the shovel, firing below the flap. No large lumps that way! They pass Hilton Junction at 49 and the reverser comes back to 20 percent. Soon they are beginning to fly – 69 on the level beyond Forgandenny, 74 by Forteviot and 76 by Dunning at the foot of the bank. Speed tails off on the 1 in 100 and Dewar gives the reverser a quarter turn; by the time they pound over the Crieff branch connections at Gleneagles they are down to 56 and the thin, chiffly noise from the double Kylchaps is quite pronounced. Now Dewar must shut off for a 20mph relaying slack by the crest.

He wastes no time once his tail is by the T-board, and opens up strongly again. It is gently falling for the next nine miles; they speed over Blackford level crossing at 51 and by the time that Kinbuck's distant comes into view the speedometer is saying 78 and Dewar must shut off and put the brake in to steady the train just below the 70 mark and let her coast down to Stirling. An occasional touch of the brake keeps things within bounds. They stop in Stirling's spruce station – it is too early for the floral display – in 34 minutes, a gain of two in spite of the Gleneagles slack.

Now it is a very bitsy road to Glasgow. The wait for the rightaway seems endless, but they are away to time. Dewar goes at the 1 in 118 up to Plean energetically, making 58mph, and reaches 66 at Alloa Junction before coasting and braking to 40 for the Larbert restriction. 60009 has steam to spare and blows off hard through the station, but an open regulator soon puts a stop to that. The engine is worked quite hard on the steep rise to Greenhill past the sleeper creosoting plant, and tops the crest at 56. The sharp dip to Castlecary box brings them up to 68, and then Dewar sets her first to 22 percent and then to 25 percent as the train winds up Cumbernauld Glen. By the top of the 1 in 128 they are down to 53, and a mere breath of steam keeps her from exceeding the 60 limit through the junction at Garnqueen North.

McKay has put his shovel away and they are home and dry. Easy steaming on the level past the new Gartcosh strip mill (there are too many lorries outside the works for a railwayman's liking) brings them up to 68 by Robroyston, where Dewar closes the regulator for the last time. Now it is steeply down into Buchanan Street, and the brakes are kept rubbing all the way. McKay watches from his seat as St Rollox shed and then Sighthill Goods slide by; on the driver's side St Rollox works yard attracts mild interest. A blast on the chime whistle and they dive into the tunnel, brakes firmly holding the train. They emerge into the light and roll gently to a stop in platform 3. The station clock says 10.06.

McKay gets a bucket of hot water ready for them to wash their hands. Dewar is just getting a lather when a voice from the cab doorway says 'Nice work, driver. Thanks.' No passenger complaints from that train, anyway.

When the engine is released they will take it up to St Rollox shed and hand it over to a disposal crew; it will work the 17.30 back to Aberdeen. They will take their 'piece' in the bothy before preparing another engine for their return working. Home for tea, a day's work well done. Not even the Super in Aberdeen will be able to fault the record for that day!

> *continued*
> The fireman read until his eyes were sore, then he had a stroll around. He lifted the lock of the tablet instrument and pulled out the slide – and there was the missing tablet. In her hurry the girl had grabbed the hoop and forgotten that she had never put the tablet in the pouch!

Cock O' The North

What a splendidly evocative name that is – even though very few Scots can tell you to whom the nickname belonged (George, fifth Duke of Gordon, 1770–1836). It had first been applied to a new North British Atlantic, No 903 (LNER No 9903) in August 1911, and was picked for Gresley's *magnum opus* when it appeared in May 1934. An inspired choice!

Clearly it was a name which only the largest and most prestigious locomotives could be trusted to carry with distinction. (It is now borne by Class 87 electric locomotive No 87022).

The class P2 2–8–2s, of which No 2001 *Cock O' The North* was the first, were built specifically for the Edinburgh–Aberdeen route, though early on there were thoughts that the Waverley route to Carlisle might be included in their ambit. And if ever a route justified horses-for-courses, the Aberdeen road was the one. Gresley clearly thought so, anyway.

The Aberdeen route was not of course built as a single entity but made up of a series of short lines strung together. From where it parted company with the Edinburgh–Glasgow main line at Saughton Junction, three mile out, to joining the Caledonian main line at Kinnaber Junction, north of Montrose, 102 miles later, the line had been built up from parts of nine separate undertakings – and it showed. There was a seemingly endless succession of severely speed-restricted junctions from which, in one

Fighting Cock. Gresley's great passenger 2–8–2 (class P2) No 2001 Cock O' The North *in original form with Lentz rotary cam poppet valve gear and smoke deflectored front end. The tender is already equipped with the necessary support for the tablet catcher required for its Scottish duties.*

While waiting to pass a train bound for Oban, Stanier Class 5 No 45357 takes water at Taynuilt station on 17 May 1960. These mixed traffic 4–6–0s were the mainstay of all services on the line from their introduction in the 1930s until dieselisation. Tall lattice post signals add their own special character to the scene.

A little snow still remains on Ben Lawers as ex-CR 0–4–4T No 55217 basks in the sunshine ready to take its one coach train from Killin to Killin Junction on a May day in 1960. The line closed prematurely on 28 September 1965 due to a landslide on the mainline and was steam worked until the end.

Butlins Holiday Camp at Heads of Ayr had its own purpose-built station next door. A typical return working is seen leaving Ayr for Newcastle behind ex-LMS 'Crab' 2–6–0 No 42737 and an unidentified Class 5 on a September Saturday in 1962.

A Stranraer-bound local leaves Barrhill to tackle the next three miles of 1 in 67 towards the summit of this renowned 37 mile line from Girvan to Stranraer in January 1963. The view gives some impression of the desolate nature of this part of the Glasgow & South Western territory.

Thompson rebuild (class A2/2) No 60505 Thane of Fife leaves Edinburgh (Waverley) in the early 1950s with the 10.10am to King's Cross. Note the small smoke deflecting plates alongside the chimney, which remained a feature of these engines throughout their rebuilt life. The leading coaches are still in LNER teak livery including the NER designed brake composite which heads the rake. Although originally their home it was most unusual to find one of the rebuilt P2s in Waverley.

direction or both, trains were faced with a tough climb on 1 in 100 or steeper – in two cases at 1 in 70. Just for good measure there was a two-mile stretch of single line south from Montrose, where tokens were normally exchanged by hand, and a severe long-standing colliery subsidence restriction at Thornton. Then there were the two major bridges: that over the Forth limited to 40mph, over the Tay bridge to 25mph. Little wonder that Gresley's A3 Pacifics, introduced here in 1928, were limited to 480 tons northbound and 420 tons southbound. As for timings, it was not until 1960, with diesel traction, that the 130½ miles were brought down to 3 hours.

A curious feature of the Edinburgh–Aberdeen trains under steam was that engines were invariably changed at Dundee, though it was only 59¼ miles from Edinburgh (71¼ miles from Aberdeen). This was governed by water supply; there were no troughs and the columns at Dundee were so slow filling up a 5,000 gallon tender that it was quicker to provide a fresh engine! Footplate crews changed at Dundee, anyway.

For such a road Gresley had to meet five main requirements:-

1. High tractive effort for acceleration from slacks and for climbing with a 550 ton train,
2. Adequate adhesion (the climb out of Aberdeen can be particularly difficult with gale-driven salt on the rails),
3. Ample boiler power to back the tractive effort, while recognising that the demand tended to be intermittent and in relatively short bursts,
4. Flexibility of wheelbase for the very extensive curvature, and
5. Ability to fit on existing 70ft turntables.

The engine that was designed for the job was the most powerful passenger locomotive to run in Britain, with a tractive effort of 43,462lb. Its three cylinders were 21in diameter and the eight coupled wheels were 6ft 2in diameter. The boiler was essentially that of the A3 Pacific, working at 220lb per sq in, but the firebox was lengthened by 1ft 3¼in to give a grate area of 50sq ft.

Cock O' The North had a form of Lentz rotary cam poppet valve gear with continuous cams giving infinite adjustment of cutoff, but his brothers (all had profoundly masculine names with the possible exception of *Mons Meg*) were given the traditional Walschaerts valve gear with 2:1 conjugated gear for the inside valve. A double Kylchap blastpipe and chimney was fitted in a semi-streamlined smokebox.

On test on the East Coast main line before taking up duty in Scotland, No 2001 showed it could produce nearly 2,100 horsepower at the drawbar, an unprecedented figure in Britain at that time. No 2002 was no wit inferior, but brought the first problem to light; the front end design would not keep the soft exhaust resulting from piston valves and the Kylchap blastpipe clear of the driver's line of vision, whereas the rather sharper exhaust from the poppet valves did not drift down in the same way. The remaining four engines were built in 1936 with the A4-type front end (and the original two engines modified to match) to overcome this.

The continuous cams on No 2001 quickly showed excessive wear due to point contact with the cam followers, and it was necessary to fit new six-step camshafts giving fixed cutoffs of 12, 18, 25, 35, 45 and 75 percent. This selection proved rather too coarse, leading to high coal consumption, and in 1938 new piston valve cylinders and Walschaerts valve gear were fitted instead.

All the P2s could burn coal when opened out, thanks to their sheer power, and soon became known as the 'Miners' Friends'. The large grate was too big for what was mostly short intermittent effort, and made the fireman's job in controlling the boiler more difficult, as well as wasting coal during standby periods. There were superheater element problems, too.

Nor did the eight-coupled wheelbase take kindly to the curvature south of Kinnaber. The swing link leading truck gave insufficient guidance on curves, leading to heavy tyre wear on the leading coupled wheels which were having to do much of the guiding. Hot axleboxes and crankpins were frequent. What was needed was some form of articulation between pony truck and leading coupled axle, such as would have been used on the Continent, but the tight clearance between leading crankpin and crosshead dictated by the British loading gauge would not permit sufficient axle sideplay.

It had been a brave try, but fell some way short of success. So in 1941, with Gresley dead and Thompson in charge, the end came for the P2s and they were rebuilt as Pacifics with Thompson's elongated front end. They moved to England and (as their new weaknesses became apparent) gained new notoriety.

But Gresley himself had already learned the lesson of the six Mikados. Just before the war Doncaster had schemed out a high-powered 4–8–2 for heavy East Coast expresses. The boiler was that of the P2s but pressed to 250lb per sq in, a conventional Pacific-type cylinder layout with piston valves was incorporated and a leading bogie provided for guidance. But for the war this design might well have been built, and a version with 6ft 2in diameter wheels could have fitted on 70ft turntables. What a *Cock* that would have made!

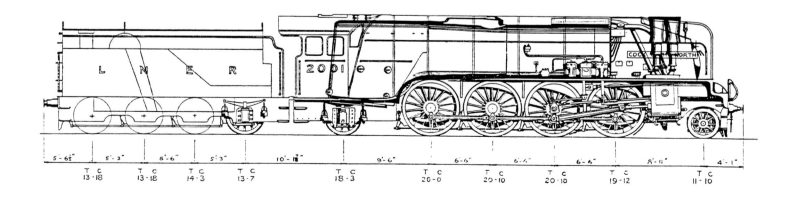

LNER Class A4 No 60026 Miles Beevor *coasts along the cliff top near Cove Bay with an Aberdeen to Glasgow three hour express. The light load made an easy swan song for the last regular workings of these East Coast pacifics.*

The twin-funnelled paddle steamer Waverley, *now the last sea-going paddle steamer in the world, calls at Dunoon on the Firth of Clyde during the early 1950s. The funnels carry the house colours of the then owners, BR, the steamer having been launched in 1947 for the LNER. Later part of the fleet of the Caledonian Steam Packet Company, the vessel is now operated privately.*

Seen from the seventh coach BR Standard Class 5 4–6–0 No 73077 and ex-GN K2 2–6–0 No 61792 rounds the horseshoe curve at Tyndrum with a Glasgow-bound train during March 1956. The maroon coach livery had recently been introduced and this colourful scene was soon to end.

Peter Drummond's 0–4–4T of 1906 now carrying its BR number 55053, brings its mixed train of one coach and three wagons tailed by a goods brake close to the A9 trunk road at Cambusavie on the approach to The Mound junction where it connected with the Highland main line from Inverness to Wick and Thurso. One of a pair remaining in traffic in the mid-fifties, they were both replaced during 1957 by two Swindon-built light 16xx pannier tanks until the line closed in June 1960.

Some Scottish Tunnels

Name		Railway Company	Lengh miles/yards
Dock Street (Dundee)		NB	620
Drumlanrig		GSWR	1410
Edinburgh			
Haymarket South Lines		NB	1009
Haymarket North Lines		NB	992
Calton		NB	510
The Mound		NB	135
Falkirk		NB	1000
Fairlie		GSWR	1000
Glasgow			
Buchanan Street		CR	
Low Level - Stobcross St		CR	640
- Anderston		CR	1 1012
- Canning Street		CR	460
- Dalmarnock Rd		CR	790
Queen St High Level		NB	1000
Low Level - Finnieston		NB	530
- Charing Cross		NB	1200
- High Street		NB	685
Greenock (Newton Street)		CR	1 350
Kippenross (Dunblane)		CR	620
Moncrieffe (Perth)		CR	1210
Mossgiel		GSWR	680
Union Street (Greenock)		GSWR	726
Winchburgh		NB	350

Some Scottish Bridges

Name		Railway Company	Height Ft	Length Ft
Blair Atholl		Highland	40	250
Borrodale Burn	(a)	NB	86	127
Connel Ferry	(b)	CR		1044
Dunkeld		Highland	67	515
Forth	(c)	Forth Bridge Co	156	8298
Glasgow (St Enoch)		GSWR		502
Glasgow (Central)		CR		700
Spey (Garmouth)	(d)	GNSR		950
Tay		NB	77	11652

Notes (a) When built, world's longest concrete span
(b) Combined road and rail bridge
(c) Towers 361ft high
(d) 7 spans, longest 350ft

Swing Bridges

Alloa	CR	Firth of Forth
Banavie	NB	Caledonian Canal
Bowling	CR	Forth & Clyde Canal
Clachnaharry	Highland	Caledonian Canal
Fort Augustus	NB	Caledonian Canal

Some Scottish Viaducts

Name		Railway Company	No of Arches	Height Ft	Length Ft
Avon (Linlithgow)		NB	23		
Almond (2)		NB	7 & 36	70	
Ballochmyle	a	GSWR	7	163	
Big Water of Fleet		PP&W	20		
Castlecary		NB	8	150	
Creagan		CR	4	40	
Culloden		Highland	28	130	1800
Divie		Highland	7	106	
Findhorn		Highland	9	144	1320
Glenfalloch		NB		144	
Glenfinnan	b	NB	21	100	1248
Glenluce		PP&W	8		
Killiecrankie		Highland	10	54	
Kilmarnock		GSWR	23	60	
Leaderfoot		NB	19		
Little Water of Fleet		P&P&W	9		
Loch Ken		GSWR			
Piltanton		PP&W	13	73	
Rannoch		NB	9		684
Solway	c	CR	193		5820
Templand		GSWR	14	145	

Notes (a) Largest single masonry arch in the Country
(b) Built on a curve, 12 chains radius
(c) Cast iron piers

Scottish Light Railways

	Light Railway order	Opened	Closed
Bankfoot	19 Nov 1898	1 May 1906	13 Apr 1931 P
extra time	10 Oct 1903		7 Sept 1964 G
Leadhills and			
Wanlockhead	5 Aug 1898		2 Jan 1939
Elvanfoot			
– Leadhills		1 Oct 1901	
Leadhills			
– Wanlockhead		12 Oct 1902	
Cambeltown &			
Macrihanish	8 May 1905	17 Aug 1906	
amended	15 May 1908		Nov 1931
Carmyllie	6 Aug 1898	1 Feb 1900	2 Dec 1929 P
			24 May 1965 G
Dornoch	13 Aug 1898	2 Jun 1902	13 Jun 1960
Fraserburgh			
& St Combs	8 Sept 1899	1 Jul 1903	7 Nov 1960 G
			3 May 1965 P

Gifford & Garvald	14 Jul 1898	14 Oct 1901	3 Apr 1933 P
			1 Jan 1959 G
Cairn Valley	29 Dec 1899	1 Mar 1905	3 May 1943 P
			4 Jul 1949 G
Maidens & Dunure	30 Sept 1899	17 May 1906	see below
Lauder	30 Jun 1898	2 Jul 1901	12 Sept 1932 G
			1 Oct 1958 G
Wick & Lybster	27 Nov 1899	1 Jul 1903	1 Apr 1944

Maidens & Dunure

	Re-opened	Closed Passenger	Closed Goods
Turnberry		2 Mar 1942	28 Feb 1955
Maidens		1 Dec 1930	28 Feb 1955
Glenside		1 Dec 1930	28 Feb 1955
Knoweside		1 Dec 1930	28 Feb 1955
Dunure		1 Dec 1930	28 Feb 1955
Heads of Ayr		1 Dec 1930	28 Feb 1955
	4 Jul 1932	31 May 1933	
Summer only			
New station on different site			
for Butlins	17 May 1947	9 Sept 1968	
Alloway		1 Dec 1930	7 Dec 1959

Railway Hotels in Scotland

Railway		Open or Purchased	Closed/ Sold
GNS	Aberdeen – Palace	1874	destroyed by fire 30 Oct 41
GNS	Aberdeen – Station	1910	sold 1983
H	Achnasheen Station	purchased 1870	sold 1969
GSW	Ayr – Station	June 1866	sold Oct 1951
GNS	Cruden Bay	March 1899	closed 1939 demol 1952
H	Dornoch	July 1904	sold April 1965
GSW	Dumfries – Station	c 1865	sold April 1972
Edinburgh			
NB	North British	Oct 1902	sold 1981
C	Caledonian	1899–1903	sold 1981
Glasgow			
C	Central	19.6.1885	sold 1983
NB	North British	May 1905 (rebuilt)	sold 1984
GSW	St Enoch	July 1879	closed 1974 demol 1977
LMS	Gleneagles	2.6.1924	sold 1981
H	Inverness – Station	1856	sold 1983

H	Lochalsh	purchased 1896	sold 1983
Jt.	Perth – Station	June 1890	sold 1983
H	Strathpeffer – Highland	June 1911	sold May 1958
GSW	Turnberry	17.5.1906	sold 1983

TARIFF OF CHARGES.

NORTH BRITISH STATION HOTEL, GLASGOW
(Adjoining Queen Street Station).

All communications to be addressed to the "Manager."

The HOTEL RESTAURANT and GRILL ROOM are open daily from 11 a.m. until 9 p.m.

QUEEN STREET STATION.
The Refreshment Rooms are under the management of the Railway Company.

MOTOR GARAGE.
There is a splendid Motor Garage adjacent to the Hotel fitted with the most modern machinery for repairs, and skilled attendants on duty night and day.

Tariff of Charges of the N.B.R. Co.'s Station Hotel, Waverley Station, Edinburgh, can be obtained at the Reception Office of this Hotel, and rooms reserved by Telegram free of charge.

HOTEL SOUVENIR BOOK ON APPLICATION.

CANCELS ALL PREVIOUS TARIFFS.

The Class 37 diesel electric represented the final years of locomotive traction on many Scottish lines. No 37405 Strathclyde Region, resplendent with large logo blue livery, complete with the Eastfield shed terrier motif makes a fine sight on 5 October 1988 hauling the 10.15 Glasgow-Fort William past Achallader.

In the spring of 1990 there were still named through trains from Inverness to both Kings Cross and Euston. The Highland Chieftain, the 12 noon from Kings Cross approaches Dalwhinnie just seven hours after leaving the London terminus. The 3,000 foot Grampian Mountains form the snow covered backdrop.

The new era on the Kyle line. Super-Sprinter No 156–457 forms the 11.35 Kyle of Lochalsh to Inverness, the blue and grey livery fitting in well with the surroundings and the Isle of Skye across the entrance to Loch Carron.

Inter City liveried Class 47 No 47595 Confederation of British Industry *leaves Pitlochry with the 12.17 Inverness to Glasgow on 26 May 1990. This section between Blair Atholl and Stanley Junction near Perth has always been single track.*

A Stranraer-bound passenger train leaving Dumfries in the early 1920s hauled by Glasgow & South Western 4–4–0 No 384 of 1905. As LMS No 14256 the engine was withdrawn in 1932.

A local unfitted freight enters Dumfries alongside the G&SWR main line to Glasgow with freight train from Castle Douglas c 1955, hauled by ex-Caledonian Railway class 2F 0–6–0 No 57378. The Dumfries shed code plate (68B) is fitted to the top of the smokebox door and the weather sheet tied forward over the cab roof to the handrail. This very useful class of 244 engines had a long life being first built in 1883 and not becoming extinct until 1962.

6
THE PORT LINE

THE Port Line, Galloway's first railway, was built primarily to carry passengers, goods and mails to and from Northern Ireland, and only secondarily to benefit the local community. Its most valued clients were those whose feet only touched Scottish ground when they walked from train to boat or *vice versa*. Those bound to and from Ireland only saw Galloway through the compartment window – a pity since almost no other part of Scotland has richer or more varied historical and literary associations, while in places its scenery rivals that of the more famous Highlands. Neolithic immigrants set up monuments here, where they worshipped their gods or buried their dead, 4,000 years ago. The Romans came, built marching camps, took tribute from the natives and then retired behind Hadrian's Wall. St Ninian established the first known monastery in Britain, at Whithorn in the Wigtownshire Machars, and from it his itinerant monks went out to Christianise the pagan Picts. The waves of the Norman Conquest reached Galloway in the early 12th century; many motte-and-bailey earthworks mark their strongholds. Bruce won his first victory over the English in the recesses of Glen Trool. Covenanters defied the dragoons who hunted them down for disobeying the Government's ban against assembling in outdoor Presbyterian conventicles during the later 17th century, and many were shot out of hand when caught; gravestones with pathetic inscriptions mark where they were martyred. R.L. Stevenson, John Buchan and Dorothy Sayers placed some of their most famous novels in Galloway settings.

The area was without doubt romantic. Can the same be said for the railway which served it for a full century?

The Portpatrick Railway, to give it its full title, certainly had a chequered history. Built to tap the potential of the Short Sea route to Ireland, it disappointed its local promoters' expectations. Once it had been completed from Castle Douglas (where it made an end-on junction with a branch of the Glasgow & South Western Railway from Dumfries) to Portpatrick on the coast of the Rhinns of Galloway in 1863, the Post Office reneged on earlier promises and refused to use it for the Northern Ireland, alleging the unsuitability of Portpatrick harbour. The Portpatrick Railway won only niggardly compensation.

The railway then rented a pier on Loch Ryan from the Burgh of Stranraer, and eventually a steamer service to Larne was established which connected with trains from Carlisle and the South. Through trains took a long while to be established, for the PR first tried to operate on its own, using its own engines and rolling stock to take passengers on from trains terminating at Castle Douglas. Perhaps not unsurprisingly, it could

Nairn

Many of the elements that make Scottish railway history so fascinating are present at Nairn from which this volume is published. Even today it is an interesting station, the Victorian buildings not only surviving but having been restored, the Highland Railway Museum housed on the Inverness-bound platform. The Forres-bound one is Scotland's longest and sees the signalman cycle up and down it on a 'company' provided machine for the passage of each train: a dozen passenger ones each way daily, the highest number in history even if most of them are two-car Sprinters. There is still a vestige of through freight and indeed until the end of the 1980s Nairn itself still figured on the freight map as a loading place for timber.

There are signalboxes at either end of the long loop, while the block instrument (and some of the signal levers) are beside the booking office. When BR provided the bicycle it was featured in a management video showing how easy it is to gain publicity and goodwill. And you can still see the signalman pedalling away from one of those famous Highland Railway bridges with see-through metal walkways, a slight hump over the tracks. Currently it is tokenless block in one direction but token in the other. And now the 16 miles to Inverness is a single section.

Joseph Mitchell, an engineer once employed by Telford who held the position of chief inspector *continued overleaf*

113

continued

and superintendent of Highland roads and bridges, saw Nairn as on a through route from Perth to Inverness. First plans for a route through the Pass of Drumochter were ridiculed, and Mitchell and his Inverness business associates settled for a start: the Inverness & Nairn, opened after delays through the mismanagement of locomotive, turntable and other tenders on 5 November 1855. That was one of the noisiest days in Nairn's history.

Thereafter the four daily passenger trains did good business, but freight was sparse, there indeed being no form of public freight conveyance east of Nairn to Forres, where Aberdeen's westerly influence petered out.

Eventually the Inverness & Nairn was absorbed into the Highland, of course, and the line completed from Perth through Aviemore and Forres, all traffic to the north coming through Nairn, in design now only a wayside station but one of the busiest north of Perth with locals and tourists visiting the 'Brighton of the North' with its renowned mini-climate, hotels and bathing beaches. Though plans for a branch to the harbour never matured, and Nairn lost out fishingwise to Lossiemouth, the goods station also was busy, specials including many of sheep from the north (mainly via Lairg) sent to winter on the pastures of the milder coastal strip.

Not until 1898 was the direct Aviemore–Inverness route via Carrbridge opened, and until the 1960s many trains to the south were still routed via Nairn, indeed on summer Saturdays starting point for two to Edinburgh, one to Waverley and the other to Princes Street. With three lightly-used intermediate stations even between Inverness and Nairn (one formerly junction for Fort George) services were slow, and

continued opposite

not make ends meet, and accepted the Caledonian Railway's offer to work the line, which it did for 21 years. But the Caledonian soon came to feel that it had made a bad bargain, and much friction ensued.

The agreement expired in 1885, by which time the PR's directors were ready to sell the company. Together with a recently-built branch from Newton Stewart to Whithorn, it passed into the hands of four other lines to become the Portpatrick & Wigtownshire Railways Joint Committee. The owning companies were the London & North Western, the Midland, the CR and the G&SWR. The last two took three-year turns to do the actual managing. At last, from 1885 to 1914, there was increasing prosperity. Holiday traffic grew, services improved and receipts were satisfactory. But World War I put an end to all this; fewer people travelled and those who did were mainly service personnel – risking submarine attack on the crossing of the North Channel. Track maintenance had to be reduced to a minimum because of shortage of labour and nothing like normality was resumed between the end of hostilities and the committee's empire becoming part of the LMS in January 1923. Control was run from England.

Under LMS management there was slow but steady improvement. Through trains from the South began to run once more, with first and third class sleeping cars. Indeed, by 1939 services were better than they had ever been. But then came World War II, affecting the line in much the same way as the first.

BR also began its ownership with arrears of maintenance, but though there were temporary improvements there was to be no general renaissance this time. Indeed, the Whithorn branch and the extension from Stranraer to Portpatrick were soon closed: Stranraer had of course long replaced Portpatrick as the port for Northern Ireland. But few people were ready for the announcement that the entire Port Line would be removed from the map – except for the short section between Challoch Junction and Stranraer Harbour, which station now had to serve the town as well as the ferries. Trains still ran from Glasgow by way of Ayr and Girvan, through traffic from the South being also routed that way (first via Mauchline and then *via* Kilmarnock), but between Dumfries and Challoch the rails were lifted, stations and signal-boxes were dismantled or sold and grass grew over the track-bed. In just over a century the Port Line had been born, flourished, decayed and died.

Always a difficult route to work, as told so vividly by David Smith, it was a delight for the interested traveller. Scenery varied from the pleasantly pastoral to the savagely wild, with occasional glimpses of the sea.

As good a way as any in which to make an imaginative journey on it is to picture oneself in a down boat train conveying a through first class sleeping car from St Pancras to Stranraer about half-way through the Edwardian decade. One is, let us suppose, a young man who has just left a public school and is shortly going to Oxford or Cambridge; in between one has been invited to spend part of the vacation with relatives living on the Antrim coast. The pater has very decently paid the first class return fare and the sleeping berth charge, so that when the overnight express to Glasgow and Stranraer had been brought into the platform at St Pancras

By 1963 passenger trains were honoured with comfortable ex-LMS corridor coaches and on 19 July LMS class 5 4–6–0 No 45485 is seen at Newton Stewart with the 1.40pm Stranraer to dumfries.

soon after 8pm, all one has to do is to claim one's single-bedded cubicle in the car labelled 'Stranraer Harbour', get undressed and go to bed. It is a little early for going to sleep, but there is the latest issue of the *Railway Magazine*, in which Mr Charles Rous-Marten entertainingly pontificates about the contemporary locomotive scene. His sonorous prose soon induces slumber, whose onset is helped rather than hindered by the gentle purr of the six-wheeled bogies, and one does not waken until Dumfries, when the coach is shunted to the Stranraer-bound line of carriages in the bay platform. The accents of the station staff indicate that we have now crossed the Border. A press on the electric bell-push brings the attendant and a cup of tea – and up goes the blind. We are approaching Dalbeattie, where the train halts briefly in the half light of summer daybreak. Lowering the window allows one to see that the Midland-liveried crimson lake engine of last night has been replaced with a green GSWR one of Mr Manson's latest four-coupled big-boilered type.

We swing towards the north-west for a few miles along the valley of the Water of Urr, and then turn to the west again. At this point one sees a sight which recalls a history lesson in prep school, a well preserved motte-

continued

until the last three decades extraordinarily sparse to Aberdeen, for a generation there being only a single daily through train. But there was a huge variety of locomotives and rolling stock over the years, including those famous lengthy caravans of assorted rolling stock coming up for the grouse shooting and GNSR/LNER stock from Aberdeen.

continued overleaf

continued

Once it looked as though Inverness–Aberdeen would close, but it came to life with faster trains calling at fewer stations, and a score of passengers on Nairn's platforms is not unusual. Like most resorts it owed everything to the railway...and people turned out in force to see a Black Five haul the first steam train for a quarter of a century in 1992.

After having left a wagon in the siding there, LMS class 5 2–6–0 No 42919 is seen drawing into Creetown station to take water on 15 July 1963. Freight traffic lasted here until April 1965 shortly before the line closed completely on 14 June 1965.

and-bailey earthwork, the Mote of Urr. Then negotiates a sequence of cuttings and Castle Douglas, where a few Kirkcudbright-bound passengers alight. Re-starting, we are now on the metals of the Port Line proper and progress briskly in a north-westerly direction along the shore of Loch Ken for several minutes. To the right are wooded hills but nothing spectacular; all is pleasantly pastoral in the morning sunshine. We slow down for tablet-exchange at Crossmichael and Parton, and then veer round to the west to go over the Ken viaduct, a 3-span bridge crossing the narrowest part of the loch. Immediately the engine's exhaust sharpens, for we have begun the climb up the valley of the Black Water of Dee. Passing New Galloway station, 6 miles from that small burgh but linked to it by a coach service, we struggle up four miles at 1 in 80 to reach the wild and barren table-land which divides the Ken valley from that of the Cree. At the top of the climb, at Loch Skerrow passing place, there is a water tower where the driver may stop to replenish his tender tank. This is the loneliest part of the line. Peaty moors extend on all sides. Away to the north west rises the whaleback of the Cairnsmore of Fleet, over 2,300 feet high. Trending south west, we cross two splendid viaducts over the Little and Big Waters of Fleet, and appear to be heading for a line of crags, the Clints of Dromore, haunt of wild goats. However, we veer south just before reaching them and come to the summit of the line at Gatehouse of Fleet station, over 500 feet above the sea. The town it serves is some 7 miles to the south, on the Fleet estuary; a horse-drawn coach service connects the two, taking an hour to make the journey.

Hard locomotive work is over for a while and speed begins to quicken as we descend to near sea-level down a 1 in 80 incline, following the

Moneypool Burn. Out into the corridor to get a splendid sea view from the other side of the train: Wigtown Bay and the coast of the Machars, Wigtownshire's long triangular extension to the south, green and inviting in the early morning sunshine. The tide is out and the Cree, Galloway's chief river, is snaking its way to the sea across the exposed sand. Then cuttings block the view after Creetown station; we cross a few fast-flowing burns by high bridges and reach sea level at Palnure. A timber-and-steel viaduct takes us across the Cree, and we begin climbing again up the flank of a hillside, to reach the second largest station on the line, serving Newton Stewart.

Here we halt for a few minutes to allow passengers to alight; some will be making for the connecting train down the Whithorn branch which is waiting in the bay beside the up platform. It consists of a motley assembly of six-wheel coaches headed by an engine about to run tender-first. We pull and begin climbing once more to cross the base of the Machars, through pastoral scenery with occasional rough moorland patches, over the Bladnoch viaduct and through Kirkcowan village and station, reaching our second summit at milepost 40³/₄ (from Castle Douglas). A brisk run down steep gradients then brings us to Glenluce station, beyond which is the high stone viaduct across the Water of Luce. Here, if one steps out again into the corridor, one can enjoy another seascape briefly, across the sands of Luce Bay towards the Lands End of Scotland, the Mull of Galloway at the southern extremity of the Rhinns, whose lighthouse blinks across the water and is always noted by the crew of the Irish cattle trains, usually double headed.

Stranraer Town was originally a through station as the line continued beyond the buffer stops on left to Portpatrick (closed in 1950). The home signal remained in situ however, now useless. On 12 July 1963 LMS class 5 4–6–0 No 45432 has just arrived on the morning train from Dumfries and is about to proceed to the engine shed behind the station to turn.

117

Another couple of miles, and the line from Glasgow and Ayr comes in from the right to join us at Challoch Junction. Time to gather belongings together, for the end of the train journey is now only a quarter of an hour away.

At 5.45, if the train is on time, we approach Stranraer, but avoid the main station by swinging off to the right. A couple of minutes later we come to a halt on the quay, where the *Princess Maud*, the newest of the steamers on this run, named after the King's youngest daughter, waits for the crossing to Larne. For a few seconds English feet tread Scottish ground...and then up the gangway and to the first class dining saloon, where the half-sovereign which the mater pressed into one's hand will buy a decent bacon-and-egg breakfast with lashings of coffee, and leave some change with which to purchase picture postcards and halfpenny stamps with which to mail them.

Of all the lesser main lines in Scotland the Port Line probably saw the largest number of steam locomotive types heading its trains during its century of active life. Probably no photographs remain of the 0–4–2s and 2–2–2s which worked during its first two years of operation. Of all the others there are plenty still to be found. From 1864 till 1885 it was Benjamin Conner's outside-cylindered 2–4–0s, with their tall stovepipe chimneys and exiguous weather-boards instead of cabs, which dealt with most of the traffic; after that came Hugh Smellie's 'Wee Bogies' and 'Big Bogies', domeless 4–4–0s, which often had to be used two at a time on the heavier trains. Later, James Manson's big-boilered 4–4–0s replaced them and coped well while he was in charge of the G&SWR locomotive department. In 1915 very briefly one of his successor Peter Drummond's large superheated 4–4–0s worked on the Port Line – performing wonders with the heavier trains, on an astonishingly low coal consumption. Alas, the pw gangs quickly reported it was too heavy for the track and it had to be taken off.

After the Grouping in 1923 former CR Pickersgill 4–4–0s predominated for a while; then came the newly-built Midland-type Class 2 4–4–0s, often used in pairs. Not till 1939, when Stranraer was given a new long turntable, was it possible to use ten-wheeled engines. Stanier's 'Black Five' 4–6–0s were then introduced; they could go anywhere and do anything, and maintained their supremacy until the end. But the most memorable feat of speed, albeit with a light three-coach load weighing less than the locomotive, was performed by a BR Clan Pacific, No 72005, *Clan Macgregor*, which on one occasion during its short life ran from Dumfries to Stranraer Harbour on the afternoon boat train, taking 88¼ minutes for the 73.8 miles of this difficult road. That included three intermediate stops and slowings at all the other stations for tablet exchange. Before Dunragit it reached 72mph – probably the only 70 the line had ever known and certainly the last. All of them, from pygmies to giants, have now gone to the scrapyard; peace to their shades. The line itself died when steam died, and never saw a diesel locomotive. With it went a daily challenge to locomotive men, signalmen who had sharp bursts of activity (especially before Christmas when the Irish cattle traffic was at its peak) between long lulls, and a whole way of life.

Face to Face

It was the summer of 1964, and there had been a major rationalisation of the provision of vans on the King's Cross and West Coast fish trains from Aberdeen to make the traffic profitable. On the Thursday (always the heaviest day) of the first week the district traffic superintendent was at the Guild Street fish loading roads. Having seen the 13.43 King's Cross away, he walked round to see how things were working out with the 14.15 Manchester.

Hearing vehement imprecations coming from an ex-LMS six-wheeler, he climbed in. Fish for half a dozen drop-off points was already piled high in stacks, and the loader was carrying more icy boxes through narrow aisles to the individual stacks.

'How is it working out?' asked the Super. 'I'd like to meet the stupid b...r who dreamed this lot up,' came the angry reply.

Eyes met, and the Super said 'Well, now you have. Provided you don't want to add another van, which we can't afford to do, I'm listening to suggestions'. The arrival of another merchant's lorry at the doorway deflected further comment.

Lattice Posts and Tablet Catchers

Scottish pre-Grouping railways saw little virtue in producing much of their signalling equipment in-house; there were insufficient economies of scale to be achieved. So they went to established private firms for their signals, lever frames and block and tablet instruments, and having a reputable firm on the doorstep in the shape of Stevens & Sons with a works in Glasgow, all but one placed orders there. Only the North British, however, took the standard Stevens spectacle with pear-shaped glasses, the others producing more traditional spectacles.

The exception to using Stevens products was the Highland, who for their own good and sufficient reasons patronised the rival firm of McKenzie & Holland. The third big signalling name, Saxby & Farmer, got no look-in north of the border.

There was universal acceptance of lattice posts in Scotland, though there was an element of backsliding by the Highland who used timber in some areas, notably the Kyle line. But there is lattice and lattice; the North British adopted a lighter form than the others, with zigzag bracing rather than the more usual crossed (at least to casual examination) type. The posts were surmounted by very distinctive finials. The prize undoubtedly went to McKenzie & Holland's elegant design some 3½ feet high, its long lance-like spike growing out of what might have been the protector on an epee. The Stevens finial was mundane by comparison and little more than half its height. It came in two forms, one centred on a hollow perforated ball, the other consisting of two profiled ribs at rightangles to give a not-very-convincing replica of the ball. Signals controlling divergences into goods loops were normally mounted on a neat strutted bracket well below the main arm.

The signal arms themselves, of wood, were unexceptional, even though some of those on the Great North and Highland Railways appeared distinctly slender for their length. Scottish signals never gave an indication that could raise drivers' doubts; they were either horizontal (or even slightly above) or they were off at something like 60°.

An unusual suspended bracket signal still with Caledonian arms, controlled the exit from Nos 2 and 3 platforms at Buchanan Street Station, Glasgow. BR Standard class 5 No 73006 and Stanier class 5 No 44705 (already fitted with a wrong type boiler with topfeed on the second row of the barrel by St Rollox works) wait for mid-morning departures on 6 May 1952.

Gleneagles was home to this splendid Caledonian bracket signal controlling the divergence to the Crieff branch. The main post is of heavy lattice construction with much lighter lattice for the individual dolls, surmounted by Stevens finials. Note the subsidiary stiffening post to which the structure is stayed.

Shunting signals were seldom on the ground but of the open 'bow tie' form, a pattern almost unique to Scotland. Lamps, too, were often very far from plain, with tall top cowls, some of 'cottage loaf' pattern. The North British and Highland, especially on tall signals, tended to eschew ladders for the lampman, preferring to lower the lamp by windlass for filling and trimming at ground level.

Special circumstances produced special signals. The Highland's unstaffed request halts were sometimes dominated by a platform signal with two arms, normally at 'off', *for operation by intending passengers* to stop the train (what a delight for small boys!). In at least one case this took a different form – a rotating disc signal atop a short lattice post. Then there were (and still are) the famous double-arm rockslide warning signals in the Pass of Brander on the Oban line, which were installed at frequent intervals for a distance of over three miles. The wire screen fence which operated them soon earned the nickname of 'Anderson's piano' after the Callander & Oban's secretary whose brainchild it was.

The Caledonian made a leap into the future in 1908 when, with the help of Stevens, it installed electro-pneumatic semaphore signalling at Glasgow Central. The number of signal arms was curtailed by the use of pneumatically operated route indicators. Even so the miniature lever frame to control the installation had no less than 374 levers in one line, the largest in the world. It continued in operation until the postwar colour light age.

The signal boxes themselves were highly distinctive. While some early Caledonian examples, especially on the northern routes, were somewhat mean in appearance, the standard format was quite elegant, as visitors to the SRPS at Bo'ness, viewing the box recovered from Gartsherrie, can testify: brick base, wooden upperworks with large sliding windows, generous roof overhang, the rather upright Stevens frame, and in some cases double line block instruments featuring *two* signal arms (facing and back) instead of needles. There were oddities, too – Glencruitten, for instance, at the summit of the climb out of Oban, which was combined signal box and signalmen's houses. It was fortunate that no signalman had to attend for the down night mail train, for there would have been little sleep for the other occupants!

The North British was less uniform. In so far as there was a standard it had a brick base (with generous windows for the locking room) with continuous stone sills and a timber superstructure incorporating sash windows; as such it needed no outside platform for cleaning purposes. But quite common was an all-brick design, still with sash windows. The G&SW went for all-timber boxes of rather nondescript design, as did the Great North of Scotland.

Highland boxes were instantly recognisable. Very dour-looking erections, their vertical weatherboarding with timber cover strips had much of the charm of an over-grown platelayers' hut built from old sleepers – though at least this style matched many of the station buildings. They were invariably economical in height and were entered by a short flight of outside stairs leading to an enclosed porch to give some weather protection. As ever there were exceptions, of which perhaps the most interesting was Keith East, perched high to see over vehicles in the Portessie bay platform. It contained an early frame with no catch handles as such, the whole lever tops being pivoted to serve this purpose.

The Highland's speciality, of course, was to be seen at its single line crossing places, the loops of which were often too long to be worked from a single box. Sometimes a signal box was provided near one end, with a ground frame to work the other (disguised as a small squat signal box but devoid of block and tablet instruments). Elsewhere there would be ground frame boxes at each end with the instruments in the booking office. The procedure for crossing trains would have done credit to a work study expert.

For many Scottish single lines, such a system was perfectly adequate; traffic levels were hardly hectic, and passenger trains tended to stop at every station anyway. Exchange of tablets in a pouch with large wire loop, hand-over-hand, was routinely undertaken by enginemen up to

A typical Caledonian box. West Street Junction, on the Glasgow freight line from Larkfield Junction to General Terminus on 17 April 1965. The wide roof overhang and the external walkway (with no outside handrail, only grab handles on the window frames) were typical Caley practice.

Ex-Caledonian Pickersgill 4–4–0 No 54471 leaving Keith Junction on the 2.15pm Aberdeen–Inverness via Mulben on 7 May 1957 diverts attention from Keith East signal box perched above the Portessie bay. Its typical Highland construction (if not its position) has a very unusual lever frame.

about 25mph (well over the official limit), even a bit more if the driver was faced with a hard climb. The signalman offered the tablet with his upper hand from either the platform, his signal box steps if within range, or from a wooden 'pulpit' if not, while the fireman concentrated on

Doing it the hard way. The fireman of the class 5 No 45179 collects the token for the section to Strome Ferry in its leather pouch from the Kyle of Lochalsh signalman by the traditional wire hoop in the early 1950s. Control of the single line is now from Dingwall by Radio Electronic Token Block (RETB).

collecting it, the while trailing the previous tablet low. But there were some routes where many stops could be omitted or where critical line capacity could not afford the constant slowing for tablet exchange. James Manson, locomotive superintendent of the Great North, designed an automatic tablet catcher which enabled the exchange to be made at speed. It was first used on the Fraserburgh line in 1889 and extended to all of the GNSR main routes. Manson – he who, soon after moving to the Glasgow & South Western handed out fierce punishments and checked his cleaners' work by running his finger along the *underside* of the engine platform – declined to patent the apparatus because of its safety benefits. This gave the opportunity for the Highland to adopt it for the Perth–Inverness, the Far North and the Keith lines.

The Ballinluig signalman has just completed the token interchange with the driver of class 5 4–6–0 No 44978 on the 3.42pm Perth to Blair Atholl local train which on 22 August 1960 included 2 ex-LNER non-corridor coaches. The one-coach Aberfeldy branch train had just arrived behind Caledonian 0–4–4T No 55212. The apparatus was that invented by James Mason of the GNSR

Drummond's big banking tank engines at Blair Atholl had *one each side* for obvious reasons. The Portpatrick & Wigtownshire Joint also used it on the Port road in preference to the Bryson 'snatcher' originally provided by the Glasgow & South Western between Girvan and Stranraer.

The North British and Caledonian had little scope for such fineries, since operating headways were not critical and climbing on the West Highland and Oban lines was done at speeds which allowed manual exchange anyway.

Small improvements such as these could hardly mask the retention of pre-Grouping practices on the single lines until the 1980s. Now it has all changed on the routes which Dr Beeching would have closed and the government disallowed. Signal boxes have gone, along with the signals. Train movement authority is now captured from the air in the form of radio signals with Radio Electronic Token Block instead of brass discs in leather pouches by the jaws of Manson catchers. Passing loops are negotiated by courtesy of automatic trailable facing points, unmoved by hand, through which the authorised speed is 15mph – the same as was laid down for manual exchange and which was pushed up to 60mph (though usually 40mph) by tablet catchers. Such is technical progress.

7
FOUR LOCOMOTIVE BIOGRAPHIES

THE individuality and soundness of locomotive design, building and performance north of the border is well emphasised by studying the lives of four individual machines.

HR No 55 *Clan Mackinnon*

The Highland Railway's isolation contributed towards the line's romantic image and as if to complement this perception it owned some of the most aesthetically pleasing locomotives ever built in Britain.

When in 1915 the civil engineer refused to allow the use of his new 'River' class locomotives, Frederick Smith resigned as locomotive superintendent. His replacement in unhappy circumstances was Christopher Cumming, a North British man from Burntisland. The Highland urgently required additional engine power and the first decision was to increase the numbers of the existing 'Loch' and 'Castle' classes.

A new class of 4–6–0 engine, needed to handle the growing traffic between Inverness and Perth, had to wait until 1919. Hawthorn Leslie & Co were largely responsible: batches of four came during 1919 and 1921. Named after well known Scottish clans they proved to be free and reliable steamers capable of very hard work – and looked extremely attractive in the unlined Highland green livery, relieved by the name on the continuous splasher and a large oval numberplate on the cabside.

From the second batch, No 55 *Clan Mackinnon* left Hawthorn Leslie's Newcastle works in July 1921 and travelled north to take up duty. The first few years of No 55's career were spent on the Inverness to Perth route, the HR having been granted running powers over the Caledonian Railway from Stanley Junction over the last few miles into Perth. In common with other members of the class allocated to regular drivers, *Clan Mackinnon*'s smokebox door was embellished with a thistle motif achieved by scraping away the door paint to leave the shape in shining bare metal.

The Grouping resulted in through engine working between Inverness and Glasgow Buchanan Street, albeit confined to one train a day in each direction, with 'Clan' class engines and Highland men throughout. They were short-lived, unpopular workings as the men had to spend nights a long way from home.

In its early years under LMS ownership *Clan Mackinnon* was turned out in red livery with Company crest on the cabside and its new number 14767 in large numerals on the tender, yet by 1929 it had been repainted in the black LMS livery with red lining. During 1934, along with three other sister locomotives, it began working over the Callander & Oban –

Seen at Montrose

April and May 1949 were interesting months in the Montrose area. On 15 April, the 6.30 fish ex-Aberdeen was hauled by 60031, painted black, an unusual visitor. On two occasions the southbound Aberdonian was double-headed, the train engine in each case being a V2, and the pilots B12 61528 and B1 61343 respectively, these engines acting as assistant up the single-line gradient to Usan.

B1s are becoming common those noted including 61133/4/47, 61242/63 (on a special from Dundee), 61342/3/6 (which worked the second portion of the Aberdonian on 20 May). This was a twelve-coach train, and it was assisted up the bank by J35 64619. Fish specials provide an occasional K3, and recent visitors have been 61909/28, both in very dirty condition. The Shire 4–4–0s have also been in evidence, and 2702/18/28 have been noted on the 3.37 parcels from Aberdeen to Kirkcaldy.

Unusual visitors were C16s 7484 (working the Inverbervie branch) and 7493 (running north light). An interesting feature has been the number of locos coming from Inverurie Works in new British Railways livery; these include J35s 64488 62A, 64490 64E; J36 65324 65C; J37s 65491 63A and 65493 62B.

Two 'crocks' were lying in the shed at Montrose for a week – J37 4611 65A and 60503, which had developed an overheated bearing and was removed from the fish
continued overleaf

continued
train. 60506 of the same class was seen in a state of complete collapse being towed northwards on LMS metals by a WD 2–8–0, and shortly afterwards two of these were noted 'on tow', one of them having a cylinder head blown right out. 60510, painted black, passed Montrose on a fish special on 21 May.

Some interchange working has been noted. Two LMS Compounds were seen working fish trains south of Montrose on the LNER section, and the 6.30 fish from Aberdeen to King's Cross was worked on 25 May by class 5 4956 65A, with LMS lettering on the tender.

A few new 5s have appeared on the main-line traffic from Glasgow (Buchanan Street) to Aberdeen, and these have included 44722/3/5, all with black tender sides. – Journal of British Locomotive Society.

FALLS ON THE SPEAN.
ROY BRIDGE.

and was soon joined by the rest of the class ousted from the Highlands by the newly arrived Stanier Class 5 4–6–0s.

Allocated variously to Balornock, Stirling and Oban sheds the 'Clans' were worked very hard during this period of their career and put in some superb performances on the challenging Glasgow to Oban line. However in the summer of 1939 the increasing numbers of Black Fives arriving in Scotland saw them displaced again – back to the Highlands where this time they were as familiar on the Kyle of Lochalsh and Wick lines as south of Inverness.

The first to be withdrawn was No 14769 *Clan Cameron* in October 1943 and the others were quick to follow. Only two survived to become British Railways property: No 14764 *Clan Munro* and No 14767 *Clan Mackinnon*, the latter being the only one to carry its allotted BR number 54767, applied during an overhaul at Lochgorm Works in September 1948. This engine had spent a large proportion of its later years working out of Aviemore but its final allocation was to Inverness where it was frequently seen on goods and cattle trains over the Kyle route, on one occasion in August 1949 being photographed leaving the western terminus of the line double-headed with 'Clan Goods' No 57951. From time to time it would still be used on the odd passenger turn and was a welcome sight for local enthusiasts in the summer of 1949 arriving at Forres with an RAF special from Inverness.

Clan Mackinnon's final journey took place on 4 February 1950 when it travelled under its own steam to Kilmarnock Works for scrapping. Externally the locomotive looked in surprisingly good condition with the name shining proudly through the grime; it was reported as still intact outside the works a month later although by 14 March cutting up had all but been completed.

CR No 903 *Cardean*

In November 1905 the forward-looking Caledonian Board authorised the construction of twenty new locomotives: among them five 4–6–0s were destined to rank among the most famous steam engines of their era.

Built to the design of John Farquharson McIntosh the first, No 903, left St Rollox Works in May 1906 at a cost of £3,500. The other four, Nos 904–7, followed quickly. Although bestowing names upon their engines was not a common practice of the Caledonian, No 903 was named *Cardean* after the estate of a director, Edward Cox, who later became deputy chairman. The name was painted on the leading splashers in gilt letters while the CR coat of arms appeared on the middle ones.

Cardean entered traffic from Polmadie shed and ousted one of McIntosh's earlier successful designs, 4–6–0 No 49, from its regular turn on the 2.00pm 'Corridor' express from Glasgow (Central) to London. This was taken as far as Carlisle where the engine then returned on the corresponding 8.13pm down train. Apart from occasional trips back to St Rollox for overhaul or repair *Cardean* worked these two particular trains almost exclusively for the next ten years.

The prestige of the Caledonian and of the 903 class in particular took a severe knock on 2 April 1909. *Cardean* was heading the down 'Corridor'

when shortly after passing Crawford at over 60mph the locomotive gave a sudden lurch that snapped the drawbar between engine and tender. The automatic brake coming into action, the engine stopped in three quarters of a mile – and investigation showed that the crank axle had fractured just inside the left hand wheel seat and the main frames were badly twisted. The tender and most of the carriages were derailed, though there were no serious injuries to the passengers. The official enquiry reported that the failure of the crank axle (which had only run 145,000 miles since new) had been caused partly by bad design leading to premature metal fatigue, aggravated by inferior quality material. Why the drawbar between locomotive and tender also broke was never satisfactorily explained.

It was only a temporary setback for *Cardean* and her four sister locomotives continued to earn good reputations. This led to a series of tests being carried out between No 903 itself and an LNWR 'Experiment' Class 4–6–0 over the Carlisle to Crewe line during a 25 day period in the early summer of 1909, just two months after the unfortunate episode at Crawford. Few details survive of No 903's exploits north of Crewe, but the run of 6 July 1909 in particular has often been used to illustrate the best of British locomotive performances in the pre-superheater era.

Around the time of these trials *Cardean's* standard whistle was replaced

The Highland Clans were the last of the family of three Hawthorn, Leslie designs, appearing in 1919 after the 4–4–0s Durn *and* Snaigow *in 1916 and the Superheater Goods in 1918. No 14767* Clan Mackinnon *(HR No 55) is seen here leaving Callander with an Oban train, a service to which the engine was transferred in 1934 after the Highland main line fell to the ubiquitous Stanier class 5s. It returned to the Highland in 1939, working mainly freight trains until called to Kilmarnock works for cutting up in February 1950.*

by a highly distinctive deep-toned version which apparently could be heard for miles. This had been supplied by Colonel Denny, a Dumbarton shipbuilder who was a Caledonian director. Another factor adding to the *Cardean* legend was the production of 30,000 tinplate clockwork $1\frac{1}{4}$in gauge models of the locomotive, ordered by the CR from Bassett-Lowke Ltd and sold to the public at half a crown ($12\frac{1}{2}$p) – a public relations gesture rivalling even the Great Western Railway's efforts. One wonders how many of the models still exist today.

The mystique surrounding *Cardean* is nicely captured by a small piece in the *Railway Magazine* for August 1932, reminiscing about West Coast services in the early years of the century:

A handsome combination *Cardean* made with the seven cars of the 2 o'clock, all twelve wheelers of a special design and some of the smoothest-riding stock that has ever run over West Coast metals. And so on a typical winter's night at Carlisle with half the city – or so it seemed – making Citadel station the venue of its evening promenade, and *Cardean* the centre of attraction…then would come a thrilling blast on the great foghorn that *Cardean* carried in place of a whistle and the shapely form of the 2 o'clock vanished into the night.

Even in LMS crimson lake, standing at Edinburgh's Princes Street station in 1927 at the head of a Glasgow stopping train, ex-Caledonian 903 class 4–6–0 No 14752 shows something of the majestic appearance that earned the class (led by 903 itself Cardean*) considerable fame. Built as a saturated engine in 1906 super-heating was applied in 1911. In the LMS scheme of things there was no place for the five engines of the class and No 14752 was cut up in December 1930.*

The 10 year association with the 'Corridor' finally came to an end during the winter of 1916–17. Then *Cardean* was used for a time on the heaviest Glasgow–Liverpool workings as far as Carlisle. Latterly it worked in a link with its successor, Pickersgill 4–6–0 No 61, on a morning train to Edinburgh and an afternoon express to Carlisle. Interestingly although Nos 903–7 had all been superheated in 1911 there was little improvement in performance, though a reduction in coal consumption undoubtedly made them more popular with their firemen.

Around 1920 it was reported that *Cardean* had lost its name and a further slip into obscurity came after the Grouping in 1923 when the celebrated No 903 became simply No 14752 in the LMS lists. In fact under this new ownership most of McIntosh's 4–6–0 designs quickly lost their importance and the former *Cardean*, now in simple black livery, finished its days in December 1930 on the Perth to Aberdeen stopping trains.

Although *Cardean's* fame still lives on, many commentators have expressed reservations as to just how good a locomotive it actually was. Its place in history is more probably as a consequence of its links with the 'Corridor' rather than achieving high quality performances on a regular basis. Without this association No 903 could well have been as little known as its four identical classmates which were rarely in the spotlight during their careers.

GNSR No 49 *Gordon Highlander*

In its entire history the GNSR did not use anything larger than a 4–4–0, a wheel arrangement which proved to be economical and capable of carrying out all but the heaviest work singlehanded. Towards the end of 1898 William Pickersgill, the locomotive superintendent, managed to get the director's cautious agreement to order ten new engines, Class V, from Neilson Reid & Co in response to an expected increase in loads. After five of them had been delivered traffic levels actually declined and the GNSR decided to cancel the order for the remaining five. Neilson Reid sold them instead to the newly formed South Eastern & Chatham Railway in England.

As part of a general locomotive renewal programme a further eight Class V 4–4–0s were built somewhat spasmodically at Inverurie between 1909 and 1915 but after World War I there was a more pressing need for new engines to replace those worn out. Accordingly eight new superheated locomotives were built in 1920–1 at the request of T.E. Heywood who had succeeded Pickersgill in 1914. These were almost identical to the earlier design but were designated Class F in recognition of their superheated boilers.

As part of this new class No 49 *Gordon Highlander* left the North British Locomotive Co's Hyde Park works in October 1920, painted in the Heywood black GNSR livery with red lining and polished brass smokebox hinges. Along with other members of the class it was employed on the most important express passenger duties, principally those between Aberdeen, Keith and Elgin although it would not have been unusual for it to take turns at the head of a goods train or venture down one of the many branch lines within the limit of its axle loading.

Quintinshill

Many of Scotland's worst disasters were at least in part the result of the elements: storms, floods and blizzards. One says at least in part because often there were contributory factors, notably the poor workmanship that went into Thomas Bouch's first Tay Bridge, which collapsed on the stormy night of 28 December 1879 with the loss of all 75 passengers and crew on board a train that plunged into the waves with it.

The elements, however, had nothing to do with the worst accident of all; in the annals of all British railway history, there is nothing that compares with the tragedy of Quintinshill, north of Gretna.

It was the height of World War I, and at this time the Caledonian was conveying thousands of tons of coal over its main line, destined for the Royal Navy's Grand Fleet at Scapa Flow. The sheer volume of this extra war traffic, made an already busy civilian main line literally groan at the seams. Prior to the war, Quintinshill had been a relatively quiet signal box controlling two passing loops where goods trains could be shunted to allow the faster express workings to pass. On 22 May 1915 the night signalman, Meakin, was officially due to be relieved at 6am, but an 'arrangement' had been made with his mate Tinsley who worked the day shift, so that by coming in a bit later they could travel from and to their homes in Gretna by train. This was completely against company rules so, to avoid being discovered, Meakin would write down any train movements after 6am on a sheet of paper for Tinsley to enter in his train register when he arrived. Now when Tinsley did arrive he found the down loop was occupied by a freight train, causing Meakin to shunt the 6.10am northbound all-stations passenger train (on which he had just travelled) on to the up

continued overleaf

continued

line in order to allow a delayed Glasgow express to pass; this it did at 6.38am. Meanwhile he had accepted an empty coal train into the up loop, leaving only the down main line clear.

What happened next is beyond belief, for not only were there two signalmen in the box, but also the guards of both freight trains. Tinsley had produced a newspaper, and it is evident that during the crucial few minutes all thoughts had turned to events proclaimed in the headlines. Even though the fireman of the stationary passenger train had come into the box to remind the signalmen of his presence on the up main line, the obligatory collar was not put over the signal lever to prevent its unauthorised movement. Despite the fact that the local still stood in full view of the box, it was forgotten by all as at 6.42am Tinsley accepted an up troop train and immediately after a second down express, the 6.05am from Carlisle, and duly cleared signals for both main lines. The 'trooper', carrying the 7th Royal Scots, came down the section at 70 mph and struck the front of the local head on with such force that the debris spilled all over the down main line. The two freight guards realised that the 6.05am was due any second and they ran down the line to warn it, but it was too late and the double-headed express flashed by them at about 60 mph straight into the wreckage. Five trains now lay strewn around Quintinshill in a mountain of rubble, and the wrecked wooden coaches of the troop train had caught fire. The flames were soon consuming everything and everyone who lay within their path. The blaze was so bad that it was still smouldering 26 hours after the crash. In that time three railwaymen and nine civilian passengers died and many more were injured, but it was the

continued on p131

In the national coal strike during 1921 *Gordon Highlander* was temporarily converted in June for oil burning using the Scarab system – the only GNSR locomotive so equipped – but the ugly tender mounted oil tank was removed in October.

Following the Grouping *Gordon Highlander* was renumbered as LNER No 6849 and continued working from Aberdeen's Kittybrewster shed. Within a few years it found itself competing for the principal express duties with five class D31 4–4–0s brought in from the North British section. But it was not until the B12 4–6–0s were imported from East Anglia from 1931 onwards that the D40s (as the GNSR Class V and F had by then been reclassified) were ousted from the heaviest turns. It was during its latter period in LNER ownership that *Gordon Highlander*, by now renumbered again as 2277 under the 1946 scheme, spent a lot of time working from the Buchan line terminus at Fraserburgh. Royal trains to Ballater were hauled by a pair of D40s. The engines allocated to this duty, including *Gordon Highlander*, were obviously kept in sparkling condition, but as it was customary to allocate the superheated D40s to regular crews anyway the standard of cleanliness of ex-GNSR engines was always very high, at least until the outbreak of World War II.

As the number of B12s increased, the D40s spent more time off their traditional duties and by nationalisation, when B1s had also arrived in the north, they were more normally seen on secondary workings away from the main line. *Gordon Highlander*, now carrying BR black livery and the number 62277, together with several of its sister locomotives came to monopolise services over the Speyside branch from Craigellachie to Boat of Garten and it was this line that saw the last regular activity of the engine prior to its official withdrawal from Kittybrewster in June 1958 as the final representative of the class.

During the following month *Gordon Highlander* was given back its old GNSR No 49 and painted at Inverurie Works in the pre-Heywood green livery of the old company. After a period back on the Speyside line it was transferred to Dawsholm shed, joining the other preserved locomotives which had been retained for special working. In the following years No 49 was utilised on a host of excursion trains which took it over the metals of the former NBR, CR, GSWR and Highland railways as well as working coupled to the preserved NBR Glen 4–4–0, the CR 4–2–2, the Highland Jones Goods 4–6–0 and even the GWR 4–4–0 *City of Truro*.

These special trains finally came to an end in June 1966 when *Gordon Highlander* dropped its fire for the last time and was placed in the Glasgow Transport Museum alongside engines representing the other pre-Grouping Scottish companies.

NBR No 875 *Midlothian*

In the early years of this century the North British Railway locomotive superintendent, Matthew Holmes, was suffering from poor health and during this protracted illness his assistant William Paton Reid regularly deputised. Shortly after Holmes's death in July 1903 Reid's appointment as his successor was ratified, some 25 years after he had entered service with the NBR at the age of 17.

It was around this time that major developments were taking place in the development of the steam locomotive north of the border. The Caledonian and G&SWR had just introduced some large 4–6–0s and the NBR could see itself lagging behind in the standard of services, their own largest engines then being the '317' class 4–4–0s. Rising to the challenge Reid initially proposed a 4–6–0 design similar to that of the neighbouring companies but this was rejected by the NBR directors who were concerned that such a long engine with a rigid wheelbase might cause problems on some of the severely curved main lines.

So the 4–4–2 Atlantic wheel arrangement was adopted. The resultant engine was truly massive. An initial order of fourteen was placed with the North British Locomotive Co in 1906. At first the class did not meet with universal acclaim; drivers complained they rolled alarmingly at speed while the civil engineer was convinced they were damaging his track. In the end however the Atlantics came good and a second lot of six appeared in 1911 with a further two entering service in 1921, bringing the total to 22.

Class D40 4–4–0 No 62277 Gordon Highlander, *otherwise known as* The Sojer, *was a North British Locomotive Company product of 1920 and was withdrawn from normal service in 1958, the last surviving GNSR engine. It was overhauled at Inverurie works and turned out as No 49 in Great North green livery – which in fact it never carried – for use on enthusiast specials until 1965, when it was retired to the Glasgow Museum of Transport. Here it is on its old stamping ground, the beautiful Speyside line, working a typical passenger train on to August 1951 near Nethy Bridge, its paintwork gleaming.*

The one that nearly survived! North British class H 4–4–2 No 875 Midlothian starts an express out of Inverkeithing station for the severe climb up to the Forth Bridge about 1922. Built by North British in August 1906, the engine was super-heated at the end of 1920 and with-drawn in December 1937, only to be reinstated in June 1938 with a view to preservation. Alas, the war caused it to go to the scrap line in November 1939. At this stage vacuum brakes had been added to the original Westinghouse brake system, which was later removed.

No 875 *Midlothian* left the NB Loco Company's Hyde Park works in August 1906 and entered traffic from St Margarets shed in Edinburgh where at first it was used on the Carlisle expresses and then on the Aberdeen line once a turntable large enough to take the Atlantics had been installed there. Within a couple of years *Midlothian* was reallocated to the newer and better equipped Haymarket shed where it continued working through to Aberdeen until shortly after World War I. At this time however the pattern of services over the Edinburgh to Aberdeen route was completely re-arranged with engines being changed over at Dundee. Thus the Haymarket Atlantics worked to Dundee and back while the Aberdeen locomotives did the same in the opposite direction.

Although superheating of the class began in 1915 No 875 had to wait until December 1920 before it was fitted with a brand new superheated boiler manufactured by Robert Stephenson & Co. Interestingly, after all the Atlantics had been withdrawn in the late 1930s this particular boiler saw further service as a stationary steam raiser at Stratford Works, surviving until June 1960.

Renumbered 9875 shortly after the 1923 Grouping *Midlothian* continued hard at work from Haymarket shed, although the arrival there of increasing numbers of the new Gresley Pacifics during the late 1920s saw it appear more frequently on the Edinburgh to Glasgow main line and on occasions this also included a run at the head of the up Queen of Scots. However the Atlantics were still regular performers on the Aberdeen line, though by now many of the trains were well above their maximum load and double-heading was not uncommon. It was this inability to cope with the increased traffic levels of the 1930s that contributed to their inevitable demise.

In September 1936 No 9875 was transferred back to St Margarets shed where the handful of Atlantics saw service principally on the Carlisle and Perth routes, the tendency being for engines to work specific trains on a regular basis. Even so the days of this famous class were now numbered and as their boilers became due for renewal the locomotives were gradually withdrawn, *Midlothian* and No 9901 *St Johnstoun* being the last examples to go at the end of 1937.

But this was not to be the end of the Atlantic story. Although *Midlothian* had entered Cowlairs Works for dismantling in April 1938, moves were afoot, supported by the LNER chairman William Whitelaw, to preserve one for posterity. Unfortunately by the time the relevant instructions found their way to the right department at Cowlairs *Midlothian* was in an advanced state of disintegration. Nevertheless orders were orders and so the task began of trying to put the locomotive back together – some parts were still lying around but many had to be made new while the boiler came from No 9876 *Waverley*, withdrawn the previous summer.

The rebuilding was complete by mid-June 1938 and resplendent once again in LNER green No 9875 re-entered traffic at St Margarets. Initially employed on an Edinburgh to Perth diagram it subsequently found a regular spot on the 4.55pm Edinburgh to Glasgow express and 8.25pm return, while in the following year it was frequently rostered on an Edinburgh to Carlisle working. Throughout this period it became a firm favourite with local railway enthusiasts.

Midlothian was still at work when World War II broke out but its journey to Cowlairs for overhaul in November that year was destined to be its last. The workshops had more important repair work to carry out and the whole question of looking after preserved locomotives seemed irrelevant in wartime. This time there was to be no miracle escape and *Midlothian* was quietly cut up for scrap by the year end.

continued

troop train which suffered the greatest casualties, with at least 215 officers and men killed an a further 191 injured. Both signalmen were tried for manslaughter, convicted and imprisoned. The engines of the local train, 4-6-0 No 907, and of the troop train, 4-4-0 No 121, were both destroyed.

Walking Scottish Railways

With an increasing spate of closures from the 1930s to the 1960s, Scotland has been left with many hundreds of miles of disused railway lines. The majority of the routes have been re-absorbed into private ownership, but an increasing mileage is being converted into public walkways, cycleways and bridleways by a combination of local authorities and private organisations.

In the Grampian Region, the erstwhile Great North of Scotland Railway system has provided several interesting walks. After closure, the first 12km from Aberdeen of the Deeside line that once took the Royal Train to Ballater were converted into a public walkway. The route starts in the Duthie Park and passes through the urban sprawl of Aberdeen before entering into the rich farming country of the Dee Valley. Sadly, many of the station buildings have been demolished, leaving only the platforms marking their location. However the station buildings at Cults, Murtle and Milltimber have survived, the first two being typical GNSR timber examples.

The walkway ends at Culter, and the continuation of the line is in private ownership, though the final 12km to Ballater are again open to the public. At Ballater it is possible to follow part of the planned extension of the line to Braemar, opposed by Queen Victoria who did not want the trains passing too close to her royal residence. Ballater station has been tastefully restored and includes a cafe conversion welcomed by those following the route of the Royals.

Refreshment of another kind is provided on Scotland's longest railway walk, also in the Grampians some 25km from Dufftown to Craigellachie and on to Ballindalloch, it passes through the wooded slopes of the valleys of the rivers Fiddich and Spey, the heart of Scotland's whisky production. The railway served numerous distilleries along the way, some of which are now open to the visitor. This line retains many railway artefacts. Several mileposts can be found in the undergrowth as well as a few faded 'Stop Look and Listen' notices, which warned former users of crossings about the presence of the railway. Several stations have survived intact, adding to the general pleasure of walking this very scenic route. The former Knockando station (now called Tamdhu) retains its signal box along with the station buildings, which now serve as a visitor centre for the nearby distillery.

Moving into Highland Region, one of Scotland's most enigmatic railways was the Invergarry & Fort Augustus, which suffered the fate of twice closing in its first ten years. Running from Spean Bridge, the line ran through the Great Glen, which forms a spectacular cleft through the Scottish Highlands. The line served more sheep than people and was finally closed to passenger traffic as early as 1933.

Unfortunately, the trackbed has not been converted into a walkway, but the section which passes through the South Laggan Forest from east of Invergarry to the Corriegour Lodge forms a forest access road. This runs on the hillside above Loch Lochy, and permits one to savour some of the rugged scenery which the railway traversed. Other parts are also walkable, and the nearby 'General Wade's Military Road' allows these sections to be linked together, as well as presenting an opportunity to view some of the many bridges and viaducts, built in concrete, that were needed to take the railway up through the Glen. There is a project to create a footpath through the Great Glen, that will no doubt use parts of the railway and the military road, to allow a safe pedestrian route from Inverness to Fort William.

Perhaps one of the most spectacular of Scotland's disused railways is the route of the former Callander &

Oban line from Dunblane to Crianlarich. The section where the line climbs up Glen Ogle, the 'Khyber Pass' of Scotland, from Lochearnhead, forms the basis of a circular walk from the small village. With the use of the railway and the former military road constructed by Major Caulfield but attributed to General Wade, Stirling District Council have created a magnificent ten kilometre circular walk.

Starting from the village, the easiest way is to follow the military road up to the head of the glen, offering views of the railway as it hugs the contours of the nearby hillside. At the head of the glen, a stile gives access onto the trackbed, permitting a return back along the railway, seen before from below, crossing side valleys by means of sweeping stone viaducts. The walk ends above the village, dropping down through the fields past the village's former station on the line to Crieff. Here a detour to view the excellent conversion work done by the Scout Group who now own the building is recommended. If only all former railway stations could have been treated like this example! A few further kilometres of the route through the Pass of Leny from Callander station (now a car park) to Strathyre have also been converted into a path.

Some of Edinburgh's once dense network of circuitous suburban lines built by the competing North British and Caledonian have been converted by the council into green, traffic-free corridors into the heart of the city. The old Caledonian route between Murrayfield and Granton is a particularly pleasant walk, as is the route of the Balerno branch from Slateford, which includes a tunnel.

Worthy of mention is the former Smeaton to Gifford line, which re-opened in 1964 as the Pencaitland Way. Walkers go through a very rural countryside which has covered over the remaining traces of the area's early industry. Further west, again on the south side of Edinburgh, can be found the Dalkeith–Bonnyrigg–Penicuik line passing through the steep sided gorge of the North Esk. Walking alongside the river, past wooded slopes and through a couple of short tunnels and over several girder bridges and viaducts, you rebuild in your imagination the railway serving the water-powered mills in the valley's industrial heyday. A recent conversion is the former line from Dalmeny to South Queensferry, which gives an unusual viewpoint of the Forth Bridge as it passes under it.

The efforts of the charitable Sustrans, are helping put the Glasgow area on the map of railway walks. The North British line from Kirkintilloch to Killearn and the continuation onto Balloch can be walked most of the way. The route curving round the foothills of the Campsie Fells gives a sharp contrast to urban development. The Glasgow & South Western line to Kilmacolm and the Lochwinnoch Loop have been adopted for walkway conversion.

From Galloway to the Far North, sections of abandoned lines wait to be explored. With charitable organisations like the Sustrans and the Buchan Line Trust taking over the initiative started by local authorities nowhere in Britain is there greater official awareness of the rich heritage of routes Remember that you need permission to explore those sections over private land beyond the official paths.

8
THE ROMANCE OF THE CALLANDER & OBAN

IT is 1959, a time we can now look back at with great affection. True, people travelling then spoke of more glamorous bygone times when service really was service, yet they realised that what they were enjoying could not last indefinitely, or indeed that much longer. After just over a decade of nationalisation, losses were mounting and the severity of closures to come was beginning to be hinted at...and it was obvious from intelligent looking at the trains and their passengers that the books could nowhere be near balancing. Moreover, as in much of the rest of Britain there was a feeling of amazing continuity...trains running much as they had in the days when the railway had a virtual monopoly, the timetables easily memorised since they changed so little season by season...and above all the war that had seemed to put an end to civilisation now just seeming a temporary interruption of the norm.

We are off to the West Coast for the weekend, still an adventure, Oban seeming in a different and far more romantic world. It is summer and will remain light throughout the journey and we have promised ourselves dinner in the restaurant car which still uses this like most of the other great Scottish scenic routes. But we do complain about the length of journey, and especially the slowness of its first part from Edinburgh.

Princes Street, perhaps the most forgotten of the former large city termini, is busy and most corner seats are already taken on the 4.23 through coaches to Oban, attached to a Perth train running the round-about route via Stirling, Dunblane (where we will be detached) and Gleneagles. There are the usual delays in the Falkirk area and our call at Grahamston is several minutes late, but at least quite a few shoppers and office workers starting their weekend early alight here. Bridge of Allan looks its best in the sunshine after a shower...and then we have an idea. We are irritated by the fact that the timetablers not only give this train 12 minutes in Stirling but even then it leaves 33 minutes ahead of the 5.15 from Glasgow to which we are to be joined at Dunblane. 'Excuse me, but I wonder if you could keep these seats for us...we'll be back at Dunblane,' has not only the people opposite but the whole compartment surprised as we alight and admire Stirling's summer floral display.

Stirling on a summer Friday evening is always busy and you can spot preparations for ever heavier traffic next day. A Black Five comes in with the 5.00 from Glasgow to Dundee West, a well-used business train sandwiched in between the Edinburgh and Glasgow portions of the Oban. And a ubiquitous Stanier Class 5, and incidentally very black, arrives with the Glasgow–Oban, on time at 5.59. Crowded too. Straight to the restaurant car where the chief steward says he will be 'coming through the train'

Daily Bread

Southerners visiting the Hebrides have always been apt to replan the islands' economies in their minds and be irritated by the apparent lack of self-sufficiency even on the larger islands such as Skye and Mull. They could therefore be quite upset at some of the things they discovered on the trains going to the ports.

Laundry baskets were one, for nearly all Hebridean hotels have for generations sent their laundry to Inverness, no laundry ever having been established locally. Milk was another. Fish might be exported but frequently milk was imported along with virtually all admittedly rare and expensive fresh vegetables. Likewise flowers for the hotels and 'big houses'. And even bread. Half a ton of bread was despatched daily from Glasgow bakehouses on the early morning passenger for Mallaig, transferring for both the Portree and Stornaway ships. Much of the rest of the Highlands had its Glasgow-baked bread sent daily by goods train.

Designed for the Oban line by McIntosh and built at St Rollox in 1902, CR 4–6–0 No 57 enters Callander with a train from Oban on 26 July 1913. The substantial corridor stock of this train makes an interesting comparison with non-corridor vehicles stabled on the far side of the platform. Note the air brake equipment on the locomotive and the safety chains provided on the non-corridor coach. A true pre-Grouping scene.

but reluctantly gives us two seats for second sitting. 'Busy tonight,' he mutters, 'and not everyone from Edinburgh will be suited.' Our decision to change at Stirling has been vindicated.

We are away sharply at 6.04; a pity we could not see the St Mungo due in seven minutes no doubt with more interesting motive power than ours. There are few spare seats, but we settle for the two middle ones in one of those half compartments (one bench seat looking at a blank wall) the LMS have at the end of many of their pre-war carriages. Did they design them that way, or just find they could only fit in a final half compartment?

When we reach Dunblane at 6.17 the passengers in the Edinburgh section which has been there since 5.43 look as though they are eager to get on their way…or is that our imagination. We decide to stay put and let those we left behind wonder what has happened to us, for dinner will start. Passengers from the first sitting are already drifting back.

Though told they are not ready, we somehow manage to remain in two window seats in the spacious restaurant car. Old fashioned it may be, but

134

it exudes comfort with its picture windows and seats designed for giants...and we soon notice it has the excellent riding quality one expects of such LMS vehicles. This is more like it. The chief steward tells the chef there are a couple of customers for a third sitting but the chef gestures not on your life. We think of at least a dozen other examples where you can change earlier than you are supposed to in order to get into the restaurant car that will eventually be on the train you left.

As we study the menu – little choice, but still a separate fish course – we cogitate that there are 82 fascinating miles from Dunblane to Oban where we are due at 9.33. This is the day's last through train, only Callander having later services tonight though tomorrow there will be a connection off the last one to Callander to Killin as the Killin branch train makes its weekly Saturday night outing along the 'main' line, giving Killin its only through service. The last train except that the first of tomorrow's really begins tonight at 10.30 from Glasgow Buchanan Street getting to Oban at 5.7am...and on a summer Saturday will no doubt be quite busy. And it will be followed a few hours later (but from Glasgow Central) by another night train conveying a sleeping car and indeed seating carriages from Euston.

In winter the sleeper only runs once a week and we discuss how the difference between winter and summer traffic is much sharper than it used

Passing trains at Strathyre. On 24 August 1960 Stanier class 5 No 45359 on the early morning Stirling to Oban goods waits in the up platform for the 7.50am Glasgow (Buchanan Street) to Oban hauled by sister engine No 45468 to clear the station and the next section to Balquhidder which until 1951 was the junction for Comrie, Crieff and Perth. The crew of the down goods can be seen seated on the far side of the decorative fountain on the up platform.

The Callander & Oban viaduct in Glen Dochart about one mile west of Killin Junction taken from a west bound train hauled by ex-Highland Railway Clan class 4–6–0 No 14769 Clan Cameron on 11 August 1937.

The 5.15pm Oban to Glasgow train in Glen Lochy photographed from the A85 across the River Lochy on 13 August 1939. The locomotive is ex-Highland Clan class 4–6–0 No 14769 Clan Cameron and the train conveys a former Pullman car running as a restaurant car.

to be. In winter indeed you can almost have a whole carriage to yourself and enjoy a good blether with the unhurried staff in the restaurant car. And in winter the following train to Callander only runs if there are passengers from south of Carlisle travelling by the 10.00 ex–Euston. The station master at Stirling has to wire Dunblane whether or not there are passengers.

Turning west from the main line, the train sets out through undulating meadowland with mountains on the horizon some ten miles ahead. We failed to spot the site of Springbank Siding, worked in the up direction by the goods from Doune, the first station, which consists of an island platform and marks the end of the double track. The signalman at Doune West hands over the single line tablet, and here we are sipping sherry heading west into the sunshine in the restaurant car of a six coach train with well over two hundred passengers on the curving single track.

The journey along the valley of the River Teith, whose waters reach the sea as the Firth of Forth, with views of Lanrick Castle on the far side, is interrupted only by the slowing of the train to pass through the loop at Drumvaich Crossing, nearly four miles beyond Doune.

The Dunblane, Doune & Callander Railway opened in 1858 and trains could proceed no further for twelve years until the first stage of the Callander & Oban proper was brought into use as far as Glenoglehead, the site of the original Killin station. The terminus at Callander was bypassed but at this time is still a goods shed.

We pass the disused ticket platform before drawing into the 'new' Callander station, reminiscent of the alpine style, with a steeply pitched roof, and made famous by the filming of the TV Doctor Finlay series.

Now the journey westwards begins in earnest with a climb through the Pass of Leny (with its waterfalls near the lineside) of 1 in 61 for more than three miles to St Bride's Crossing at the southern end of Loch Lubnaig. Ben Ledi is visible to the left and at the disused loop the driver can no doubt see Ben Vorlich (3224 feet) dominating the north east skyline.

The railway now runs along the west side of the loch, remote from the parallel main road, and at isolated Craig-na-Cailleach arrangements are made for school children to be picked up in the morning for Callander and returned at tea time. Our train also calls there on Saturdays to set down employees returning from shopping. Those at St Bride's Crossing only have this privilege officially alternate weeks.

The Working Timetable states: 'Drivers of all trains and engines must run at such a speed as will enable them to stop at once, if necessary, when passing the Craig at Loch Lubnaig' (and between the 52 and 55 milepost on Loch Aweside as we shall see later) 'as stones are liable to become detached'. Automatic stone signals are sited here and a special bell and telephone circuit connected the foreman platelayer's house there with the station master at Strathyre.

Benvane can be seen on the left when running beside Loch Lubnaig. In the early days trains stopped by request at Laggan Farm House for the benefit of trout and salmon fishers on the loch.

At the head of the loch road and rail come together again in Strathyre, nearly twenty miles from Dunblane. Tonight we stop at Kingshouse

Kingshouse Platform between Balquhidder and Strathyre closed prematurely along with the line between Callander and Crianlarich due to a landslide in Glenogle on 28 September 1965. (The advertised closure date was 1 November.) The two-coach school train hauled by BR class 4 2–6–4T No 80028 is the 4.05pm from Callander to Killin on 8 September 1965.

Platform, a request stop. The timetable warns that notice must be given to the guard at Strathyre – and no luggage or bicycles. The Working Timetable stipulates that the guard must call out the name of the halt as soon as the train stopped and collect tickets (and any excess fares). These must be handed to the station master at Balquhidder from whom a receipt has to be obtained. The platform was provided by local people, not the railway company, and was not open until June 1871. It is a fine place to wait for a train in good weather, there being a view of the hills encircling Loch Voil.

Less than a mile further and we are at Balquhidder, known originally as Lochearnhead, until that name was acquired by the last stop for the trains that came west from Crieff and Comrie between 1905 and 1951. An island platform on the up side at Balquhidder catered for the branch service. Already too late in history for a branch connection but we cross the first of the late afternoon trains from Oban to Edinburgh and Glasgow with observation car at its tail.

The climb resumes and our Black Five works hard for the six miles up to the summit of 941 feet at Glenoglehead. The view eastward over Loch Earn is truly magnificent. Then follows stony, bleak Glen Ogle with the main road on the far side of the valley. [It was hereabouts that a landslide led to premature closure of the line north of Callander, on 28 September 1965, rather than from 1 November as advertised.]

Up freight trains halted at Glenoglehead for their brakes to be pinned down.

From the loop at Glenoglehead our route (opened in August 1873 from here to Tyndrum and diverted off its intended route at Crianlarich to preserve a salmon pool) drops at 1 in 70 to Killin Junction nearly two miles further on. Killin Junction: an isolated spot high on the hillside, just an exchange station for passengers to the Killin branch train which is at the north face of the island platform. Forty passengers must be transferring tonight: all must take the connecting one-coach train as there is no road access – and as we sip our coffee the people opposite our seats we left at Stirling recognise us and wave.

To the east is majestic Ben Lawers towering to 3,984 feet; to the north west rises Beinn Cheathaich (3,074 feet), to the south west stands The Stob and ahead is Ben More (3,843 feet). A wonderful location for a junction – in fine weather like tonight's now that the showers have died away.

A down freight train with a load (in Presflo Alumina wagons) for British Aluminium Company via Ballachulish hauled by LMS class 5 4–6–0 No 45163 approaching Connel Ferry in 1960. The Connel Ferry bridge over the Falls of Lora can be seen in the background.

Late afternoon crew change at Connel Ferry on 20 May 1960. On the left hand platform ex-Caledonian class 2P 0–4–4T No 55238 has arrived with the 3.57pm from Ballachulish whilst just arrived from Oban on the right hand platform is sister engine No 55224 with a train for Ballachulish. The wide platforms and ample passenger accommodation are typical of many stations on this line.

We tipped down at 1 in 69 for the next three miles to Luib [on the formation today's straightened road uses] and cross the second late afternoon trains from Oban, the last of the day with a refreshment car to Stirling and sleeping car to Euston (in winter the sleeper only runs on Monday nights). Loch Iubhair is followed in quick succession by Loch Dochart on the north side of the line and then we reach Crianlarich Lower Level, a disappointing single-platform compared to the glories of the ex-NB Upper. [At this time an observation car from Glasgow still ran to Oban via Dunblane but from 1950 the connection from the West Highland's sixteen mile shorter route was used by a daily summer train and now all Oban trains of course use it.]

As we pay our bill, we reflect that our route's original motive power was 4–4–0s with stovepipe chimneys, inclined cylinders and rounded cabs built by George Brittain with 5ft 2in driving wheels. There were four-wheeled tenders to fit the small diameter turntable at Oban. Known as 'Oban Bogies' some ran until 1930. John McIntosh introduced a class of nine inside-cylinder 4–6–0s in 1902 which lasted until 1937. Just before the Grouping they were joined by William Pickersgill's 4–6–0 locomotives with two outside cylinders and 5ft 6in driving wheels. These were augmented by the former Highland Railway Clan class 4–6–0s which ran on the line from 1934 until 1939. Now the Stanier Class 5 4–6–0s rule supreme. Eastbound steam trains can load to eight coaches but westbound the limit is six (our load tonight) so that there is one train less from Oban. Some trains, usually the mid-day ones and several on summer

Saturdays, are double headed and strengthened and there have been many ingenious arrangements such as double heading between Dalmally and Crianlarich using an engine to take over the 2.00pm freight to Stirling.

In the summer of 1914 a Pullman car named *Maid of Morven*, designed for observation as well as catering, was introduced to the line, withdrawn during the subsequent war and operated again from 1923 on the 9.45am from Glasgow and the 3.35pm return. The agreement with the Pullman Car Company expired in 1934 but the coach was retained and repainted in LMS colours. Now, as just mentioned, a buffet observation car runs in the summer with a supplementary charge of 3s 6d each way.

Back in our original seats in the generous-size compartment with two half sliding doors to the corridor (only one of the passengers is the same as when we left at Stirling) we climb from Crianlarich to Tyndrum (5 miles) at 1 in 61, in parallel with the West Highland higher up on the mountains to the east. Trains leaving Tyndrum for Oban face a difficult start on a 1 in 49 gradient to the summit at 840 feet above sea level. Then it is downhill for fifteen miles to the shore of Loch Awe, through Glen Lochy.

Financial difficulties put a stop to the ambitions of the original Callander & Oban Company at Tyndrum and they had to look to the Caledonian Railway to complete the project and then to operate the line. It is still often nicknamed John Anderson's railway after the first secretary and manager. Construction work began again under the new management and Dalmally was reached in 1877 with the opening to Oban in July 1880.

To break up the twelve mile section of single line to Dalmally, there is a loop at Glenlochy Crossing, a little over five miles from Tyndrum. The isolated signal box is built as part of residential accommodation for the staff: the house and the box are integral, with a bow window to facilitate sight of the trains and block bells repeated in the domestic quarters. Coal is brought from Tyndrum by the morning freight on the last Saturday in the month. The box is usually switched in for one shift only from 11.15am until 7.15pm on weekdays. The 9.33am goods from Callander to Oban (timed to arrive there at 4.10pm) had to wait in the loop for thirty minutes when the 12.50pm fish special was running from Oban to Stirling but fish alas is rare on this line now.

Incidentally, years ago when elders of the Kirk thought the railway was closed on Sunday in fact a mixed train of passenger and stock crept into Oban shortly after 5.00am, having left Stirling at 12.15am. It called at all tablet stations (except Connel Ferry) to enable the guard to exchange and lock up tablets. The load was not to exceed 18 vehicles unless double-heading was provided when four more could be added. It called at Crianlarich at 2.53am to detach livestock and perishable traffic for the West Highland Line. A strict order of preference was laid down for traffic by this train. Priority was for Oban except minerals; then livestock and perishables for the West Highland and beyond Dalmally; then for Connel Ferry and Ballachulish goods; then Taynuilt goods; and lastly minerals for Oban.

The unique Connel Ferry bridge on 18 July 1961 with the usual branch train hauled by CR design 0–4–4T No 55263. The rail-road bridge was closed to cars and lorries when a train was due. It is now a single track road bridge controlled by traffic lights.

Soon after leaving Dalmally we cross a viaduct over the River Strae and then turn to follow the shore of Loch Awe, with a picturesque station where once you could change for the railway steamer to Ford and the steam launch to Taycreggan and Port Sonachan. The railway-owned *Countess of Breadalbane* was built at Dumbarton shipyard and reassembled on the loch in 1936 after transport by rail.

The second location at which 'stones are liable to become detached' is in the Pass of Brander after the River Awe has left the main loch. Here there are 14 automatic stone signals, an up and a down arm on each post normally in the off position but if one or more of seven wires on the hillside above are broken by a rock falling then all the signals go to danger. A signal linesman who checked the signals is picked up at Awe Crossing early on Wednesdays only.

The north side of the line is dominated by Ben Cruachan (3,689 feet).

An unusual view of Oban with the approach to the engine shed in the foreground. The locomotive is one of William Pickersgill's 4–6–0s built specially for the C&O, LMS No 14620. Just peeping into the picture on the left is one of McIntosh's small wheeled 4–6–0s also built specially for the line.

Then Taynuilt and tonight even a request stop at Ach-na-Cloich, also with a pier: you used to be able to sail the length of Loch Etive, take a bus up Glen Etive to the Pass of Glencoe and return from Ballachulish on the branch train, a pleasant day out from Oban.

As we emerge from the trees towards Connel Ferry the bridge, designed on the lines of the Forth Bridge, which carries road traffic north to Fort William as well as the Ballachulish trains, comes into view. The last train for Ballachulish left four hours ago though tomorrow there will be a sharp Saturday connection for the fish-and-chip brigade.

The remaining seven miles to Oban: a climb of nearly four miles to the loop at Glencruitten Summit and then a three mile drop all at 1 in 50 virtually to sea level during which the train almost encircles the town, so as to enter the station from the south. Tonight's views are enhanced by the bright westerly light. Prior to the final overbridge, sprung from the rock, there used to be a ticket platform near the engine shed. We breathe the salt air as we take in the scene outside the entrance: lively lads and lasses, a pipe band in the distance, the Macbrayne steamers waiting for tomorrow. It has not been a quick journey yet now Edinburgh seems in a different world.

The classic view of Oban station on 19 May 1960 with McCaig's Folly overlooking the town on the left. LMS class 5 4–6–0 No 45443 is waiting to depart with the 5.15pm to Glasgow (Buchanan St) and Edinburgh (Princes St). The pilot locomotive has yet to be attached on this normally double-headed working. On the right ex-Caledonian Railway 0–4–4T No 55224 waits with the 4.55pm local to Ballachulish.

Beyond Aberdeen

Aberdeen is the natural terminus of the East Coast Main line. Yet the LNER did not end there. Those who carved up the country at the 1923 Grouping put the Great North of Scotland Railway in the Eastern Group, so the new LMS did not dominate Scotland. The old GNSR was a compact, self-contained, and independent railway. Just in case its general manager should be under any illusions about his status, the general manager of the dying North British Railway, who was taking over as LNER general manager (Scotland) on 1 January 1923, wrote to his opposite number in Aberdeen: 'I have no doubt that you will advise the GNSR officers that I will take full executive responsibility in Scotland for current business as from 1st proximo.' Yet in many ways – 'full executive responsibility' or not – the old GNSR remained independent. Part of the reason was geographical: 38 LMS miles from Kinnaber Junction separated GNS territory at Aberdeen from the rest of the LNER.

But there was another reason why the former GNSR continued to be very independent: Inverurie Works. In the nineteenth century a penurious GNSR carried out its engineering tasks wherever it could (and sometimes in the open air), but between 1901 and 1905 all locomotive, carriage and wagon, and permanent way efforts were transferred to a brand new, electrically-lit works complex at Inverurie. And so it continued right into the 1960s. In

In 1931/2 the LNER transferred five former Great Eastern Railway 4–6–0s, LNER class B12, to the Great North of Scotland section followed by further batches of these useful machines in 1933, 1939 and 1940/42 making a total of 25. No 61528 eases a substantial north bound freight out of Kittybrewster yard in September 1949. The engine, in unrebuilt condition, is painted in LNER apple green, with black and white lining but with 'British Railways' on the tender. Many of the open wagons are empty and are probably destined for the whisky traffic from Speyside.

LNER days it made no sense to transfer work arising in the Northern Scottish Area (as the old GNSR was now styled) to workshops further south, so Inverurie in more senses than one maintained the distinct identity of LNER lines north of Aberdeen.

Away down south the new masters had problems enough of their own, welding together the parts of their new railway, and as long as there was no trouble north of Aberdeen they were content to let the locals get on with it. And that is what they did. How many years was it before Gresley LNER carriages appeared regularly north of Aberdeen? They got no engines from the new owners until 1931, and *they* were ex-GER B12 Class 4–6–0s dating from 1912. It was 1947 before *new* engines actually appeared in the shape of some B1 Class 4–6–0s. One has the impression that the GNSR section did not mind this Cinderella status. They had their own stock and Inverurie to look after it. At the ending of wartime austerity Inverurie was far ahead of Stratford in restoring the LNER apple green livery to its B12s. When BR introduced the 'blood and custard' livery for corridor stock, Inverurie applied it to GNSR carriages that were nearly half a century old. The parallel separateness which comes most readily to mind is the unlikely one of the Isle of Wight.

The old GNSR had been a railway of branches. They fed its portion of the Aberdeen–Inverness main line, and it fed them. The only casualties of the depressed 1930s were the passenger services on the Old Meldrum and Boddam branches. At Cruden Bay on the latter the old GNSR had optimistically built the Cruden Bay Hotel and Golf Links, hoping to generate revenue from the affluent, but even before 1914 the venture did not prosper. With the withdrawal of the passenger services on the branch in 1932 the prospects for the hotel nosedived, the nearest station now being at Ellon, a full ten miles away. LNER Headquarters was slow to react, but for the 1934 season the railway provided a rescue package in the shape of a limousine which would carry hotel-bound passengers all the way from Aberdeen. And it was a Rolls Royce. That the idea of such opulence originated from careful Aberdeen beggars belief, but the Rolls operated until the outbreak of war, which put paid to the Cruden Bay Hotel and its electric tramway.

The GNSR had originated as a line toward Inverness, the Highlands due north of Perth being considered impenetrable for the railways of the 1840s, and down the years traffic between Inverness and Aberdeen was a major concern, though the Highland prevented the GNSR itself getting beyond Elgin. Demand for meat and fish brought prosperity to Aberdeenshire, and little by little the branches came. They reached out to the sea coast at Boddam, Peterhead, Fraserburgh, Macduff, Banff and Portsoy, and inland to Alford. Most of them ended in small stations where passengers could shelter under an overall roof, Banff, Fraserburgh and Peterhead remaining into the 1960s. Generations of travellers blessed them, for a north-easterly gale in winter can be a fearsome thing. Having trudged up from the town through wind and rain

The quayside lines at Aberdeen were originally shunted by horses but to cater for increased traffic the GNSR purchased four small 0–4–2Ts from Manning, Wardle & Company of Leeds in 1915 which lasted well into BR days. No 68192 is seen on Trinity Quay in May 1957 together with, rather amazingly for such a late date, a horse drawn lorry. The second shop from the left rejoices in the name of 'Baltic Boot Store'.

the station was a snug haven, not exactly draught-proof, but a great deal better than waiting on some windswept open platform. Of course they were dark, and smoky when the branch train arrived, and not at all up to date.

Portsoy on the coast of the Moray Firth was for some years the terminus of the resoundingly named Banff, Portsoy & Strathisla Railway, which became part of the GNS in 1867. Along the coast from Portsoy west to Elgin the Coastal Route served a string of fishing villages and small towns which the GNS decided to take possession of before its Highland rival got its hands on them. However, it was a close-run thing for the Highland's branch from Keith was into Portessie, looking for the Buckie fish traffic, nearly two years before the GNSR opened at that port with its completed Coastal Line.

There were some notable bridges (and viaducts) along the coast you can still see at Cullen, and an oddity of a station only accessible by rail: Cairnie Junction near Keith on the main line existed purely for the interchange of passengers, and shunting. Opened in 1898 it first appeared in the timetable in 1965, and closed in 1968. Most trains from Aberdeen to Inverness via Elgin were in three portions and at Cairnie Junction that for the Coast Line stations was detached. It made a sedate passage along the heights above the Moray Firth and rolled into Elgin's

handsome GNSR station, still intact, but now in other use. By some careful timetabling passengers from Keith and places beyond were brought to Cairnie to connect with the Coast Line portion. The other two portions went forward to Keith Junction where they split again. One went straight on over the LMS (ex-Highland) metals to Elgin, which was quick but boring and the only route to survive today. The other set off up Strathisla to Dufftown and down the whisky glen to Glenfiddich and Craigellachie, passing through a countryside which was noticeably less pastoral and definitely more pine and heather than most of the GNSR. Many of the stations seemed to be in sight of a substantial chimney and malting cowls belonging to the local whisky distillery, and on a calm day it was worth lowering the carriage window to have a sniff of the local aroma. Few lines could tickle your taste buds like the Craigellachie route – except perhaps the Speyside line which began its pilgrimage to Boat of Garten there.

There was a time when north of Aberdeen was 4–4–0 country. The coming – under LNER management – of 4–6–0s and ex-NBR 0–6–0s began to dilute the locomotive flavour, but it lasted well into the 1950s. The GNSR itself never possessed an 0–6–0 tender engine and its 4–4–0s worked passenger and goods trains without discrimination. Their shapely general outline added to the distinctive general appearance of trains beyond Aberdeen and drew the discriminating observer. Not that there were many of them. The very slow pace of change was probably why reports of happenings on the old GNSR did not appear often in the rail Press. They generally seemed to be written by a southerner who had made a visit in the summer holidays.

Fraserburgh was at the northern end of the Buchan lines, a sort of Second Division of the old GNSR, devoted very largely to carrying fish and beef cattle. In this century the GNSR began to have ambitions for Fraserburgh and its coastal environs, the first (and only) fruit of them being the Fraserburgh & St Combs Light Railway of 1903. Now when we consider the fact that most branches beyond Aberdeen received no more than the most basic three trains a day provision, the service provided to St Combs was almost overwhelming in its lavishness: seven trains a day. The St Combs Light Railway really was a light railway, laid through the machar on the sandy ground stretching down to the coast with a complete disregard for the normal proprieties of railway life. There were no fences, no bridges, no earthworks. Just a cleared strip of land with ballast and track. There were Halts, of so basic a nature as to be invisible from any distance. So the St Combs Light Railway threaded its way up and down the sandy heath in the top right hand corner of Scotland for over 60 years. The engines, which were at the last BR Class 2 2–6–0s, had cowcatchers. The St Combs train was known locally as the Bulger trainie, trainie being the word

Opposite The Great North of Scotland approached Aberdeen Joint Station from the north with a line through the Denburn Valley. Class B1 4–6–0 No 61308 passes Union Gardens with the 12.9pm arrival from Elgin (dep 9.25) on 7 May 1957.

Evening Rush Hour. As the 5.50pm to Dufftown leaves Elgin, only the Gresley carriages intrude into a scene which, on 6 August 1953, looks pre-Grouping in every other aspect. The leading coach is a GNSR bogie of the 'toplight' era, c 1910, with a Gresley brake third behind. Lower quadrant signals abound, all by Stevens & Sons of Glasgow who supplied most of the Scottish railways. No 62264 is an 1899 member of the GNSR class V (LNER D40), its Manson tablet catcher out ready for duty as they approach Elgin East signalbox. Typical of things beyond Aberdeen, the only other engines in sight are 4–4–0s. No 62265 in the distance is getting ready to work the 6.00pm Coast Line train to Buckie, and No 62272 is shunting the goods yard.

used hereabouts for a train, and like the locomotives, the tiny corridor coaches and so many other things, the word contributed to the sense of difference north of Aberdeen.

The weather ever exerted its influence. Storms meant a break in the fish business, while snow frequently needed ploughing off the Buchan line – and at the 476ft peak at Glenbarry on the Coastal Line where it was the signalman's duty to determine whether or not to plough.

Below *At Fraserburgh the Great North of Scotland Railway provided this splendid overall roof to protect both passengers and stock from the North Sea wind and rain. On 21 July 1954, class D40 No 62279* Glen Grant *waits with the three coach train to St Combs; a five mile journey with two halts and a station en route. The locomotive is fortunately fitted with steam heat pipes at the front end as the return workings are tender first. The 4–4–0s on this service were shortly replaced by BR Standard class 2 moguls which were in turn replaced by DMUs before the eleven return trips (twelve on a Saturday) were withdrawn in May 1965.*

9
VERY CAREFUL BUT NOT MEAN

THE title for a piece by an English writer on Scottish coaches comes from the late and inimitable David L. Smith quoting from correspondence by one Scottish railwayman about another. The coaches were indeed carefully, economically produced but for the most part not mean.

There were some fine vehicles but the majority were no more or less than adequate for their tasks. When it came to the Anglo-Scottish trains, then, East or West Coast, comparatively few vehicles were built by the North British, Glasgow & South Western and Caledonian companies. The East Coast Joint Stock comprised ordinary carriages, dining cars and sleeping cars working the principal East Coast day and night trains. There was no separate ECJS capital account and each company managed its share in its own way. The capital account of each had a portion allotted to the ECJS and when new vehicles were built, each company contributed a proportion of the cost and debited its capital account with that amount. When carriages were taken out of the ECJS fleet, each company took a proportionate share. The shares as between the three East Coast companies were Great Northern 40 percent, North Eastern 35 percent and North British 25 percent. Yet, after the turn of the century, there was virtually nothing that could be attributed to the NB's influence.

The same was true for the West Coast Joint Stock (LNWR and Caledonian), Midland & Scottish Joint Stock (Midland, North British and Glasgow & South Western) or Midland and North British or Midland or G&SWR. These last-named succeeded the MSJS c1897. The dominant partner was always the English company and its design practices prevailed. The result was that all the experience and prestige associated with the Anglo-Scottish rolling stock was vested in the English partners. Doubtless there was a careful judgement by the Scottish companies as to the costs and benefits of their contributions.

So in talking of Scottish passenger carriages one is talking of stock built for service largely within Scotland although there were through coaches that were not in Joint stocks. Also Scottish vehicles were loaned to English lines. E.L. Ahrons records, for instance, that the G&SWR provided the Midland with stock for excursion traffic between Bradford and Morecambe.

If we return to the earliest days of railways we find the use of fourth class by Scottish companies. This was a feature of both the Glasgow, Paisley & Greenock Railway and the Edinburgh & Glasgow Railway. In the 1840s, they were in competition, the former with Clyde steamers, the latter with passenger boats on the Forth & Clyde Canal. Hamilton Ellis engagingly describes the E&GR fourth-class carriages as 'like elongated

---

Grand Splash

Gerry Fiennes tells how in 1939 a partly-fitted freight came to a standstill in Haymarket Tunnel near Edinburgh Waverley. When the fireman, Charlie, failed to find where air was getting into the vacuum pipe, the driver also got off the footplate.

Eventually they found what Charlie should have found, a vacuum hose pipe not properly seated on the plug. Charlie reseated the plug and emerged into the darkness of the tunnel.

As he did so, he heard from the front end: 'Ch...ch...ch.' Not only had the driver left the big ejector on but the regulator open – or so we found at the inquiry I took next day. The driver and Charlie set off to catch the engine but the wagons began to shoulder past them; anyway Charlie caught his hand-lamp between his knees, came a purler and the driver fell over him.

They clawed their way to the nearest signal and telephoned the
continued overleaf

In 1905 the Caledonian Railway introduced some magnificent corridor coaches for the Glasgow and Edinburgh to Aberdeen services. They were 68ft 6in long and ran on two six-wheeled bogies. The standard formation appears to have been a very lightweight one by modern standards, three coaches from Glasgow and one from Edinburgh. It was obviously not intended to use such fine vehicles in a common pool as they had the route painted on the upper panels 'Corridor Express Glasgow (or Edinburgh), Perth and Aberdeen'.

continued

signalman at Waverley. He, good lad, had three choices: first to let the train go on its way to Portobello but the line was full of trains; secondly to direct it to the line to Granton Dock which was empty; third to turn it up a dead end and wreck it against a wall of rock. He rightly chose the second. Next, how to warn the guard. So he rang the station inspector who gathered a posse of carriage cleaners, mainly female, ticket collectors and porters and posted them half-way along the platform.

The train emerged from Haymarket tunnel, now going strong. The guard emerged from his brake and leaned over the rear rail, his cap on the side of his head and his pipe drawing sweetly. It was Angus Panton's day. He had an early turn. He would be at Portobello about noon. He had arranged to take his wife and kids out. It was his birthday. Therefore when the mob on the platform screamed in every key: 'Ye're on the road to Granton. There's naeone on the fuitplate' he thought they were shouting: 'Hurrah for Angus Panton. Many Happy Returns, mate.'

The engine, 37 wagons and brake ended up beneath the water.

cattle wagons'. Talking of class, the Great North of Scotland never had second-class and charged third-class passengers a rate per mile between second- and third-class on other railways.

When it comes to innovation, the North British built the first sleeping car to run in Great Britain. This Cowlairs product was placed in service on 31 July 1873 and was a six-wheeler, 30ft in length. It ran from Glasgow to King's Cross returning the following night. The interior is said to have been furnished with crimson velvet, ebony panels and silver-plated metal fittings. No bedding was provided. The North British was a fairly early user of bogie carriages and built some in the late 1870s to work with Midland stock on Edinburgh–St Pancras expresses.

At this time the Highland creditably produced three bogie sleeping cars to work between Inverness and Perth. These were the first British side-corridor carriages as far as interior layout is concerned - they did not have gangway connections. For a while these Highland pioneers were used between Wick and Inverness but not in the down direction; somewhat uniquely the night trains on this route conveyed goods wagons. In 1885, the Highland's sleepers were converted to ordinary first-class coaches and replaced by Pullman-owned vehicles.

David Jones of the Highland is known on account of that railway's six-wheeled main line stock of the late 1880s/early 1890s which had straight sides and chariot-shaped half-compartments at the ends. Even as late as this period, they were originally oil-lit. Vehicles for purely local traffic were particularly spartan. But many of the railway's passengers seldom travelled in Highland compartments, in view of the number of through carriages from other railways conveyed on its trains. When one looks at Anglo-Scottish and internal Scottish passenger traffic, it is amazing just how it was dominated by midsummer and the shooting season. Ahrons coined a memorable phrase when he talked of 'a landslide' of rolling stock returning southwards at season's end. In these days of fixed formation trains it is almost impossible to imagine the complexity of passenger train marshalling with trains such as the 7.50am Perth- Inverness with 36 vehicles from nine companies in its formation. These would include horse-boxes, saloons and luggage vans, giving some clue to the well-off family groups and their servants aboard.

To take stock of the Scottish railways' carriages in the last decade of the nineteenth century, it is worth taking the companies in turn. The G&SWR had neat and well-finished stock which until the late 1880s was painted dark-green, that colour being shared with the Highland. The dark-green of the Sou'West then became something near the Midland's red. Some MSJS coaching stock was built by the G&SWR. One claim to fame of that company was its trial of a novel carriage heating system in the 1880s. Above the flame of the compartment oil-lamp was a small wrought-iron boiler serving a pipe-circuit that ran down underneath the seats. But if the lamp was unlit there was no heat!

The Caledonian also experimented with train heating, using the exhaust steam from the locomotive's Westinghouse brake-pump to heat radiators in the carriages. Its efficacy must be in some doubt. The Caley's main line stock was generally six-wheeled but elsewhere the majority were

The Caledonian Railway built some very fine 12-wheel coaches, both corridor and non-corridor, which, late in their lives, were dispersed far and wide over the former LMS system. Corridor brake composite No Sc7385 was on an enthusiasts' tour round Lancashire when photographed at Bolton Great Moor Street (ex-LNWR) on 26 July 1953.

Some Glasgow & South Western Railway coaches also lasted into BR days and corridor brake composite No Sc7396M was at Dingwall on 12 July 1955.

four-wheeled. At this stage the livery adopted was not far off a dark-purple. One rather curious survival from the CR's contribution to the WCJS is to be found today in the saloon, very much rebuilt, known as CR No 41 which originated as a Joint Stock dining car in 1893 but passed to the Caley when displaced from West Coast use.

Speaking of WCJS stock, one of the most attractive carriages from the turn of the century that has survived with a Scottish connection is the Fourth Duke of Sutherland's private saloon of 1899/1900 built at Wolverton. This handsome clerestory-roofed vehicle is not only of interest for its original owner's sake but was effectively the progenitor of a whole sequence of WCJS carriages and, indeed, Royal saloons.

6

GREAT NORTHERN NORTH EASTERN AND NORTH BRITISH RAILWAYS

THROUGH AND TOURIST TICKETS

are issued between stations in Scotland and stations on the Great Northern, North Eastern and North British Railways, and the railways in connection. For full particulars as to fares, etc., see the time tables and tourist programmes issued by the above-named Railway Companies.

PRIVATE OMNIBUSES.

The Great Northern Railway Company provide a limited number of omnibuses, at reasonable charges, to meet the trains at King's Cross station, London, when previously ordered.

Omnibuses will also be sent to the hotels or residences of parties leaving London by the Great Northern Railway, on application, stating the train by which they will travel.

THROUGH CARRIAGES.

Carriages of the most improved description, fitted with lavatories, lighted by gas, and heated by steam in winter, are attached to all the express trains from London, King's Cross, and run through to the principal places on, and in connection with, the Great Northern, North Eastern, and North British Railways.

DINING ARRANGEMENTS.

Passengers travelling by the Scotch day express trains which leave London before 11·15 a.m. have time to dine at York, where hot dinners are provided at 2s. 6d. each.

LUNCHEON BASKETS

are provided at the Refreshment Rooms at Perth, Edinburgh, Newcastle, York, Doncaster, Retford, Newark, Grantham, Peterboro', and King's Cross. Any passenger desiring to have one of these baskets should give notice to the guard of the train, or to one of the station staff at the previous stopping station.

7

GREAT NORTHERN NORTH EASTERN AND NORTH BRITISH RAILWAYS

SLEEPING CARS

are run in all the night express trains between Scotland and England. For ladies travelling alone a separate saloon is reserved.

PILLOWS AND RUGS

may be hired by passengers (first and third class) by the night trains between Scotland and London (King's Cross Station) at a charge of 6d. each pillow or rug.

SALOON AND FAMILY CARRIAGES

have been constructed expressly for the accommodation of families, and can be secured by giving timely notice to the Superintendent of the Line at Edinburgh (North British Railway), York (North Eastern Railway), and King's Cross (Great Northern Railway). The exclusive use of a first class compartment (the minimum payment being four first class fares) may be secured by giving notice at a terminal station two hours before the starting of the train; or, if at an intermediate station, by giving notice the previous day.

CONDUCTORS

in charge of baggage travel in each direction by the day and night trains between London and Scotland.

8

GREAT NORTHERN NORTH EASTERN AND NORTH BRITISH RAILWAYS

DINING CARS
(FIRST AND THIRD CLASS)

connected throughout by covered gangways are run in the undermentioned through express trains.

LONDON (King's Cross)	dep.	2 20 p.m.
NOTTINGHAM		3 0 "
GRANTHAM		4 27 "
YORK		6 15 "
DARLINGTON		7 12 "
NEWCASTLE		8 7 "
BERWICK		9 29 "
EDINBURGH	arr.	10 45 "
EDINBURGH	dep.	2 20 p.m.
BERWICK		3 37 "
NEWCASTLE		5 5 "
DARLINGTON		5 54 "
YORK		6 50 "
DONCASTER	arr.	7 29 "
NEWARK		8 15 "
NOTTINGHAM		9 8 "
PETERBORO'		9 8 "
LONDON (King's Cross)		10 45 "

* On Saturdays leaves Nottingham 3·45 p.m.
The up express is in connection with express trains leaving Inverness 6·0 a.m., Aberdeen (via Forth Bridge) 10·20 a.m., Dundee (via Forth Bridge) 12·15 noon, Perth (via Forth Bridge) 12 30 noon, and Glasgow (Queen Street) 1·0 p.m.

There is not much to say about the general run of North British carriages until the building of the bogie saloons built for the opening of the West Highland Railway. These were 50ft 1in over the buffers and had a combination of saloon and compartment accommodation. To permit passengers to see the glories of the scenery, side and observation windows were as large as possible. There were first and third-class vehicles. Hamilton Ellis was to note that they displayed ' great superiority to anything else in the carriage line on NB internal services'. In original condition, none of the windows was able to be opened; this was changed to the detriment of the external appearance, but the relief of passengers. It is easy to forget that the Forth Bridge opened as late as 1890. Its absence had hampered the NB's access to Dundee and Aberdeen; through carriages had to be worked to Larbert, to be conveyed northwards by the CR. Once the Forth Bridge was opened the service north of Edinburgh was transformed.

As with the rest of the British railways, the new century saw investment in rolling stock. The Caledonian was justifiably proud of its 65ft 'Grampian' corridors running on six-wheel bogies. Their roofs were more a three-centred curve than elliptical. Twelve-wheeled non-corridor stock was built as well for services such as Edinburgh-Glasgow. The longer vehicles, as on other railways, were somewhat unwieldy and so the remainder of Caley pre-Grouping main line carriages were to a 57ft length. Fortunately, a pair have survived in preservation as they were appropriated to run with Single No 123 in the late 1950s. The CR built some of the very last four-wheeled carriages for main line service as suburban block trains.

The Caledonian entered into a 20-year contract with the Pullman Car Co in 1914 and introduced Pullman dining cars on several principal services. There was also the famed Pullman observation car *Maid of Morven*, built by Cravens just before the outbreak of World War I. Curiously, the seating at the observation end faced inwards. Intended for working between Glasgow and Oban, the *Maid* was stored from 1915-19. When the agreement with Pullman had run its time, the LMS let it lapse and used the Pullmans as restaurant cars; incidentally, some new Pullmans had entered service on LMS trains in Scotland in the mid-1920s. At any rate, the former Pullmans survived in Scottish Region use until the early 1960s.

The North British was not to be outdone by the Caley and built some handsome corridor stock to work behind the Reid Atlantics in 1906/7 on Glasgow-Aberdeen trains. Just before World War I, similar carriages were built for the West Highland line. They had side corridors but no vestibules as the end coupé compartments had scenic windows. As an example of early twentieth century NB stock there is a former invalid saloon of 1919 preserved by the Scottish Railway Preservation Society. In that year, some rather monstrous all-steel dining cars were built by Cravens, notable for a tare weight of 47 tons.

The older NB carriages were long-lived. Hamilton Ellis wrote a

The LMS imported many 'cascaded' coaches from England to Scotland including dining cars. M289 was a former London & North Western Railway first and third class composite car with central kitchen, built at Wolverton in 1910. It was photographed at Inverness in May 1949. A very fine scale model of one of these cars is displayed in the National Railway Museum. Note the recent damage to the 3rd class end-footsteps, grab rails and adjacent panelwork.

Opposite above The Midland Railway was also represented at Inverness in May 1949 by third class dining car No 157 seen in one of the north platforms. It ran to The Mound or Helmsdale where it was detached and returned on a southbound train. This was one of six built at Derby in 1903. It was running on borrowed time, being scheduled for withdrawal in 1948 (as indicated by the figure 8 in the bottom left hand panel). It was withdrawn later in 1949.

Opposite, below The Caledonian Railway contracted the Pullman Car Company to supply coaches to run as dining cars in various internal Scottish services. When the contract expired in 1933 the LMS took over the vehicles and used them mainly on their former routes. One such was on the Highland 'Further North' line and car No SC219M was photographed at The Mound in October 1951 having worked down on the 6.25am from Inverness. It will be attached to the rear of the 8.40am from Wick for the return journey.

characteristic essay about an overnight journey from King's Cross to Mallaig in 1924. As the East Coast train was badly delayed by engine failure, the connection at Fort William was missed. A scratch train was provided: 'as battered and shaky a collection of vintage '85 six-wheelers as you might find in Great Britain.'

The Highland had undergone a revolution, too, and some decent carriages were produced under the aegis of Peter Drummond, including some composite sleeping-cars in 1907; composite in that there were first-class berths and third-class seating compartments. Third-class sleeping-cars were not to come until 1928. In 1916, the Highland received some TPO vans which were probably the last pre-Grouping examples in service on BR.

Drummond moved from the Highland to the G&SWR where whatever he may have done to the engines, at least some pleasant and tidy elliptical roofed coaches were put in service. That leaves the GNSR where the older rolling stock was not of a high order. This company's modern stock was perfectly acceptable and the toplights above the main side windows were reminiscent of GWR practice. One problem of this railway was that it was unable to accept stock of more than 12ft 11in height.

And so the LMS and LNER took over. The Anglo-Scottish services received the first call on new stock. However, the LNER built over 370 non-corridor coaches for the South Scottish Area (as the former NB was now termed) and gradually standard Pullman gangwayed, buckeye coupler stock took over the principal services. Yet, as late as 1938, pre-Grouping vehicles were still rostered for the LNER set working between

LONDON MIDLAND AND SCOTTISH RAILWAY

Pullman Car Services between GLASGOW, EDINBURGH, OBAN, CRIEFF, DUNDEE and ABERDEEN

SUNDAYS

	Breakfast Car, Glasgow to Dundee and Aberdeen.	Breakfast Car, Glasgow to Oban until 31st October.		Luncheon Car, Glasgow to Aberdeen.		Luncheon Car, Glasgow to Oban until 8th October	Luncheon and Tea Car, Glasgow to Aberdeen.	Tea and Dining Car, Glasgow to Aberdeen.		Tea and Dining Car, Glasgow to Oban.		Breakfast Car, Perth to Aberdeen.
	a.m.	a.m.		a.m.		p.m.	p.m.	p.m.		p.m.		a.m.
GLASGOW (Buchanan St.) dep.	—	7 15	8.0	—	10.0	—	12.15 a.m.	1.30	5.0	—	6.5	—	g7.15
EDINBURGH (Princes St.) ..	—	7.0	7.0	—	9.25	—	11.30 p.m.	1.10	4.25	—	5.31w	—	7.10
Stirling .. .. „	—	8.6	8.52	—	10.45	—	1.9	d2.21	5.47	—	7.0	—	8.18
Callander .. rr.	—	8.49	9.26	—	—	—	1.43	—	—	—	7.32	—	9.27
Gleneagles ..dep.	—	8.37	—	—	11.10	—	—	2.48	6.13	—	—	—	8.50
Oban .. ..arr.	—	—	12.35	—	—	—	4.48	—	—	—	10.16	—	12.30
Perth .. .. „	—	9.4	—	—	11.32	—	—	3.13	6.37	—	—	—	9.10
dep.	—	9.20	—	—	11.40	—	—	3.19	6.45	—	—	—	9.26
Dundee West ..arr.	—	9.40	—	—	12.34	—	—	3.55	7.14	—	—	—	10.3
Forfar .. .. „	—	10.10	—	—	12.23	—	—	4.6	7.25	—	—	—	10.9
ABERDEEN	—	11.40	—	—	1.58	—	—	5.40	8.55	—	—	—	11.30

d—On Saturdays calls only when required at 2.17 p.m. to pick up passengers for North of Perth.   g—Central Station.   w—Waverley Station, Edinburgh.

These Pullman Restaurant Cars are available for First and Third Class Passengers for Meals and other Refreshments without Supplementary Fare, except where otherwise specified.

LMS   RESTAURANT   CAR   157   3

RESTAURANT   CAR   ScM219   BRITISH RAILWAYS

The two LNER observation cars from the pre-war Coronation sets were sent to Scotland in the 1950s and after rebuilding to improve visibility they were used inter-alia on the Fort William–Mallaig service. Car No E1719E is being positioned by class B1 4-6-0 No 61342 for its return working from Mallaig at 5.42pm on 26 May 1961, after being turned on the locomotive turntable.

Busy Junction

Of the numerous different worlds conjured up by less than half a page in *Bradshaw*, the Buchan system and the main junction within it at Maud did not disappoint in reality. Here was a totally different world brim full of variety and individuality with as responsive and responsible staff as you could find anywhere, ready to walk long distances through snow and stay up all night to keep the wheels moving.

Roughly 30 miles from Aberdeen, 16 from Fraserburgh and 14 from Peterhead (the latter usually regarded as the 'branch'), Maud had a signalbox, platform bookstall, refreshment room, large goods depot, and a curious layout including separate up and down platforms for the Fraserburgh and Peterhead lines.

While Maud was of course well inland, it thought constantly of the sea. For example, a light engine on its way back to Kittybrewster shed meant poor landings at the 'Broch'; one in the other direction showed that an extra train was needed. Specials (fish, fishermen and fisherwomen going for the season's herring gutting, cattle and summer evening excursions to Aberdeen) abounded. Extra traffic was indicated on a large board 'Train Following'.

This was no byway. Freights and even fish trains were often double headed, especially before the arrival of the B12s from the
continued opposite

Edinburgh and Inverness. LMS and LNER kept a close watch on what each other was doing on the Anglo-Scottish routes and within Scotland. The LNER was conscious that the LMS had more open stock suitable for excursion traffic in the early 1930s and justified the building of new stock to work in Edinburgh - Glasgow sets when it believed its competitor had better. Pre-Grouping joint working continued so that there were still through LNER carriages between Edinburgh and St Pancras and, less well-known perhaps, through from Aberdeen overnight on the 5.45pm, returning on the 9.15pm from St Pancras. One of the show inter-war through workings was with carriages that made the Aberdeen to Penzance run, introduced in 1921.

To the LMS Pullman cars were added those in Pullman stock on LNER services in Scotland such as between Edinburgh and Perth, Edinburgh and Glasgow (and for a short time to North Berwick) and Edinburgh and Carlisle. The LMS built carriages steadily for Scottish workings not least for suburban services and these included some articulated non-corridors.

Both railways were withdrawing passenger services in the 1930s which enabled them to dispose of some of the more decrepit examples in their fleets. Both brought in steam railcars although the LMS had few. Yet when a special meeting was held at King's Cross in 1934 with Gresley in the chair to review the numbers of four and six-wheeled stock still in service, the figures were staggering. The Southern Scottish Area had 272 six-wheelers while the Northern Scottish Area had 301 six-wheelers and 24 four-wheelers with over 130 of both types still oil-lit. This was in the same year that *Flying Scotsman* achieved 100mph.

On the East and West Coast routes there was eager competition and fast trains and novelties were to be found on the principal services. Then came the streamliners. Only Glasgow and Edinburgh were to be served but the LNER had considered a fast train to Aberdeen before finalising the Coronation. In 1936, timings were got out for a 9-hour run in each direction from/to King's Cross.

Under Nationalisation, much of the enterprise was missing until the 1950s were well under way. Then there were belatedly, observation cars on the West Highland line, the Callander & Oban line and between Inverness and Kyle of Lochalsh. Meanwhile, part of the former Silver Jubilee set had trundled between Glasgow and the Fife Coast and probably hundreds of carriages of all ages had been under-employed. There were wandering sets of Scottish Region vehicles which were wont to help the Western out of a sticky patch. In pre-war days they would have been employed on the many excursions run by both railways; now potential passengers went by road. A BR rolling stock man once told the writer that three new standard vehicles had been allocated to Scotland but there were no duties for them and they did no work before being sent south again. Perhaps it can serve as a comment on those wasted years while traffic was deserting to road.

The luxury Observation Cars are attached to the rear of certain trains on routes through some of the most delightful scenery in the Scottish Highlands.

In the comfort of your armchair you can sit back, relax and view the ever-changing panorama of mountain, glen, loch and river unfolding as the train speeds on.

A conductor in the car describes the many points of interest en route.

There is, in addition to the three Observation Cars featured in this folder, an Observation Car on the Inverness — Kyle of Lochalsh route. For details of dates of operation, etc. please see last page.

GLASGOW-OBAN
Buffet Observation Car

Mondays to Saturdays
3 May to 18 September 1965

GLASGOW			OBAN			
(Buchanan St.)	lve	07 55	STIRLING	arr	20 44	
STIRLING	„	08 49	GLASGOW			
OBAN	arr	12 13	(Buchanan St.)	„	21 34	

A conductor travels in the car between Stirling and Oban. Light refreshments can be obtained in the Buffet Observation Car.

5/- Supplementary charge for the single journey in either direction.

*Glasgow-Fort William Observation Car →
passing Arrochar, Loch Long*

*Cover: Fort William-Mallaig Observation
Car on the Lochy Viaduct*

GLASGOW-FORT WILLIAM
Observation Car

Mondays to Saturdays
14 June to 4 September, 1965.

GLASGOW			FORT		
(Queen St.)	lve	10 05	WILLIAM	lve	17 10
FORT			GLASGOW		
WILLIAM	arr	14 05	(Queen St.)	arr	21 10

A conductor travels in the car between Glasgow and Fort William.

5/- Supplementary charge for the single journey in either direction.

FORT WILLIAM-MALLAIG
Observation Car

Mondays to Saturdays
3 May to 2 October, 1965.

		A	B	C
FORT WILLIAM	leave	09 55	10 28	14 45
MALLAIG	arrive	11 25	12 04	16 27

		C	D
MALLAIG	leave	12 30	18 25
FORT WILLIAM	arrive	13 52	20 02

A — 31 May to 25 September.
B — 3 May to 29 May and 27 September to 2 October.
C — 14 June to 4 September.
D — 3 May to 25 September.

A conductor travels in the car between Fort William and Mallaig.

3/6 Supplementary charge for the single journey in either direction.

continued
Great Eastern section. They enabled the 10.00 express to Aberdeen to be accelerated to 50 minutes for just over 30 miles with three stops. Saturday lunch time brought a non-stop from Aberdeen, while on Saturday evenings in pre-radio days the young blood of the village came to the station to wait the 8.20 arrival from Aberdeen bringing 'Green Finals' with details of football results. Later, indeed in the 1950s, there was a half crown excursion for the locals to see the match at Pittodrie themselves.

The red letter days were those when drovers brought huge quantities of cattle to the market at Maud for sale and onward train journey. The station was then truly at the heart of the local economy, though throughout the year it brought in just about everything needed by farmers for miles around and was a favourite meeting point.

As on many lines, the great days were surprisingly close to the end. Postwar locomotive power peaked with a batch of B1 4–6–0s and an assortment of LMS 2P 4–4–0s. Passenger services were dieselised first, and it was as late as 1960 that a DMU with 57 passengers spent 15 hours locked with a ten-foot snowdrift at New Machar, 20 miles toward Aberdeen. The timetable was not especially imaginative in the DMU era, and the especially keen local esprit de corps – you could have eaten off the floor of any signalbox on the system, and even the gents were spotless – survived ever more inward looking as it was plain that distant management neither understood or cared about the Buchan system's potentials and problems.

Busy Junction. On 13 July 1957 the Peterhead services were shared by two 4–4–0 designs, the NB Glen and ex-LMS class 2Ps, while the Fraserburgh trains were in charge of BR Standard 2–6–4Ts. Kittybrewster allocated 2P No 40603 is seen entering Maud with the Peterhead portion of the 12.25pm from Aberdeen which had been detached from the Fraserburgh train outside the station. Another Class 2P No 40648 worked the 2.30pm fish from Peterhead to Aberdeen and No 40603 worked the 3.10pm passenger train back to Maud Junction. No 62479 Glen Sheil *was provided to work the evening trains.*

Watching The LMS At Elderslie

You will look in vain for Elderslie in recent BR Passenger Timetables. Even to railwaymen, as they rush past in their electric multiple units on the way from Glasgow to Ayr or Largs it is little more than a name. There is an up goods loop and a siding, perhaps full of Cartics, with runround; that is all. But redundant earthworks make it clear that Elderslie was once something much more.

Indeed it was. Its up and down island platforms 2½ miles from Paisley (Gilmour Street) may not have been the most important on the line passenger-wise, but its pair of signalboxes, No 1 at the Glasgow end and No 2 at the country end, were immensely important traffic regulating points. Elderslie sat in the middle of a railway crossroads. To the east there was a choice of two routes into the city, the Joint Line from Gilmour Street (much of it with four tracks) or the curvaceous Canal line. To the west it was the junction for the coast line to Ayr, Girvan and Stranraer or the Greenock Princes Pier route. There was also the alternative route to Ayr via Lochwinnoch, a late comer which swung off the Greenock line at Cart Junction, ¾ mile from Elderslie No 2, to rejoin the main Ayr line with a flyover at Brownhill Junction 11½ miles further on. Unusually, the up direction at Elderslie was *from* Glasgow; a straightforward Ayr-bound train started at St Enoch as an up train, became a down train at Shields Road, and then between Gilmour Street and Elderslie reverted to being an up train for the rest of its journey. Confusing!

Over time Elderslie had been adapted to carry the heavy commuter and seasonal traffic which these routes generated with a minimum of conflict. At the Glasgow end, after the Canal line came in, up and down slow lines skirted the outer platform faces. An up slow line from the Canal route, which had started at Ferguslie (little more than ¼ mile from Elderslie No 1) gave direct access to the up slow platform clear of movements on the fast line from Gilmour Street, and a comparable parallel move in the down direction from the fast line was provided for. The up Greenock slow line from No 2 box dived under the mains and there were thus four tracks, fast and slow in each direction as far as Cart Junction box, again with provision for parallel working. There were separate up and down goods loops, the up loop only being accessed from the Canal line, and a small goods yard on the down side.

The LMS Sectional Appendix was much less detailed in regard to speed restrictions than the BR Appendices have

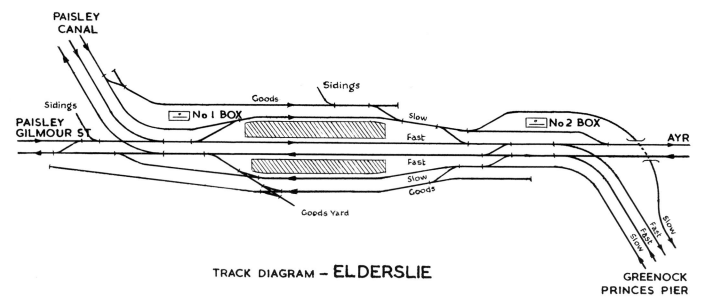

TRACK DIAGRAM – ELDERSLIE

become, but in general the junction divergences and the fast/slow turnouts were authorised for 30mph; the turnouts for the Lochwinnoch line at Cart Junction were much sharper and were specified for 15mph only. But in those days long before speedometers, what speeds drivers *actually* took these junctions at depended much more on their confidence in the riding of their engines!

At the Grouping in 1923 the entire traffic through Elderslie was in the hands of Glasgow & South Western Railway locomotives, of which 528 were bequeathed to the LMS; 84 percent of them were tender engines, some of considerable antiquity. The Sou'West, never the prosperous railway that its near neighbour and deadly rival the Caledonian was, tempered its new locomotive building with a fair amount of rebuilding of older classes, often with bigger boilers. Under Peter Drummond, locomotive superintendent from 1911 to 1918, the railway was very slow to recognise the advantages and adopt superheating; when the LMS came into being only 26 engines were so fitted, and even afterwards only five more were given superheaters.

On the Ayr and Largs trains, a lasting impression was being made by the six Whitelegg 4-6-4 tanks (Nos 540-5), which at this time were brand new. They were exotic in some of their equipment – witness the duplicated regulator, brake and whistle controls on each side of the cab – and their lined green livery with the unpainted boiler clothing in blue planished steel matched the design features. In 1923 they were allocated to Ayr, Fairlie Pier, Corkerhill and Hurlford, which meant that five of them were through Elderslie virtually every weekday. The Corkerhill engine worked the 16.10 St Enoch–Stranraer as far as Girvan for a time (the limit of its route availability) while one of the Ayr engines would be on the 17.10 out of St Enoch, the prime Ayr commuter express. They were allowed to work to Greenock also, but did not do so.

The Baltics did some fine work; they were powerful,

reasonably economical and had a good turn of speed. But they had an Achilles heel – two, in fact. They suffered from a spate of hot bogie axleboxes, and they *rolled* if the track was other than good. No high speeds through the junctions with *them*; their rough riding soon kept them off the Ayr–Girvan section. They worked turn-and-turn-about with the four-cylinder 4-4-0 oddity *Lord Glenarthur* which Whitelegg had rebuilt in 1922 with a large boiler. More accurately it could be described as a new engine mounted on the old wheels. It was hardly a masterpiece but it did some sound work on the Ayr expresses before being demoted by the arrival of new and simpler LMS engines.

The Greenock line passenger trains were in the hands of

Elderslie station, looking towards Glasgow, with a city-bound train via Paisley Gilmour Street passing on the fast line. The buildings and platforms were demolished after closure in 1966 and only the main running lines, now electrified, survive.

159

a group of Manson's 350 class 4–4–0s. They were getting long in the tooth, having been built in 1895 and 1899, but were holding their own over this hard road with its six mile climb out of Princes Pier, much of it at 1 in 70. Whitelegg had modified their Stephenson valve gear, which was unfortunate, and rebuilt six with larger boilers, which made them worse, but they more or less monopolised the route throughout the 1920s.

On the freight side the main interest centred on the 'Long Road Goods' trains to Carlisle, which took the route via Elderslie and Dalry to Kilmarnock to avoid the severe gradients of the Joint Line over Shilford. By the amalgamation these were mostly in the hands of the eleven 'Austrian Goods' 33 class 2–6–0s (whose link with Austria was tenuous in the extreme) working from the Carlisle end. They were essentially superheated versions of the sluggish and coal-hungry 71 class 0–6–0 'Pumpers', which at 58 tons (nine tons heavier than a Midland 4F) were too heavy to bear the additional weight of a superheater

Power to spare for what is probably a St Enoch–Largs train. Whitelegg's big Baltic No 543, piloted by what appears to be a Whitelegg rebuild of Manson's class 8 4–4–0 crawls out of Fairlie station and into the 1,000 yard Fairlie Tunnel in the early days of the LMS. No 543 was shedded at Fairlie Pier for Largs had no shed.

without an additional carrying axle. It made all the difference to the performance. By contrast the arduous 01.00 Glasgow College–Stranraer through freight and its return working at 18.35 were still being run by small Manson 86 class 0–6–0s which the LMS classified – rightly – 3F. 'Pumpers' took over the jobs within eighteen months.

Change in the locomotive department under its new standardising management set in quite quickly. Euston decreed that Midland types, 4–4–0 compounds and 4F 0–6–0s, with cut-down boiler mountings to comply with the Northern Division loading gauge, were what was needed in place of indifferent or inadequate Sou'west engines. The first to be seen at Elderslie, just two years into grouping, were occasional 4Fs working through from Carlisle, but by 1926 new 4Fs were coming to Ayrshire sheds; they were seldom seen on the Glasgow approaches, being mainly occupied working coal south to Carlisle, but at the beginning of 1928 Corkerhill got a first allocation to work the 01.00 from College; they were some of the last new engines to be built at St Rollox. The compounds were the next arrivals, though numbers were limited. Most were earmarked for Carlisle–Glasgow expresses via Kilmarnock, on which Manson's 495 class saturated 4–6–0s were increasingly outclassed. Elderslie saw them in ones and twos now and again. But by 1927 Nos 910–914 arrived on the Sou'West, brand spanking new from Vulcan Foundry,

and were stabled in penny numbers at Fairlie Pier, Ardrossan and Corkerhill, joined two years later by Nos 915/6 transferred to Ayr. In 1928 another four were grudgingly given, Nos 1179–1182, now three years old, and split between Corkerhill and Ayr. Suddenly, to the observer at Elderslie, they became almost commonplace.

These 4–4–0s took over some of the heaviest Ayrshire Coast workings, though there was still plenty for the big Drummond engines (by now almost all superheated) to do. Compounds even started to work through to Stranraer, and in pairs ventured down the hill into Portpatrick on the Sunday excursions. But by 1928 another newcomer had arrived on the scene in the form of the Fowler class 2P 4–4–0; eighteen came in that year (Nos 570–4/7–9/90–9) and two years later they were augmented by another sixteen (Nos 606–11/17–26); a further ten came new in 1931 to the Ayr road (Nos 636/40/3–50).

Now the 2P was quite a small engine; it only weighed 54 tons, of which only 35 were on the coupled wheels. Knowing the uninspiring performance of the Midland engines from which they were derived, it seemed a peculiar choice for the Sou'West. All right, it was a level route to Ayr, apart from the Lochwinnoch loop which rejoiced in 1 in 100 grades, but beyond Ayr it was a story of unremitting slog and the Greenock line was no better.

Yet suddenly the little 2Ps were the flavour of the month on the Sou'West. Enough redesign had been incorporated – smaller cylinders, double-ported piston valves, higher boiler pressure – to make them very competent in the hands of Scottish men who were used to hard work and were not above driving an engine all out, full regulator and full gear, if the need arose. No Midland man would have dared to treat an engine so. But the Sou'West men took to the 'wee black 'uns' as ducks to water and coaxed or drove them to give of their all on the taxing Ayr–Girvan–Stranraer banks; 180 tons was their official limit. They also took over much of the Greenock service for a while, where the trains were comparatively light.

But in 1933 a new and altogether more staccato exhaust sound was heard over Elderslie as the Greenock trains pounded up the 1 in 80 from Cart Junction, for Princes Pier shed had become the proud owners of four Fowler 2–6–4 tanks, Nos 2419–22 with side window limousine cabs. At last the Sou'West's reluctance to use tank engines for main line work, only modestly breached by the Baltics, was to be exorcised. And how the enginemen exulted them! With light loads they were flyers; on heavy trains they proved to be giants. There was no such help for the Ayr–Stranraer section for a couple of years. Given a good rail the 4–4–0s could time the trains, even going a little over the permitted loads. But for all-weather reliability six coupled wheels were essential. The Stranraer turntable, a 50 footer, was not long enough to turn 4–6–0s. What to do?

It took until 1935 for headquarters in Glasgow to realise that they had a solution in their own hands. The Hughes 2–6–0s had been working the Highland main line for some years, and were now being displaced there by Stanier Class Fives. Cyclic workings were set up for engines from Kingmoor and elsewhere to handle the hardest jobs, particularly south of Ayr though they also did some working through to St Enoch. In fair nick they would produce 70mph between Ayr and Paisley at the drop of a hat despite their 5ft 6in wheels. But they were common user engines, by now doing a lot of freight work also and they soon became run down – to the extent that compounds made a partial comeback.

By now Stanier's locomotive re-equipment programme for the LMS was getting well into its stride, and inevitably some of it rubbed off on the Sou'West. First was Corkerhill's use of Jubilees to Ayr; they had always been adept at using English engines on fill-in turns during their layovers in Glasgow, but in 1936 they received a small Jubilee allocation of their own which, when they had any spare moments from the Carlisle road which was the reason for their presence, would be seen bowling through Elderslie with Ayr commuters in tow.

At last, just as war started, the Stranraer turntable was replaced by a sixty-footer, enabling class 5s and 5Xs to be turned there. Many were the sighs of relief from the operators and of pleasure from the observers as a whole new panoply of larger engines was able to parade before them. In fact, the products of Fowler and Stanier were now in total charge, for the G&SW locomotive fleet was by now little more than a memory.

There were some other replacements, too, particularly as the exigences of war brought unprecedented demands for power. Blacked-out Paisley and Elderslie were assailed from time to time by the sounds of Caley 60 class 4–6–0s – the old enemy had finally got a foot in the Sou'West's door in the shape of Greybacks – struggling with trains of troops and munitions. Later the last survivors of the Highland Rivers, Nos 14758/60 were rescued from the St Rollox scrap line, given a lick and a promise and despatched to the Sou'West to help out with the torrent of military traffic. There were other occasional unexpected appearances, too, such as a new WD 2–10–0s out of the North British Locomotive works at Queen's Park running in or working to the military port at Cairnryan.

The postwar LMS years brought little change – a diet of Black Fives, 5Xs, 2Ps, 2–6–0s, compounds and 2–6–4 tanks. When Ayr races were on almost anything might be commandeered for working the specials, even Scots and Duchesses on occasion. All was fair game if it was available.

Midnight on 31 December 1947 produced the universal cacophony of factory sirens and engine whistles. They might be bringing in the New Year with traditional noise and revelry, but a few were ringing out the old LMS, perhaps hoping that the new regime would show itself less lethargic to change and more responsive to the real needs of the job. Maybe after a while, it was. And yet there was a certain sameness, too – grimy engines being worked hard to the limits of their ability by hard-bitten enginemen, remarkably tolerant of the conditions produced by indifferent maintenance and overhaul. It had all been seen before.

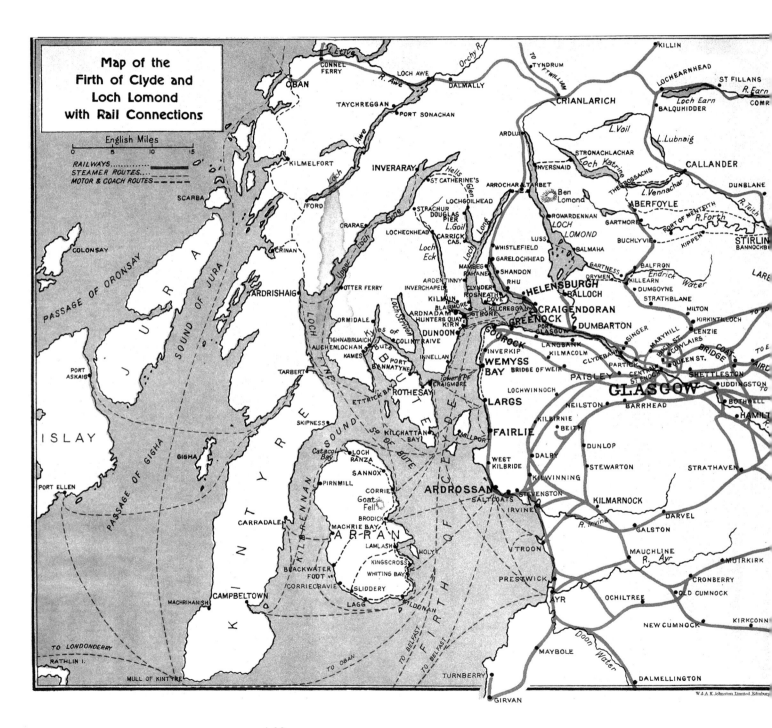

Map of the Firth of Clyde and Loch Lomond with Rail Connections

English Miles

RAILWAYS...............
STEAMER ROUTES.......
MOTOR & COACH ROUTES....

W.& A.K.Johnston Limited, Edinburgh

10
DOON THE WATER

AS late as 1949 the summer traveller to the Clyde was offered a choice of steamers – six paddlers and eight turbines, with two more paddle steamers on Loch Lomond. In addition there was a diesel electric paddler, and in high summer, another steam turbine operating day trips to Belfast from Ardrossan. If the visitor was from afar and chose to stay overnight in Glasgow all three of the railway hotels offered boat trains – steam hauled of course – from the adjacent station to the steamers on lower Clyde.

Although there were plenty of ex-Caledonian and ex-North British Railway locomotives about the boat trains were chiefly the preserve of post-Grouping designs. The Glasgow Central services to Gourock and Wemyss Bay were usually 2–6–4 tank hauled – Stanier and Fairburn, with a leavening of the earlier, and very speedy, Fowler design. The St Enoch services had their own taper boilered 2–6–4 tanks, augmented by LMS 4–4–0s, both 2P and Compound, and a sprinkling of Class Fives and even Jubilees on the longer distance services. All the ex-Glasgow & South Western locomotives had gone, remembered in the immortal writings of the late David L Smith, but St Enoch had a good supply of ex-Caledonian four-coupled engines. In addition to the McIntosh 0–4–4 tanks on shunting and short distance services there were a number of the later 4–4–0s of both McIntosh and Pickersgill designs – the original superheated Dunalastair IV, CR number 139, now BR 54440, was a well cared for and sprightly performer on the steeply graded ex-G&SWR line to Greenock Princes Pier. These trains were so much the preserve of the pre-grouping 4–4–0s that at Paisley Gilmour Street they were nicknamed 'Caleys'.

On the North Bank the traveller could expect to be hauled by the LNER equivalent of the ex-LMS classes, although one at least of the very racy looking NB 4–4–2 tanks would likely be seen at Craigendoran on the push-pull service to Arrochar & Tarbet on the West Highland Railway, within walking distance of piers on salt-water Loch Long (Arrochar) and fresh-water Loch Lomond (Tarbet). Tarbet, or Tarbert, means 'land across which boats can be dragged'; this particular isthmus was used by Vikings to make use of Loch Lomond from which they ravaged the unprotected and unsuspecting fertile central Scotland. From the Low Level station at Central there was the chance of an LMS 2–6–2 tank or even an ex-Caledonian 0–6–0.

Gourock – 45 minutes from Glasgow Central – was the principal departure point. The two ex-LMS turbines *Duchess of Montrose* and *Duchess of Hamilton* departed every day on full-day cruises to such distant destinations as Campbeltown and Inverary, at opposite ends of the

Wrong Line

The Aberdeen District was recruiting a new operating inspector, and the applicants were being interviewed by the district traffic superintendent and his chief inspector. One of the four candidates was a relief stationmaster from a Glasgow district. It was at the time when the North British Loco class 21 diesels were handling much of the traffic and their unreliability was notorious.

'Here's the picture,' said the Super. 'A single line, electric tablet working, and a diesel loco on a passenger train becomes a total failure in mid-section. An assistant engine is needed. What is the procedure for getting it to the failed train?'

The candidate thought for a moment: 'The driver will issue a Wrong Line Order Form which the secondman will take to ...' 'Just a moment,' burst in the Super. 'Before I ask you *which* wrong line order, which would be regarded as the wrong line?' Hesitation...and no promotion.

163

832/34. Wemyss Bay Station.

Wemyss Bay station in Caledonian Railway days. This was the showpiece station of the Clyde where the concourse and the covered way were in season decorated with hanging baskets of flowers and there were decorative paddle box covers from long departed steamers in glass cases.

Kintyre peninsula, to the islands of Bute, Cumbrae and Arran, whilst smaller units of the fleet provided shorter cruises to places like Tighnabruaich, Lochgoilhead and Arrochar. There was also the red-funnelled MacBrayne interloper, the *Saint Columba* sailing each weekday from Gourock to Tarbert and Ardrishaig with connections to Islay, Jura, Oban and the rest of the Western Isles.

Afternoon and early evening cruises were available on the all-year-round ferry services to the Holy Loch, Cowal and Bute. Middle aged men can still recite the litany of Kirn, Dunoon, Innellan, Rothesay, Tighnabruaich; senior citizens would add the prewar piers of Toward, Craigmore, Port-Bannatyne, Colintraive, Auchenlochan and Ormidale.

Glasgow Central offered a steam worked service to Balloch for the Loch Lomond steamers from the Low Level station but the better service was from Queen Street also Low Level, but not quite so primeval. Queen Street provided services on the North Bank to Craigendoran where the ex-LNER paddlers sailed to Loch Long and Loch Goil, to Rothesay and Tighnabruaich with longer cruises on Sundays.

The third departure point was the grandest of all – St Enoch, partner to St Pancras in the Midland/Glasgow & South Western Railway competition to the older established West and East Coast routes to London. From this great trainshed boat trains departed for Ardrossan – the main port for Arran, to Fairlie and Largs for Millport, Kilchattan Bay at the south end of Bute and the Kilbrannan Sound, and Stranraer for Larne. Ayr and Troon, on the same line, gave the opportunity over a number of

164

days of cruising on another ex-LMS turbine, the *Marchioness of Graham* to virtually every port on the Clyde. The Bridge Wharf services apart, and with the possible exception of the almost new paddler, the *Waverley*, on the Loch Long sailings, this was the only truly 'cruise' service on the Clyde. It might be only the MacBrayne flagship, the *Saint Columba*, which claimed the title 'Royal Mail Steamer' but all the others carried freight and mails and there were many regular travellers who depended on the steamers to get to work each day.

The morning and evening services were as tightly timed as anything out of Liverpool Street in Great Eastern days. Though schedules had

---

Steward Department

This Department is under the management of the Company, and the catering is suited to meet the requirements of all classes of the Travelling Public

---

BILL OF FARE

First Class Saloon

BREAKFAST - 3s.
From 7.0 until 10.0 a.m.
Porridge and Milk. Fish. Ham and Egg. Sausage. Cold Meats. Tea. Coffee. Toast and Preserves.

BREAKFAST - 2s. 6d.
Porridge and Milk.
With Single Dish as above.

LUNCHEON - 2s. 6d.
Excursion Steamers from 10.15 a.m. until 11.0 a.m. other Steamers 10.15 a.m. until 3.15 p.m.
Soup. Cold Joints. Sweets or Biscuits and Cheese.

LUNCHEON - 3s. 6d.
From 11.45 a.m. until 3.15 p.m.
Soup. Fish. Cold Joints. Roast Beef. Lamb. Braised Ham. Ox Tongue. Pressed Beef. Vegetables and Potatoes. Sweets. Salad and Cheese.

TEA - 3s.
From 3.45 p.m.
Fish. Cold Joints. Boiled Eggs. Toast. Biscuits. Preserves

TEA - 2s. 6d.
With Single Dish as above.

PLAIN TEA - 1s. 3d.
Toast, Biscuits and Preserves.

SUNDRIES.

Plate of Meat and Potatoes	1s. 6d.
Plate of Soup, with Bread	6d.
Sandwiches, small and large	6d. and 1s.
Biscuits and Cheese	6d.
Cup of Tea or Coffee	3d.
Cup of Tea with Biscuit or Slice of Bread and Butter	6d.

Second Class Saloon

BREAKFAST - 2s. 6d.
From 7.0 until 10.0 a.m.
Porridge and Milk. Ham and Egg. Sausage. Tea. Coffee. Toast and Preserves.

BREAKFAST - 2s.
Porridge and Milk.
With Single Dish as above.

LUNCHEON - 2s. 6d
From 10.15 a.m. until 3.15 p.m.
Soup. Cold Meat and Potatoes. Sweets. Biscuits and Cheese.

LUNCHEON - 3s.
From 11.0 a.m. until 3.15 p.m.
Soup. Fish. Cold Meat and Potatoes. Sweets or Biscuits and Cheese.

TEA - 2s. 6d.
From 3.45 p.m.
Fish. Cold Meat. Toast. Biscuits and Preserves.

TEA - 2s.
With Single Dish as above.

PLAIN TEA - 1s. 3d.
Toast, Biscuits and Preserves.

SUNDRIES.

Plate of Meat and Potatoes	1s. 6d.
Plate of Soup, with Bread	6d.
Sandwiches, small and large	6d. and 1s.
Biscuits and Cheese	6d.
Cup of Tea with Slice of Bread and Butter or Biscuit	6d.
Cup of Tea or Coffee	3d.

Sundries served in Dining Saloon when accommodation is available
Tearooms are provided on all Steamers
Tea. Cakes. Teabread. etc., at reasonable charges

Modification

A certain assistant general manager had recently come to Glasgow and decided to familiarise himself with one of the Districts by a two-day tour of inspection. The superintendent himself organised a programme using his car which (fortuitously) opened with an early afternoon visit to a whisky distillery.

Having seen all the production processes, the newcomer was escorted to the manager's office and offered the traditional 'wee refreshment'. A tumbler was put in his hand and the golden liquid poured; unfortunately he was already in animated discussion with another member of the group on malt deliveries, and before he realised that the tumbler was getting heavy it was full.

The rest of the afternoon's programme was 'modified' on the hoof so that he did not need to get out of the Super's car or meet any other railwaymen.

been eased out since the palmy days of competition, after World War II the best services still meant no more than six or eight minutes for transfer from ship to train. The Glasgow shipbuilder or tobacco baron had the prospect of silver service breakfast (3s 6d = 17½p) on his way to town in summer and winter; on his return the same sum purchased High Tea. In 1949 the pernicious English habit of dinner had not yet reached the West Coast. The traveller on a day cruise could lunch for 4s (20p) and for both lunch and high tea could expect to find the more usual austerity menus augmented by the prospect of cold salmon – usually skilfully laid out in the galley where it could tempt the most fastidious palate. On most of the steamers the galley was artfully sited to let tasty aromas whet appetites already sharpened by keen sea air.

The most expensive day return fare from Glasgow was 14s 2d (71p) first class on the train and saloon on the steamer. Since the equivalent – to Campbeltown, Inverary, Tarbert or Ardrishaig – with 3rd class on the train was 12s 9d (64p) the traveller could have a day out with lunch and high tea and still have change from a pound note, although he or she might find it cost 2d in pier dues to go ashore at his destination.

The railheads apart, the piers were privately or municipally owned and, both on the mainland and on the islands, duplicated exactly the functions of the contemporary railway station – serving towns and villages for both passengers and freight. If our traveller was from south of the border he would have been delighted to find that not one Scottish pier was polluted with dance hall or amusement arcade. But both aboard the steamer and on landing might find that he was taking second place to the luggage and goods which was the lifeblood of these maritime communities.

A number of piers along the Firth of Clyde enabled passengers to make direct interchange between rail and ship. Some, such as Gourock, were used by trains throughout the day serving the local community in addition to the ship connections. Others saw only boat trains which ran to connect with specific sailings. Among the latter was Fairlie Pier seen here about 1955 with LMS class 5 4–6–0 No 45266 on a train for Glasgow. The motor coach outside the station is a Midland Red vehicle no doubt on an extended tour.

Most cruises involved a departure from Glasgow between 8.30 and 9.00am; although the lieabed could take a later train to a second railhead such as Fairlie since the routes skilfully criss-crossed the Firth to duplicate the ferry services which before the war had been provided by the smaller vessels which had either been lost on war service or had come back so battered that they and been broken up. The return to Glasgow would be by 8.30 or 9.00pm since most ships were tied up by 7.30. The working day started early and overtime rates of pay discouraged the owners from making use of the long northern summer evenings for the evening cruises which had been so popular before the war. It was only when motor car-ferries relieved the excursion ships of the early morning sailings that such luxuries could be restored. Forty years on most of the above sailings can still be savoured on the sole survivor, the LNER paddle steamer *Waverley*, now privately preserved. It offers a programme covering all the routes mentioned, although many of the piers are derelict or demolished and there is the world of difference between dense regular services and the occasional cruise.

The boat trains to Gourock were among the last steam expresses in Britain and till the end conveyed ship-bound passengers in style. but you can of course still catch boat trains of a sort, to Stranraer and Ardrossan where the Arran boat now docks as opposed to Fairlie Pier on the Largs line which has joined the long list of places where no longer is there that well-paced hectic activity as train and boat connect. Each had its own distinctive flavour, the most relaxed of all perhaps being Balloch where even the latter-day electrics made occasional forays down the over-signalled extension from Central to Pier carried an exclusively fun-seeking crowd for the *Maid of the Loch*.

Helpful Foreman

Early on a warm summer's day in 1960, two National Servicemen from the Midlands, their leave tickets made out for Wick, presented themselves at the foreman's office in Perth shed. They wished to reach Inverness by steam and sought advice as to which train to catch. Little hope was offered as all were booked for diesel haulage. The foreman advised them to catch the after-noon Blair Atholl local and thus get part way with a Class 5. After a short wait on Blair Atholl platform the Inverness train arrived with 45366 at its head. The two enthu-siasts were overjoyed as they realised they could now complete their whole journey with steam. When they had recovered enough to speak to the crew they found the Class 5 was an unexpected replacement for which they were also pleased. The Perth foreman was a wonderful friend that day.

Inverness – The Mound

It is the late spring of 1949 and little has changed in Scotland to show that for just over a year the railways have belonged to the Nation. True the words 'British Railways' are emblazoned on tender and tank sides and some coaches are appearing in the new 'blood and custard' livery, but these are just outward visible signs that a new socialist government has made its mark. The Scots are proud of their heritage, Inverness is still the capital of the Highlands, and constant reminders of the old Highland railway are firmly in place. Lochgorm works continues to service a handful of Small Ben 4–4–0s and Clan Goods 4–6–0s as well as the sole surviving Clan which seems to be kept as a form of pet whilst the impressive semi-circular loco shed is straddled at its entrance like a triumphant arch by a massive water tower of smoke-blackened stone. The Station Hotel even has plumbing which appears to have been installed by Lochgorm fitters.

Like men of an older race hard pressed by an alien invader most of the smaller ex-Highland engines that survive today have retreated to the far north to work trains from The Mound to Dornoch and Georgemas Junction to Thurso. So it is the early morning train, a camera, some HP2 film and a notebook. Depart from Inverness is at seven.

Once clear of the station environs the train rumbles over the Caledonian Canal swing bridge just as dawn is breaking and one can hear the clear bark of Stanier Class 5 No 45120, as she gets into her stride for the long journey, stopping at most stations. The tail end coach is an old Pullman car which first saw service on the Caledonian Railway representing the acme of comfort on wheels in those 'good old days'. Oval and bevelled plate-glass lights in the vestibule ends, moveable arm chairs, the rich deco-ration scheme of inlaid veneer and the smell of gas from the kitchen stir nostalgic memories of early journeys long ago. Until recently an old Midland Railway twelve wheel diner performed this duty. Breakfast is fair with only an egg and a small piece of bacon accompanied by a burned sausage – never so good in Scottish cars as it is in England. But there is some compensation looking out of the huge windows as the sun rises over the Black Isle waking to sparkling life the waters of Beauly Firth.

At Dingwall there is a meet with a train hauled by one of

Highland Railway Drummond Castle class 4–6–0 No 14676
(ex-HR 141) Ballindalloch Castle now in lined out LMS
maroon livery, enters The Mound with a train from Inverness
on 19 May 1928. The barrows and mail sacks were always a
feature of this junction station, as were the mail and parcels
vans that served it.

The 8.40am stopping train from Wick to Inverness arrives at
The Mound on 12 August 1959. While the barrow and local
dress have remained very much unaltered over the years, the
branch train was now hauled by an imported Pannier tank
and the station sign of the standard Scottish Region pattern.

A mixture of ancient and modern at The Mound in 1951. The engine is ex-HR 0–4–4T, BR No 55053 which is working the Dornoch branch and acting as station pilot between duties. The signals are latter day LMS upper quadrants while the branch coach is an ex-LMS Stanier composite corridor brake in early BR 'blood and custard' livery. The barrow on the platform is a relic of the 1920s while the station's gas lamp dates back into Queen Victoria's reign.

Later the same day the branch train waits departure for Dornoch with the customary van, provided because the very small brake compartment in the single composite coach was inadequate for the parcels and mail carried to and from the county town of Sutherland. When sister engine No 55051 was withdrawn in June 1956, No 55053 became the sole surviving ex-Highland Railway engine in working order and after overhaul at St Rollox Works in July 1955, the only ex-HR locomotive to receive lined BR black livery. Unfortunately, while working the mixed from Dornoch to The Mound in January 1957 the leading axle broke – one wheel careering along the ballast until hitting a lineside gatepost. The train was not derailed. A replacement, 0–6–0 Pannier tank No 1646 ex-Croes Newydd arrived at Helmsdale on 11 February 1957 after a four-day journey.

the last five Clan Goods, No 57956, which has just come off the Skye line curving away to the west: these are now very non-standard and their continued life expectancy is short – although one, No 57954, is presently undergoing overhaul in Lochgorm works. A quick nip on to the platform confirms even earlier history than that of the Highland Railway for the crossbar on the lamp standard bear the initials I&A.J.R. thus perpetuating its predecessor.

While the East Coast Route owned by the profitable southerly companies could afford to fling great bridges over the Firths of Forth and Tay, this northern line of the Highland with its sparse traffic could never be so bold. At Tain where the line meets the southern shore of Dornoch Firth the train is but five miles as the crow flies from the small cathedral town of Dornoch which is the capital of Sutherland and surely the smallest capital town in our Islands. Yet to get there the passenger has to cover no less than forty-four. The deep inlet of the Dornoch Firth determines the course ahead.

The route now follows the southern shoreline through scenery of striking beauty to Culrain where one looks out over the still cluttered breakfast table to the Kyle of Sutherland before No 45120 crosses the Invershin viaduct high above the River Oykell and opens up for the climb inland to Lairg. There is a view up the gorge to a wild prospect of mountain loch and moorland to the west. At Lairg there is a swing eastwards and the engine coasts down the long gradient by the edge of Loch Fleet to The Mound station where the memory of the Sutherland Railway is perpetuated by the initials SR set into the brickwork of the gable end of the station building.

At the Mound there is a very Highland whistle echoing over the trees as Peter Drummond's little 0–4–4 tank No 55053 draws her mixed train made up of a coach, four vans and a brake across Telford's causeway over Loch Fleet sending a plume of white steam from her safety valves against the dark background slopes of Cambusmore.

The connection having been made with the northbound train which waits patiently, the little tank fusses its way to back on to the Pullman which it proceeds to shunt onto an adjacent siding to replenish water and gas ready for its return journey to Inverness behind the morning southbound. No 45120 gives a hoot on her Stanier whistle and makes for Golspie, Helmsdale with its sweep back inland to climb Strath Ulle, Altnabreac to Georgemas Junction, Britain's most northerly railway junction where a Small Ben, either *Ben Alder* or *Ben Wyvis* with its ugly stovepipe chimney will take the Thurso portion on. These veterans, too, will not be around much longer and the journey to see them must be the next stop after the ride to Dornoch and back.

God's Treasure House In Scotland

Three miles north west of Beattock Summit is Elvanfoot, a one time junction for an ex-Caledonian branch line, unusual in that its seven miles to Wanlockhead passed over the highest point on the LMS at Hillend 1,498ft above sea level and that it was worked as a Light Railway.

Until its demise in the 1930s the area was the centre of the Scottish lead mining industry lying at the foot of the Lowther Hills. Long ago, as far back as 1125 gold was found there and by 1661 King Charles I had taken the lead mines under his special care exempting them from 'all taxes in peace and war' though this generosity failed to exempt the populace from 'such proportions of excise for ale and beer brewed in their houses'. Not surprising the hills and glens around were known as 'God's Treasure House in Scotland'.

No line of railway reached these parts until the advent of the Light Railways Act of 1896 enabling the use of cheaper lighter materials, sharper curves and steeper gradients than usual taking into account a statutory speed limit and limited loadings. With this form of construction available the lead and sheep traffic became worth fighting for and the battle was joined by the Caledonian and Glasgow & South Western companies with the more aggressive Caledonian taking the prize. As was so often the case the promoters hoped that tourist traffic would evolve in abundance: as usual, it did not. The result was a typical Light Railway.

For example there were no raised platforms on the line; even at Elvanfoot the platform was at rail level at the back of the Caledonian down main line platform. There was a single train staff kept in the custody of the stationmaster at Wanlockhead when out of use except when the last train of the day ran, when it was retained by the engine driver and locked up in the loco tool box until needed next morning. Because this was a Light Railway in unfenced sheep country engines in early days had cow catchers fitted front and rear. The train would stop anywhere to pick up and set down with the guard attending to monetary matters, though the rules stated that 'Railway Servants were not bound to provide money change to intending passengers'.

Locomotive power was latterly the McIntosh 439 class 0–4–4 tank including Nos 15181, 15217 and 15238 though a Beattock based celebrity in the form of now preserved No 15189 replaced the resident engine occasionally. Perhaps the most interesting steam on the branch appeared in the form of two LMS Sentinel railcars Nos 29910 and 29913 which were built 1929–30 but not introduced on the branch until the mid thirties, probably due to the age and condition of the original coaching stock coupled with the already declining passenger numbers. The Sentinel cars differed, No 29913 had a six cylinder 100hp geared unit with cardan shaft drive whilst No 29910 was two cylindered with a chain drive. Each seated 44 passengers. They were the last two LMS Sentinels in use and provided a passenger service of four trains a day.

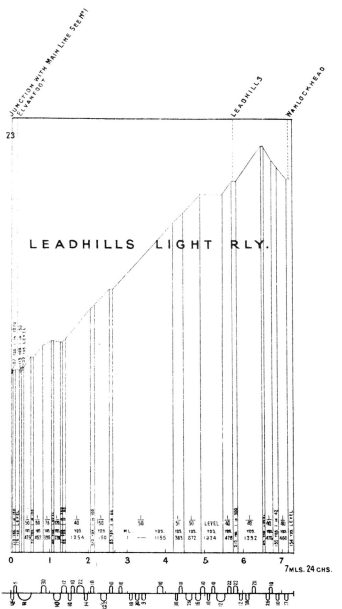

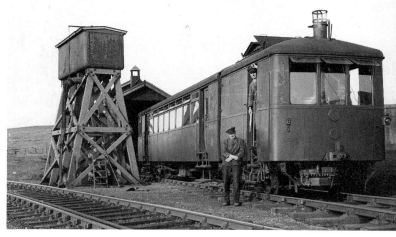

The branch line from Elvanfoot to Leadhills and Wanlockhead was worked for a time in the mid 1930s by one of the LMS Sentinel Railcars. No 29910 is seen outside the small shed at Leadhills on 19 June 1936. Note the water tank mounted on a wooden trestle.

Brake 3rd. It is thought that one of the Sentinels probably replaced the Garstang and Knott End coach.

The Glengonnar mine was closed in 1929 though many mining engineers thought this ill-considered. The branch staggered on until 31 December 1938 when all traffic ceased. 'God's Treasure House in Scotland' was now all but empty.

At other times the Wanlockhead branch was worked by Caledonian Railway 0–4–4Ts which was more convenient operationally as it was possible to run mixed trains with goods wagons behind the passenger coach. Such a train is seen here passing Glengirth Farm beyond the level crossing on the A702 Dumfries road. The coach came from the Knott End Railway in Lancashire.

On the closure of the Garstang & Knott End Railway in March 1930 some of its stock was transferred to the branch including the 'American type' coach, a composite vehicle built by the Birmingham Carriage & Wagon Co about 1908 now numbered LMS 17899. This had end roofed platforms complete with railings, hence its nickname. It met the needs of the branch admirably after the fitting of additional step boards. Certainly No 17899 gave a far better ride than the Sentinels which were less than smooth at any speed. In later days when mixed trains were normal the consist was often the Garstang coach coupled to a four wheeled brake van also from Garstang with a number of mineral wagons behind. The final train was made up of ex-Caledonian 0–4–4T No 15217 and a CR

11
GHOSTS IN THE SPRINGBURN ROAD

TURN off the M8 motorway at junction 15, on the north side of Glasgow, and take the A803 for Kirkintilloch. This is the Springburn Road, now a dual carriageway, and it starts straight as a die and rising gently. Within half a mile are the wrought iron gates and ornate stone lodge of Sighthill Cemetery on the left. Its grassy knoll, covered with blackened memorials, looks out over the sprawling city, with the Clyde 250ft below.

It is a place recording individual deaths, and yet it is the focus of an even more widespread mortality, the demise of a railway legend that grew within a few hundred yards of its boundary walls, flowered for many years and then, suddenly, wilted and withered away. For this small area centred on Sighthill Cemetery once contained the greatest concentration of railway manufacturing industry in Europe. The author John Thomas christened it the Scottish Railway Metropolis.

It takes only the barest imagination to conjure up the ghosts of Springburn's past, serried ranks of them. Ghosts of men by the thousand in soiled blue boiler suits and cloth caps, of men in navy serge uniforms, peaked caps and those distinctive black-sleeved waistcoats, of men in bowler hats set in authority over them. And ghosts, too, of long departed 'high-heid-yins', the bosses who came along the Springburn Road in their carriages to preside over the legend. Their names were household words in Springburn; Drummond, McIntosh and Pickersgill of the Caledonian, Holmes and Reid of the North British, Neilson, Lorimer and Arbuthnott at Hyde Park and Atlas.

To most drivers on the A803, Springburn is a suburb that you can be into and out of in a couple of minutes. No longer do they struggle along the *old* Springburn Road, a twisting canyon between shops and four-storey stone tenements. But for those sensitive souls with a degree of railway engineering interest it is still worth taking a look around. The evidence of the manufacture of locomotives, carriages and wagons is there for the observant. And you can still imagine the Springburn men driving, servicing and repairing them, the roar of a train ascending Cowlais Incline, the ceremonial occasions when a locomotive for India or Argentina was despatched from works to docks, the ceaseless coming and going of freight.

Barely off the motorway slip roads, a rising concrete footbridge spans the road to give access to tower blocks of flats on the left. Just past that footbridge it is easy to miss a bridge abutment in the retaining wall on the right, for the road level has been raised substantially on the rubble of demolished tenements. Once a railway crossed the road here by the Inchbelly level crossing, later replaced by an unremarkable steel bridge;

172

North British Locomotive Company order number L883 comprising eight Pacifics was completed in July 1933 and the locomotives are seen at Stobcross Quay being loaded aboard the SS Beldis for their journey to China

the road was lowered under it to give clearance for double-deck trams. The railway was the pioneering Garnkirk & Glasgow, opened in 1831 to the Scottish gauge of 4ft 6in, and terminating at Townhead (Glebe Street) station and at Port Dundas on the Forth & Clyde Canal. It had a brief moment of importance when in February 1848, after regauging, it served as the destination of the through trains from Euston via Motherwell and Coatbridge. But after only four months the London trains were diverted to South Side (Gushetfaulds). Latterly it was a haunt of Caley 'Jumbos' and wee Pugs.

As the road climbs and the retaining wall tapers to nothing, a redbrick office building with yellow brick quoins appears. Signs on its frontage

A general view of the main erecting shop at St Rollox in 1893 showing in the foreground of one of the 2–4–2Ts originally intended for the Oban line when built by Neilson & Co in 1880. Due to derailments attributed to the radial axles, they were transferred to the Glasgow area for use on local work for which condensing apparatus (part visible above the side tank) was fitted. Three were involved in accidents (one twice) and none of the fifteen locomotives lasted in traffic after 1912.

Opposite, below Built by Sharp Stewart and Company in September 1894, Highland Railway No 103 was the first 4–6–0 type to run in Great Britain. As LMS No 17916 this Jones Goods engine was withdrawn in July 1934 and preserved in St Rollox works (repainted into Highland Railway green livery) where she remained until 1959. Then, following full restoration to working order and painting in Stroudley yellow, a livery probably never carried before, she was returned to service to haul mainly special trains. HR No 103 is now in the Glasgow Museum of Transport. This rare photograph was taken inside St Rollox works during 1938 with the engine not on the rails but packed and scotched on the wooden floor.

identify it as St Rollox House, occupied by Glasgow North Ltd, Development Centre, though the gates on the carriage entrance have 'BREL' incorporated in their ironwork. Look more closely and you will see an oval plaque by the entrance door which proclaims:-

Springburn Heritage Trail
St Rollox Railway Works
Founded in 1854 by the Caledonian Railway to build
locomotives, carriages and wagons.
Greatly extended in the 1880s by Dugald Drummond.

This building is no longer the offices of St Rollox Works, let alone those of the Locomotive Superintendent; the works offices are an unimpressive modern block in a side street. Not even the title survives; under BR's Workshop Division it became Glasgow Works in 1962. Now its status has sunk to that of the Springburn Depot of British Rail Maintenance Ltd, repairing diesel locomotives, multiple units and coaches largely by component exchange. And as if in sympathy with its decline, the nearby church of St Roche, from which the works took its name, has also gone, to be replaced by a modest and modern redbrick St Rollox Church of Scotland, its peaked roof surmounted by a short spike for a tower. It lurks behind the Cawder Vaults, which must have given solace to many a St Rollox man in the past.

From the works came a never-ending stream of new and repaired locomotives and rolling stock. It made its name with the 'Dunalastair' 4–4–0s of 1896 and the '903' class 4–6–0s of 1906, of which *Cardean* became a

Above *Posed in mid-air at St Rollox an unidentified LMS class 2F 0–6–0 hangs freshly repainted in the early style livery of the new owner. The locomotive number appeared on the tender sides in large numerals. (The cabside panel was 32 × 11 inches with a vermilion background, edging and lettering gold leaf and the shading black.) The two locomotives in the background still remain in the lined blue livery of the Caledonian Railway.*

Breakfast Sojourn

The Devon secretary who had literally never been north of Watford had joined her boss in Liverpool and then had a fine dinner on the evening express from Exchange to Glasgow Central. Reminiscent of the American reported in *Punch* as being nervous of British train speeds not because American trains were not as fast but because our small land area would surely run out, the young lady was amazed when on approach Glasgow the Scot in the opposite corner said he was off to see if he could book his sleeper north. When you had already come that far, how could you possibly need a sleeper to go further?

The Glasgow and Edinburgh to Inverness sleepers were vital commercial institutions for years, and while today's first and last trains are earlier and later (and faster) the comfort of the sleeper is still missed.

Not, however, that it was prolonged comfort for those destined for all stations. Take those bound for Nairn, who might have caught the 1.35 lunch time from Euston (change between Central and Buchanan Street in Glasgow). Even if they were asleep on departure from Buchanan Street at 11.15 and not woken by the train's frequent stopping in the early hours of the night, they were decanted at Aviemore at 4.14am, departing at 4.25 in fact six minutes before the sleeper continued on its way to an unready Inverness. Come 5.28 it was out on the platform again, this time seeing the arriving train off on its way to Elgin after a 12 minute sojourn all but half an hour before the connection to Nairn, depart 6.08, terminate 6.24. You would no doubt hanker after the days before the completion of the direct route via Carr Bridge when the sleeper from London as well as mere Glasgow

continued opposite

legend on the West Coast 'Corridor'. And the impressive blue passenger livery, generously lined out in black and white and set off by footplate valances, footsteps and tender frames in Indian red, was a legend in itself. On the carriage side the mind goes back to the magnificent 12-wheeled 'Grampian' stock, used not just to Aberdeen but wherever a premium service was required – to Edinburgh and to the Clyde Coast ports – to beat the competition.

Immediately beyond the works and its offices Springburn Road spanned the Caledonian's main line into Buchanan Street station and goods depot, nearly a mile away, which had opened in 1849 as the third successive Glasgow terminus for trains from across the border. The line climbed out of Buchanan Street at 1 in 79 through a ¼-mile tunnel; alongside the works, in a shallow, overgrown and cheerless cutting, can be seen the platform edges of St Rollox station. Just over a mile further east was St Rollox shed, latterly code 65B. Until LMS days it was Balornock, home depot of the famous driver James Grassie. But Buchanan Street closed in November 1966, when the Aberdeen, Inverness and Dundee trains were diverted to Queen Street. All trace of the line towards the terminus has been obliterated under landscaping round the tower blocks.

Perhaps on a quiet night, though, those of the faith can still discern the pounding beat of a Pickersgill '60' class or a Black Five fighting the grade, or the melodious organ pipe whistle of a Caley engine or the chime of an 'A4' sounding a warning at the tunnel mouth.

Beyond the cutting again, a large level area surrounded by steel railings lies disused. A cursory inspection reveals a pattern of raised platforms, roadways and unmade parallel strips, which could only have been a large goods depot. This was Sighthill Goods, a North British Railway facility just a short distance from the main Glasgow–Edinburgh line. It competed with Buchanan Street for the freight traffic of the north of Glasgow, and through its entrance gates passed a steady stream of horse-drawn drays, mechanical horses and lorries. Under the 1955 modernisation plan it was turned into something of a showpiece with a new shed for sundries traffic, but with the gradual rundown in the handling of small consignments and the intrusion of National Carriers Ltd its deathknell was sounded. The depot was closed and the shed demolished, and no proposals for alternative use of the site have come to fruition.

Leaving Sighthill behind to its memories you are on to the *new* Springburn Road. Beyond the cemetery wall traffic lights guard a crossroads, where the *old* road goes off on the right; it even has a new name, Atlas Road, which becomes Springburn Way once past the mouldering Springburn station and peters out in a derelict dead-end, blocked by a new road. Symbolic? Gone is the lengthy frontage of the Cowlairs Cooperative Society, founded by men from that works; the whole area is given over to small modern shops, a health centre and a shopping mall with extensive car parks. How Springburn has changed!

At those traffic lights the eye will be drawn to a signboard implanted by the building contractors Barratt's, advising that in their new Hyde Park development, two-bed apartments are on offer. There is no such park in the vicinity, so it can only perpetuate the name of the one-time Hyde Park

Locomotive Works of Neilson, Reid & Co and (from 1903) the largest component of North British Locomotive Co. But why Hyde Park?

Probably not even Barratt's know, or care, that Walter Neilson and others founded an engine-building works in 1837 in Hydepark Street, two miles and more away, downstream from the M8 motorway bridge over the Clyde. Initially it concentrated on stationary and marine engines, the most notable of which was the winding engine for the Queen Street–Cowlairs incline, which operated until 1909. As the locomotive business grew the small works could not cope, and Neilson found a new site in Springburn, taking the name with him. The new Hyde Park Works opened in 1860, and with steady growth was employing 3,500 men by 1900 and was producing a locomotive each working day.

Nearby another builder, the Clyde Locomotive Co, set up a works in 1884, but had barely become established before being bought out by Sharp, Stewart & Co, who were anxious to escape the constrictions of their Manchester works. So another famous name moved to Springburn in 1888, bringing the Atlas Works name with them. By the turn of the century they had over 1500 men turning out 150 locomotives a year.

1903 was a momentous year in Springburn. The firms of Neilson, Reid and Sharp, Stewart combined forces, along with Dübs at Queen's Park (across the city) in a new company, the North British Locomotive Co. A happy feature of this amalgamation was that each works retained its distinctive builder's plates, circular at Hyde Park, oval at Atlas and diamond-shaped at Queen's Park. They were attached to locomotives great and small, from 0–6–0 pannier tanks for the GWR to massive Beyer-Garratts for South Africa.

Perhaps the most visible sign of activity, apart from the crowds of artisans hurrying to and from work, was not with the locomotives built for use in Britain; *they* slipped out of the back door by Springburn station to be hauled, motion dismantled, to their new owners – G&SWR 'Baltic' tanks, 'King Arthurs', 'Royal Scots', A3s, 'Jubilees', B17s, Stanier 2–6–4 tanks, large numbers of 2–8–0s and 2–10–0s for the War Department, and B1s. They only made up about a third of production anyway. Rather , as has already been hinted, it was with the exports, which could seldom move on British rails because of track gauge or height or width. So at quiet times of the day or night, the 1920s and 30s would see the main gates of Hyde Park works, in Ayr Street opposite the library, open for a pair of steam traction engines hauling a multi-wheeled low loader on which the latest giant, cab windows boarded up and with a temporary 'North British Locomotive Co' sign on each flank, was taken up Vulcan Street on to Springburn Road with police escort at walking pace and down to the hammerhead crane at Finnieston Quay, where a heavy lift 'Bel' ship would be waiting.

In a generally quieter inter-war market there was not room for three separate erecting shops, and Atlas built its last engine, a 4–6–0 for India, in 1923 and was advertised for sale in 1927; part was retained to service Hyde Park, notably the flangeing shop producing boiler components. But it was a bad time to seek a buyer, and only World War II saved it from early extinction. Part was used for the manufacture of shells and bombs,

continued
took the coast route.

If however you were going even further north, you could stay on the Glasgow sleeper until a moment or two before the departure of the 6.40 to Wick, making an across-platform transfer since the arriving train had conveniently backed in to be beside the departing one.

What's In a Name?
Many of the Scottish locomotive names, such as *Baron of Bradwardine*, *Wizard of the Moor* and *The Fiery Cross* are satisfyingly impressive and perhaps the extremely Scottish ones like *Glen Sloy*, *Glen Gloy*, *Loch Oich* and *Loch Quoich* do not convey to the local inhabitants quite the same suggestion of paddling in wet mud as they do to the finnicky Southron. *Wandering Willie* conjures up a vision of an overgrown youth with a drooping lower jaw and a vacant expression, while *Luckie Mucklebackit* seems like a puckish anticipation of the rhythmic sound of the engine's motion when it gets into bad condition. – W.A. Tuplin.

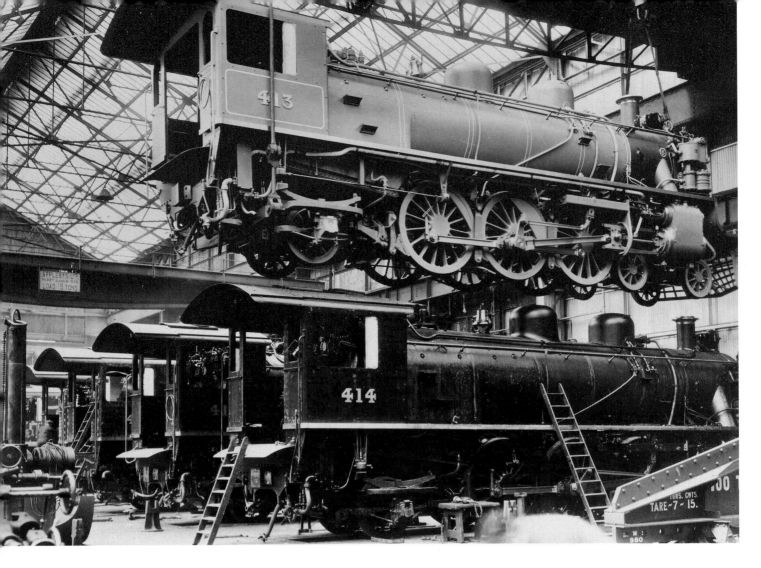

In less than seven months from the date of order, in 1932 the North British Locomotive Company's Hyde Park Works completed and shipped eight Pacifics for the Tientsin–Pukow Railway, China, based on an American design of 1920. The first No 413, is lifted ready for placing on a low loader for its road journey behind two Burrell traction engines to Stobcross Quay for shipment on the SS Beldis. The overall height of these engines brought major problems with bridges during their passage of Springburn Road.

part as a US Army store. During 1952 a section was used as the erecting shop for forty electric locomotives for South Africa, and was later retooled to produce MAN diesel engines under license.

Hyde Park built its last steam locomotives, four 2–8–2s for Nyasaland, early in 1958. By this time diesel locomotives were in production, mostly for British Railways but almost all built at Queen's Park. Hyde Park had a thin time on components and steam spares. In retrospect it was a great pity that of the 163 main line diesels built for BR, all but ten were fitted with the German MAN engine built at Atlas, for it proved totally unsatisfactory in British service and was eliminated after a life of only 7–11 years.

In the circumstances it was almost inevitable that the company would founder, and this it did in 1962, bringing locomotive building in Springburn to an unhappy end. Many of the machine tools were purchased for shipment to South Africa, and both Hyde Park and Atlas works were totally demolished about 1965. The Atlas site is now occupied by small industrial units, and Atlas Place at the end of its access road is the only link with the past. The Hyde Park site is now split up, with Barratt's busily encroaching from the Ayr Street end with 3- and 4-storey blocks of flats and a cash-and-carry warehouse at the other.

Nothing remains but the company's four-story sandstone head office

178

building at 110 Flemington Street, now (somewhat anonymously) a further education college. During World War I part of it was used as a Red Cross hospital. Another of the oval Springburn Heritage Trail plaques identifies it as:-

Springburn College
Built in 1909 as the headquarters of the
North British Locomotive Co, then the largest
firm of its kind in Europe. Architect, James Miller.

Above its pillared entrance is a coat of arms and the letters 'NBLC', flanked by the words 'Speed' and 'Science'. It could perhaps be seen as an epitaph; not enough speed in the changeover from steam to diesel and electric traction, not enough science in picking a winner when the changeover belatedly came.

On the opposite side of the dual carriageway Springburn Road, a little further on and only reached indirectly, Cowlairs Road goes off. At one time it led to Cowlairs station on the Edinburgh and Glasgow line, an elevated and curved island platform, but this closed in 1964 and was demolished. The access subway was also a pedestrian entry into Cowlairs Works, established for the opening of the Edinburgh & Glasgow Railway in 1842. NB Loco and Cowlairs constituted the hub of the 'North British' end of Springburn.

Cowlairs was the first railway-owned works of any consequence in Scotland; hitherto all new locomotives and rolling stock had been bought from outside suppliers. When the E&G was absorbed into the North British Railway in 1865 the works was expanded to take over the locomo-

An Egyptian State Railways 4–6–0 locomotive leaves Hyde Park works of the North British Locomotive Company for Glasgow Docks hauled by two traction engines and escorted by a Police motor cyclist. One of an order of thirty two standard gauge oil burning locomotives built 1947-8. The substantial tenders had a water capacity of 5,500 gallons and could carry 9 tons of fuel oil.

Opposite, above *Traffic congestion 1930s style. Local children watch as Benguela Railway 4–8–0 No 230 is halted at Aikenhead Road, Glasgow for the tramcar to pass the parked car blocking the road in front of the two traction engines. Meanwhile a horse drawn milk float – with churns – moves 'wrong road' past the tram. Note both gas and electric street lighting. Eighteen locomotives of the 9th class were constructed at the Queen Park works for this Angolan railway. Examples remained in use until the mid-1970s.*

Birthday Boy

After the one coach came into the platform by gravity, and the BR 2–6–0 tender locomotive which had 'run round' it by the simple expedient of tucking itself into a siding backed onto it, the enthusiast realised he was the only passenger on the August evening's last train from Banff to Tillynaught on the Coastal route from Aberdeen to Elgin.

The crew had noticed this, too. 'I'd be happy to switch you to first class, or the engine driver says you can join him,' was the guard's unprompted offer.

It had of course to be the footplate. Who was this traveller, what was he doing, how old was he? 'Twenty eight today,' resulted in a friendly hand directing his to the regulator. And the 40 minutes spent at the junction involved the nearest thing to a signalbox caelidh. Few birthday evenings were more memorable.

tive building activity of the cramped St Margarets (Edinburgh), but for its size – after World War II it was employing 2,500 staff – it was very hemmed in by housing and road access was difficult.

It always seemed a somewhat prosaic works, with little of the aura of its Caledonian rival down the road. Its grey stone walls effectively hid its activities from the passing traveller. By the time that new locomotive building ceased in 1924 (boiler construction continued for some years more) it had turned out about 900 new engines, solid workaday four-coupled passenger machines and six-coupled freight types, sober in their dark brown livery with red and yellow lining. Not even Sir Walter Scott's· provision of fascinating names could arouse strong partisan feelings. Cowlairs also produced some very good coaches, but stock for its prestige Anglo-Scottish services was jointly owned with its English partners and was to their designs.

Cowlairs had, perhaps, two claims to modest fame. In the early days of World War I the drawing office undertook much of the design work for F G Smith's 'River' class 4–6–0s for the Highland Railway, splendid engines exiled from their native heath for thirteen years. It also possessed an unusual traverser for moving coaches, which travelled up and down a gradient to allow for an 18in difference in floor levels of two workshops.

The rundown of steam, and of passenger and freight services, had its inevitable result. Cowlairs closed completely in 1968 and was razed to the ground. In its place has grown the Springburn Cowlairs Industrial Estate, an unexciting huddle of metal-clad buildings of which the most prominent is a whisky depot which proclaims its links to 'Bowmore, Auchentoshan and Glen Garioch Scotch Malt Whiskies'. Instant steadying of the nerves for those of us who would commune with Springburn's spirits! Even Cowlairs Road itself is now being truncated by construction of the new direct chord line from the Edinburgh route to Springburn station. There is at least *one* new railway development in the place.

Besides the ghosts of works and depots, there is another which exemplifies the North British Railway itself and which must lurk reproachfully around Springburn. No wasted wraith, this, but that of the big Reid Atlantic *Midlothian*, which contrived to beat the breaker's hammer in 1937 and was reconstituted at Cowlairs from parts with a view to preservation. Alas, in November 1939, with World War II in its phoney phase, the order was rescinded and the engine was broken up again.

Finally, at the far end of Springburn, Hawthorn Street bridges the dual carriageway and leads past Eastfield depot. This was the principal locomotive shed for the North British's Queen Street High Level services (Parkhead looked after the Low Level passenger workings and Kipps some of the freight business), and at nationalisation had an allocation of 165 locomotives, down somewhat on its peak. It was the last piece of the Springburn jigsaw, having opened in 1904 to replace the old Cowlairs shed attached to the works. It had 14 roads and (necessarily) a very long coal stage. It also boasted an elegant clock tower over the offices which figured in many a locomotive portrait. Eastfield's great excitement came on 28 June 1919, when the shed roof was burned off in a spectacular fire

Left *The North British Works had a long history of supplying steam locomotives for the Egyptian State Railways going back to 1901. Twenty modern 2–6–2 tanks were supplied from Hyde Park in 1926, and are here being loaded transversely on board ship at Stobcross Quay by a 130 ton crane of 1895. This operation would involve warping the ship along the quay several times to keep within the crane's reach. These locomotives may well have been brought by rail from Springburn.*

which left 19 engines badly damaged. In the early 1930s a 500 ton concrete mechanical coaling plant was installed, but the old coal stage remained as an emergency backup, looking increasingly derelict, until BR days.

With the extinction of steam, and full dieselisation, Eastfield was first adapted, then demolished and rebuilt, as a modern diesel depot, losing its clock tower at the same time. Its locomotives proudly wore the West Highland terrier logo – but no longer. With the gradual reduction in freight traffic in the Glasgow area, and the takeover of almost all Scotland's internal passenger services by class 158 diesel multiple units maintained at Haymarket, Scotrail has recently closed the depot. Another ghost will haunt Springburn's northern fringe.

So Springburn's life as Scotland's railway metropolis hangs by its St Rollox thread. If that goes the place will have severed its last railway connection and become just another Glasgow suburb with a station. Memories will soon fade as a generation takes its place in Sighthill cemetery. And the dual carriageway of the Springburn Road will be just a means of getting through this haunt of ghosts, spirits of a great past.

A proud group of Cowlairs carriage builders pose with their foreman (the only one without a cap) in front of a new wooden North British corridor brake coach in the 3-road carriage shop sometime before World War I.

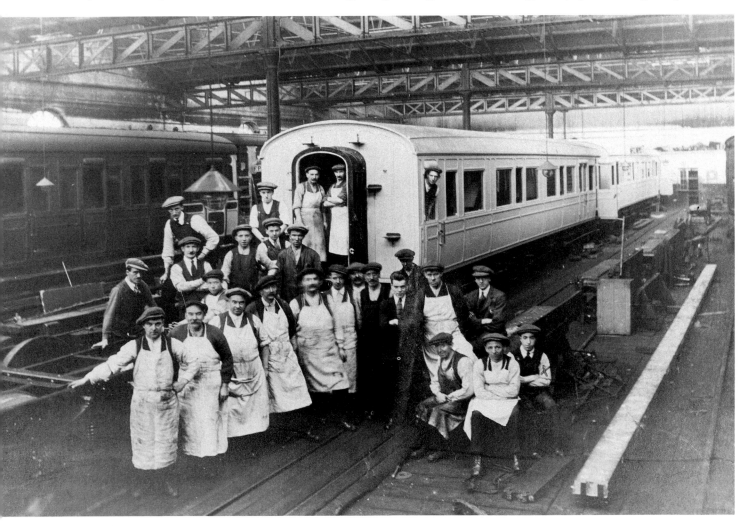

Not Springburn Built

Springburn may well have been the locomotive capital of Scotland but it was far from being the only place north of the border where steam locomotives were built. It is impossible to be precise, but early railways which became part of the five principal Scottish companies built something over 600 locomotives when Springburn was nothing but a village, while private builders (some catering purely for industrial engines but others operating in world-wide markets) built well over 8,000 in workshops from Ayr to Aberdeen.

The most productive were undoubtedly those of Dübs & Co at Polmadie, Glasgow, later the Queen's Park works of North British Locomotive Co. Its first locomotive, carrying the distinctive diamond-shaped builder's plate which was the company's hallmark, emerged in 1865, an outside cylindered 0–4–2 for the Caledonian Railway, and by 1867 Dübs was exporting to a variety of countries including India. By 1903, when the merger forming NB Loco took place, Dübs had built nearly 4,500 locomotives.

Kilmarnock Works in the last years of the Glasgow & South Western Railway. The erecting shop is full of locomotives in various stages of repair with many of the dismantled parts alongside on the wooden block floor. Identifiable are No 506, a 4–6–0 of 381 class, built in 1910 at Kilmarnock, Nos 391 and 396, both 4–4–0s, which used the 6ft 9½in wheels, a pair of which can be seen on the middle road complete with axle-boxes. The overhead crane was manufactured by Craven Brothers of Manchester in 1902 and limited to 35 tons. A Glasgow & South Western worksplate is on the splasher of the left hand engine whilst the diamond of the North British Locomotive Co makes an interesting comparison on the right hand locomotive.

One of the best markets was with the Midland Railway. When diesel traction came in the 1950s, Queen's Park did almost all the erection, in many cases using MAN engines built under licence at the Atlas works in Springburn. When North British closed down, part of the works was sold to Voith Engineering Co to produce their hydraulic transmis-

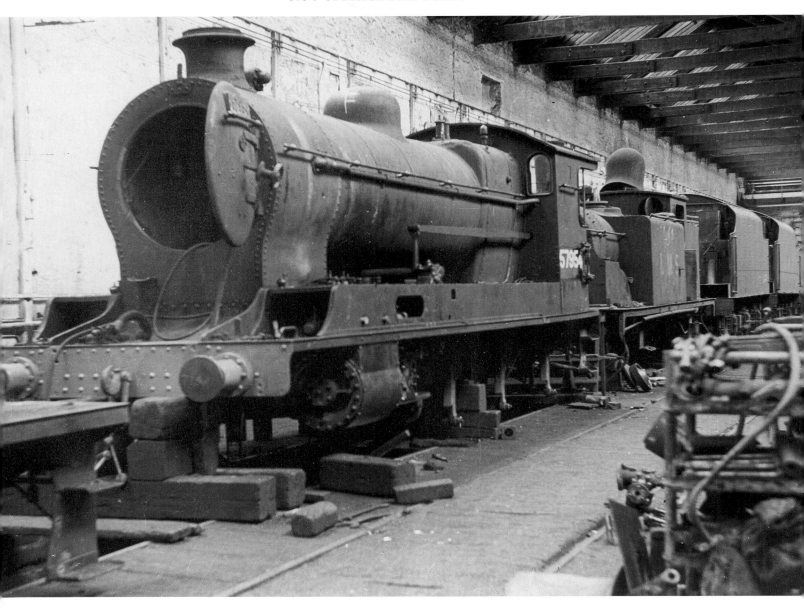

Final repairs. Cumming superheated goods 4–6–0 No 57954, the last survivor of the class of eight engines undergoes an intermediate repair in the Lochgorm erecting shop at Inverness in 1949. Behind is an ex-CR 0–4–4T still in LMS black livery. This 4–6–0 was withdrawn three years later.

sions, but this work is now undertaken elsewhere. Part of the works has changed from heavy engineering to produce...aluminium foil!

Kilmarnock had two main locomotive works, that of the Glasgow & South Western Railway and, close by, the Caledonian works of Andrew Barclay, Sons & Co. The G&SW works during the 46-year reigns of James Stirling, Hugh Smellie and James Manson (1866–1912) built new locomotives at an average rate of seven or eight a year but

had a perpetual struggle to cope with repairs, let alone build new. In the last eleven years of the G&SW, under Peter Drummond and Robert Whitelegg, it could only muster fifteen, or 1½ a year. The works was cramped and never really modernised. In all, since the first 2–2–2 it produced in 1860 it had 392 new locomotives to its credit, but the last appeared in 1921 and the final rebuild, of the four-cylinder 4–4–0 *Lord Glenarthur*, only appeared days before the LMS took over. Thereafter it was used for repairs only until closure in 1959.

By contrast, Barclays had more modest aspirations, building little but 0–4–0 and 0–6–0 industrial shunting tanks and latterly, comparable diesels. In all they churned out well over 2,000 of them. Andrew Barclay & Co merged with Hunslet in 1972 and it is perhaps ironic that as a

184

result the works, enlarged with a new erecting shop and other facilities, has progressed from simple, rugged steam shunters to become an important builder and rebuilder of sophisticated diesel multiple units.

In the north, the Highland Railway's Lochgorm works in Inverness was quite small, its two-road erecting shop and other buildings being surrounded by the two approaches to Inverness station and the Rose Street connecting line. Mainly a repair shop, between 1869 and 1905 it built a total of 41 locomotives, mostly small. The Highland had a strong affection for the products of Dübs and went there or to their successors for many of their larger engines, though for the last three new classes favours were switched to Hawthorn, Leslie & Co at Newcastle. Lochgorm remained as a repair works until 1959, when it closed its doors, but the erecting shop was subsequently taken over and continues in use as a diesel maintenance depot.

The last but not least among railway workshops was Inverurie, opened in 1901–2 on a green field site to replace the appalling conditions in the 'works' at Kittybrewster, where only four locomotives could be worked on under cover . (The rest of the repairs and rebuildings were done in open sidings!) Coming late on the scene, Inverurie built only ten new locomotives in its erecting shop between 1909 and 1921; naturally, for a railway which since 1862 had ordered nothing bigger than 4–4–0 tender engines, these new machines were of the same arrangement. But if this was the works' only incursion into the field of new building, it quite happily survived on its bread-and-butter work of locomotive, carriage and wagon repairs. It earned an extensive modernisation in 1955. Closure took place with great sorrow at the end of 1969, and it is now the nucleus of an industrial estate.

One other important firm must not be overlooked, even though locomotive building activities flowered for only eleven years and then withered away. This was William Beardmore & Co with works at Parkhead (Glasgow) and Dalmuir. It was a firm with wide engineering interests, comparable in many ways with Armstrong, Whitworth on the Tyne, and like that company turned to locomotive building and repair after the rundown of armaments contracts at the end of World War I in order to maintain its skilled workforce. Dalmuir was converted at considerable cost to handle the new construction, and its locomotives numbered nearly 400, though there were some very lean years. One of their products, LMS No 5845, the 'Tishy' 'Prince of Wales' 4–6–0, was shown at the Empire Exhibition at Wembley in 1924. An interesting feature of Dalmuir works was that export locomotives could be hauled direct from the erecting shop to a ship alongside. Parkhead busied itself with some locomotive repairs to eat into the postwar backlog. But the depression of the early 1930s put a swift end to locomotive work.

The fifty-odd other Scottish firms which produced locomotives were mostly small beer in the early days of railways, and only about a dozen were still in the business into this century. Only three built steam engines into the 1920s; they were based in Kilmarnock and Airdrie. They faded from the picture because by that time the industrial steam shunting tank had proved very long-lived and what few replacements *were* needed were provided by Andrew Barclay, who could offer steam or – if you were brave – diesel. The versatile back street foundry had no continuing part to play in this field.

The sawtooth roof of the Inverurie erecting shop forms a backcloth to newly-overhauled ex-CR Jumbo 0–6–0 No 57273 and 0–4–4T No 55238 on 13 July 1957. Integration within Scotland had already turned the works into a facility for repairing engines in central and northern districts rather than for purely ex-LNER engines.

Shed and Locomotive Allocations
31 December 1947

North British Railway

Class C 15

7452	Thornton Jct	7462	Stirling	7472	Hawick
7453	Dunfermline	7463	Polmont	7473	Hawick
7454	Parkhead	7464	Polmont	7474	Carlisle
7455	Perth	7465	Hawick	7475	Kipps
7456	Eastfield	7466	Dunfermline	7476	Thornton Jct
7457	Hawick	7467	Eastfield	7477	Hawick
7458	Carlisle	7468	Polmont	7478	Dunfermline
7459	Hawick	7469	Dunfermline	7479	Parkhead
7460	Eastfield	7470	Parkhead	7480	Hawick
7461	Dundee	7471	Dundee	7481	Carlisle

Class C 16

7482	Eastfield	7489	Dundee	7496	St Margarets
7483	Dundee	7490	Dundee	7497	St Margarets
7484	Dundee	7491	Dundee	7498	Dundee
7485	Eastfield	7492	St Margarets	7499	Dundee
7486	Dundee	7493	St Margarets	7500	Eastfield
7487	Parkhead	7494	St Margarets	7501	Eastfield
7488	Parkhead	7495	St Margarets	7502	Eastfield

Scott Class D29

2400	Rob Roy	St Margarets	2406	Meg Merrilies	Thornton Jct
2401	Dandie Dinmont	Thornton Jct	2409	Helen MacGregor	Dundee
2402	Redgauntlet	St Margarets	2410	Ivanhoe	Dundee
2403	Sir Walter Scott	Haymarket	2411	Lady of Avenel	Polmont
2404	Jeanie Deans	St Margarets	2412	Dirk Hatteraick	Dundee
2405	The Fair Maid	St Margarets	2413	Guy Mannering	Haymarket

Scott Class D30

2417	Hal o' the Wynd	Hawick	2429	The Abott	Thornton Jct
2418	The Pirate	Dundee	2430	Jingling Geordie	Thornton Jct
2419	Meg Dods	Thornton Jct	2431	Kenilworth	Thornton Jct
2420	Dominie Sampson	St Margarets	2432	Quentin Durward	Hawick
2421	Laird o' Monkbarns	St Margarets	2434	Kettledrummle	Dundee
2422	Caleb Balderstone	Hawick	2435	Norna	St Margarets
2423	Dugald Dalgetty	Hawick	2436	Lord Glenvarloch	Thornton Jct
2424	Claverhouse	St Margarets	2437	Adam Woodcock	Haymarket
2425	Ellangowan	Hawick	2438	Peter Poundtext	Dundee
2426	Cuddie Headrigg	Perth	2439	Father Ambrose	Bathgate
2427	Dumbiedykes	Perth	2440	Wandering Willie	Hawick
2428	The Talisman	Hawick	2441	Black Duncan	Dunfermline
			2442	Simon Glover	Thornton Jct

Class D 31

2059	Carlisle	2064	Kittybrewster	2072	Bathgate
2060	Carlisle	2065	Kittybrewster		
2062	Kittybrewster	2066	Kittybrewster		

Class D 32

2443	St Margarets	2447	Thornton Jct	2451	St Margarets
2444	St Margarets	2448	Blaydon	2453	St Margarets
2445	St Margarets	2449	Blaydon	2454	St Margarets
2446	Thornton Jct	2450	St Margarets		

Class D 33

2455	Dunfermline	2460	Eastfield	2464	Bathgate
2457	Perth	2461	Stirling	2466	Perth
2458	Bathgate	2462	Eastfield		
2459	Dunfermline	2463	Bathgate		

Glen Class D 34

2467	Glen Finnan	Thornton Jct	2482	Glen Mamie	Eastfield
2468	Glen Orchy	Thornton Jct	2483	Glen Garry	St Margarets
2469	Glen Douglas	Eastfield	2484	Glen Lyon	St Margarets
2470	Glen Roy	Fort William	2485	Glen Murran	Dundee
2471	Glen Falloch	St Margarets	2487	Glen Arklet	St Margarets
2472	Glen Nevis	Eastfield	2488	Glen Aladale	St Margarets
2473	Glen Spean	Eastfield	2489	Glen Dessary	Eastfield
2474	Glen Croe	Eastfield	2490	Glen Fintaig	St Margarets
2475	Glen Beasdale	Thornton Jct	2492	Glen Garvin	Thornton Jct
2476	Glen Sloy	Polmont	2493	Glen Gloy	Eastfield
2477	Glen Dochart	Eastfield	2494	Glen Gour	St Margarets
2478	Glen Quoich	Thornton Jct	2495	Glen Luss	St Margarets
2479	Glen Sheil	Eastfield	2496	Glen Loy	Eastfield
2480	Glen Fruin	Fort William	2497	Glen Mallie	Eastfield
2481	Glen Ogle	Eastfield	2498	Glen Moidart	Eastfield

Class J 35

4460	Kipps	4488	Thornton Jct	4514	Thornton Jct
4461	Stirling	4489	St Margarets	4515	St Margarets
4462	St Margarets	4490	Polmont	4516	Thornton Jct
4463	Hawick	4491	Bathgate	4517	St Margarets
4464	Thornton Jct	4492	St Margarets	4518	St Margarets
4466	Thornton Jct	4493	Dundee	4519	St Margarets
4468	Bathgate	4494	Hawick	4520	Stirling
4470	Kipps	4495	Thornton Jct	4521	Thornton Jct
4471	Stirling	4496	Dunfermline	4522	Thornton Jct
4472	Kipps	4497	Stirling	4523	Dundee
4473	Kipps	4498	Kipps	4524	St Margarets
4474	Thornton Jct	4499	Carlisle	4525	Stirling
4475	Dunfermline	4500	Thornton Jct	4526	Carlisle
4476	Dunfermline	4501	Stirling	4527	St Margarets
4477	Thornton Jct	4502	Polmont	4528	Polmont
4478	Carlisle	4504	Bathgate	4529	Bathgate
4479	St Margarets	4505	Dunfermline	4530	Dundee
4480	Dunfermline	4506	Dunfermline	4531	Polmont
4482	Dundee	4507	Kipps	4532	St Margarets
4483	Dunfermline	4509	Hawick	4533	St Margarets
4484	Polmont	4510	Bathgate	4534	Bathgate
4485	Dundee	4511	Carlisle	4535	St Margarets
4486	St Margarets	4512	Dundee		
4487	Dunfermline	4513	Dunfermline		

Class J 36

5210	Kipps	5239	Dunfermline	5267	St Margarets
5211	Bathgate	5240	Haymarket	5268	Polmont
5213	Perth	5241	Polmont	5270	Eastfield
5214	Parkhead	5242	Hawick	5271	Bathgate
5215	Kipps	5243	Haymarket	5273	Eastfield
5216	Carlisle	5244	Polmont	5274	Parkhead
5217	St Margarets	5245	Kipps	5275	Polmont
5218	Thornton Jct	5246	Polmont	5276	Bathgate
5220	Polmont	5247	Kipps	5277	Bathgate
5221	Eastfield	5248	Bathgate	5278	Bathgate
5222	Polmont	5249	Kipps	5279	Hawick
5224	St Margarets	5250	Bathgate	5280	Bathgate
5225	Bathgate	5251	St Margarets	5281	Stirling
5226	Kipps	5252	Dunfermline	5282	Bathgate
5227	Eastfield	5253	Dunfermline	5283	Parkhead
5228	Eastfield	5254	Bathgate	5285	Kipps
5229	Bathgate	5255	Kipps	5286	St Margarets
5230	Bathgate	5256	Kipps	5287	Kipps
5231	Bathgate	5257	Polmont	5288	St Margarets
5232	Hawick	5258	St Margarets	5289	Kipps
5233	Polmont	5259	Hawick	5290	Polmont
5234	Bathgate	5260	Kipps	5291	Thornton Jct
5235	Bathgate	5261	Bathgate	5292	St Margarets
5236	Kipps	5264	Kipps	5293	Carlisle
5237	Fort William	5265	Bathgate	5294	Kittybrewster
5238	Kipps	5266	Kipps	5295	Hexham

5296 Eastfield	5314 Bathgate	5330 Dundee
5297 Perth	5315 Eastfield	5331 Reedsmouth
5298 Parkhead	5316 St Margarets	5333 Dundee
5300 Eastfield	5317 Hawick	5334 St Margarets
5303 Bathgate	5318 Bathgate	5335 Eastfield
5304 Carlisle	5319 Dundee	5337 Eastfield
5305 St Margarets	5320 Dunfermline	5338 Polmont
5306 Polmont	5321 Carlisle	5339 Eastfield
5307 Stirling	5322 Stirling	5340 Hawick
5308 Eastfield	5323 Dunfermline	5341 Bathgate
5309 Perth	5324 Parkhead	5342 Bathgate
5310 St Margarets	5325 Kipps	5343 Reedsmouth
5311 St Margarets	5327 Bathgate	5344 Bathgate
5312 Carlisle	5328 Dundee	5345 Thornton Jct
5313 Polmont	5329 Polmont	5346 Stirling

Class J 37

4536 Perth	4571 Polmont	4606 St Margarets
4537 Dundee	4572 St Margarets	4607 St Margarets
4538 St Margarets	4573 Parkhead	4608 St Margarets
4539 Hawick	4574 Dunfermline	4609 Parkhead
4540 Eastfield	4575 Dundee	4610 Eastfield
4541 Eastfield	4576 St Margarets	4611 Eastfield
4542 Stirling	4577 St Margarets	4612 Thornton Jct
4543 St Margarets	4578 Eastfield	4613 Polmont
4544 Stirling	4579 Eastfield	4614 St Margarets
4545 Dunfermline	4580 Eastfield	4615 Dundee
4546 Thornton Jct	4581 Eastfield	4616 Thornton Jct
4547 St Margarets	4582 St Margarets	4617 Dunfermline
4548 Dundee	4583 Eastfield	4618 Thornton Jct
4549 Thornton Jct	4584 Parkhead	4619 Dundee
4550 Thornton Jct	4585 Stirling	4620 Dundee
4551 Polmont	4586 St Margarets	4621 Polmont
4552 St Margarets	4587 Dundee	4622 Eastfield
4553 Thornton Jct	4588 Perth	4623 Eastfield
4554 Dunfermline	4589 Polmont	4624 St Margarets
4555 St Margarets	4590 Dunfermline	4625 St Margarets
4556 Stirling	4591 Perth	4626 Parkhead
4557 St Margarets	4592 St Margarets	4627 Dundee
4558 Eastfield	4593 Dundee	4628 Dunfermline
4559 Parkhead	4594 St Margarets	4629 Thornton Jct
4560 Dunfermline	4595 St Margarets	4630 Dunfermline
4561 Dunfermline	4596 Thornton Jct	4631 Dundee
4562 St Margarets	4597 Thornton Jct	4632 Eastfield
4563 Parkhead	4598 Thornton Jct	4633 Eastfield
4564 Thornton Jct	4599 St Margarets	4634 Dundee
4565 Thornton Jct	4600 Thornton Jct	4635 Thornton Jct
4566 St Margarets	4601 Eastfield	4636 St Margarets
4567 Dunfermline	4602 Thornton Jct	4637 St Margarets
4568 Dunfermline	4603 St Margarets	4638 Eastfield
4569 Stirling	4604 Dunfermline	4639 Eastfield
4570 Polmont	4605 St Margarets	

Class Y 9

8092 St Margarets	8103 Eastfield	8114 Dundee
8093 St Margarets	8104 Polmont	8115 St Margarets
8094 Kipps	8105 St Margarets	8116 Kipps
8095 St Margarets	8106 Kipps	8117 Kipps
8096 St Margarets	8107 Dundee	8118 Eastfield
8097 St Margarets	8108 Dundee	8119 St Margarets
8098 St Margarets	8109 Eastfield	8120 Kipps
8099 St Margarets	8110 Dundee	8121 Kipps
8100 Dundee	8111 St Margarets	8122 St Margarets
8101 Dunfermline	8112 Kipps	8123 Dundee
8102 St Margarets	8113 Polmont	8124 Eastfield

Class J 83

8442 Kipps	8455 Dundee	8469 Perth
8443 Kipps	8456 Thornton Jct	8470 St Margarets
8444 Kipps	8457 Haymarket	8471 Polmont
8445 Kipps	8458 Thornton Jct	8472 St Margarets
8446 Dundee	8459 Thornton Jct	8473 Haymarket
8447 Eastfield	8460 Haymarket	8474 St Margarets
8448 St Margarets	8461 Kipps	8475 Eastfield
8449 St Margarets	8463 St Margarets	8476 Eastfield
8450 St Margarets	8464 St Margarets	8477 St Margarets
8451 Thornton Jct	8465 Dunfermline	8478 Haymarket
8452 Dundee	8466 Dundee	8479 Eastfield
8543 Thornton Jct	8467 Thornton Jct	8480 Eastfield
8454 St Margarets	8468 Eastfield	8481 Haymarket

Class J 88

8320 St Margarets	8332 Thornton Jct	8344 Kipps
8321 Thornton Jct	8333 Thornton Jct	8345 Eastfield
8322 Thornton Jct	8334 St Margarets	8346 Stirling
8323 Thornton Jct	8335 Thornton Jct	8347 Eastfield
8324 Polmont	8336 Eastfield	8348 St Margarets
8325 St Margarets	8337 Thornton Jct	8349 Eastfield
8326 Eastfield	8338 St Margarets	8350 Polmont
8327 Eastfield	8339 Haymarket	8351 Stirling
8328 Haymarket	8340 St Margarets	8352 St Margarets
8329 Kipps	8341 Thornton Jct	8353 Thornton Jct
8330 Eastfield	8342 Stirling	8354 Polmont
8331 Eastfield	8343 Kipps	

Class N 14

9120 Eastfield	9124 Eastfield	9125 Kittybrewster

Class N 15

9126 Eastfield	9159 Bathgate	9192 Dunfermline
9127 Eastfield	9160 Dunfermline	9193 Parkhead
9128 Aberdeen	9161 Parkhead	9194 Parkhead
9129 Aberdeen	9162 Polmont	9195 Parkhead
9130 St Margarets	9163 Eastfield	9196 Kipps
9131 Eastfield	9164 Dunfermline	9197 Carlisle
9132 Thornton Jct	9165 Eastfield	9198 Parkhead
9133 St Margarets	9166 Eastfield	9199 Parkhead
9134 St Margarets	9167 St Margarets	9200 Polmont
9135 Dunfermline	9168 St Margarets	9201 Dunfermline
9136 Dunfermline	9169 Haymarket	9202 Dunfermline
9137 Polmont	9170 Eastfield	9203 Eastfield
9138 Eastfield	9171 Parkhead	9204 Dunfermline
9139 Carlisle	9172 St Margarets	9205 Eastfield
9140 St Margarets	9173 St Margarets	9206 Kipps
9141 Kipps	9174 Carlisle	9207 Kipps
9142 Bathgate	9175 St Margarets	9208 Eastfield
9143 Parkhead	9176 Eastfield	9209 Parkhead
9144 St Margarets	9177 Eastfield	9210 Parkhead
9145 Parkhead	9178 Eastfield	9211 Thornton Jct
9146 St Margarets	9179 Eastfield	9212 Parkhead
9147 St Margarets	9180 Eastfield	9213 Parkhead
9148 St Margarets	9181 Eastfield	9214 Parkhead
9149 St Margarets	9182 Eastfield	9215 Carlisle
9150 Thornton Jct	9183 Eastfield	9216 Bathgate
9151 Parkhead	9184 Eastfield	9217 Parkhead
9152 St Margarets	9185 Carlisle	9218 Carlisle
9153 Thornton Jct	9186 St Margarets	9219 St Margarets
9154 Dunfermline	9187 St Margarets	9220 Haymarket
9155 Carlisle	9188 Eastfield	9221 Dunfermline
9156 Bathgate	9189 Eastfield	9222 Eastfield
9157 Bathgate	9190 Parkhead	9223 Thornton Jct
9158 Bathgate	9191 Eastfield	9224 Thornton Jct

Great North of Scotland Railway

Class D 40

2260	Kittybrewster	2271		Kittybrewster
2261	Kittybrewster	2272		Kittybrewster
2262	Keith	2273	George Davidson	Kittybrewster
2264	Keith	2274	Benachie	Kittybrewster
2265	Kittybrewster	2275	Sir David Stewart	Kittybrewster
2267	Keith	2276	Andrew Bain	Kittybrewster
2268	Kittybrewster	2277	Gordon Highlander	Kittybrewster
2269	Kittybrewster	2278	Hatton Castle	Kittybrewster
2270	Kittybrewster	2279	Glen Grant	Kittybrewster

Class D 41

2225	Kittybrewster	2235	Keith	2248	Keith
2227	Kittybrewster	2238	Keith	2249	Keith
2228	Kittybrewster	2240	Keith	2251	Keith
2229	Kittybrewster	2241	Keith	2252	Keith
2230	Kittybrewster	2242	Kittybrewster	2255	Keith
2231	Kittybrewster	2243	Keith	2256	Keith
2232	Kittybrewster	2246	Keith		
2234	Keith	2247	Keith		

Class Z 4

8190	Kittybrewster
8191	Kittybrewster

Class Z 5

8192	Kittybrewster
8193	Kittybrewster

Caledonian Railway

Class 2P 4-4-0

14363	Aviemore

Class 3P 4-4-0

14434	Aviemore	14462	Motherwell	14486	Forfar
14438	Carstairs	14463	Carstairs	14487	St. Rollox
14439	Carstairs	14464	Motherwell	14488	Inverness
14440	Greenock	14465	Motherwell	14489	Perth
14441	Motherwell	14466	Stirling	14490	Carstairs
14443	Greenock	14467	Perth	14491	Stirling
14444	Greenock	14468	Greenock	14492	Greenock
14445	Greenock	14469	Perth	14493	Aviemore
14446	Carstairs	14470	Inverness	14494	St. Rollox
14447	Perth	14471	Inverness	14495	Inverness
14448	Perth	14472	Inverness	14496	Stirling
14449	Carstairs	14473	Forres	14497	Greenock
14450	Forfar	14474	St. Rollox	14498	Motherwell
14451	Dalry Road	14475	St. Rollox	14499	Perth
14452	Dalry Road	14476	Perth	14500	Perth
14453	Motherwell	14477	Carstairs	14501	Perth
14454	Forfar	14478	Dalry Road	14502	Perth
14455	Stirling	14479	Greenock	14503	Perth
14456	Hurlford	14480	Inverness	14504	Hurlford
14457	Greenock	14481	Forres	14505	Carstairs
14458	Perth	14482	Inverness	14506	Motherwell
14459	Perth	14483	St. Rollox	14507	Dalry Road
14460	Motherwell	14484	Inverness	14508	Greenock
14461	Carstairs	14485	Stirling		

Class 4P 4-6-0

14630	Carstairs	14640	Motherwell	14648	Hamilton
14631	Motherwell	14641	Motherwell	14649	Motherwell
14634	Motherwell	14642	Motherwell	14650	Motherwell
14635	Motherwell	14643	Motherwell	14651	Motherwell
14636	Motherwell	14644	Dalry Road	14642	Motherwell
14637	Motherwell	14645	Motherwell	14653	Motherwell
14638	Hamilton	14646	Motherwell	14654	Motherwell
14639	Hamilton	14647	Motherwell		

Class 2P 0-4-T

15116	Polmadie	15122	Stirling	15126	Stirling
15117	Stirling	15123	Polmadie	15127	Polmadie
15119	Grangemouth	15124	St. Rollox	15129	Dawsholm
15121	St. Rollox	15125	Dalry Road	15130	Manningham

15132	Ayr	15181	Beattock	15217	Dundee
15133	Aviemore	15182	Corkerhill	15218	Perth
15134	Motherwell	15183	Polmadie	15219	Corkerhill
15135	Corkerhill	15184	Forfar	15220	Aberdeen
15136	Dawsholm	15185	Forfar	15221	Polmadie
15138	Motherwell	15186	Dundee	15222	Stirling
15139	Dalry Road	15187	Oban	15223	Dundee
15140	Corkerhill	15188	Motherwell	15224	Polmadie
15141	Polmadie	15189	Dalry Road	15225	Corkerhill
15142	Grangemouth	15190	Forfar	15226	Dundee
15143	Corkerhill	15191	Motherwell	15227	Manningham
15144	Perth	15192	Manningham	15228	Polmaddie
15145	Dawsholm	15193	Corkerhill	15229	Dalry Road
15146	Hamilton	15194	Forfar	15230	Forfar
15159	St. Rollox	15195	Forfar	15231	Dundee
15160	Forfar	15196	Dundee	15232	Beattock
15161	Forfar	15197	Polmadie	15233	Dalry Road
15162	Forfar	15198	Forfar	15234	Aberdeen
15164	Beattock	15199	Inverness	15235	Corkerhill
15165	Dalry Road	15200	Forfar	15236	Hurlford
15166	Dalry Road	15201	Polmadie	15237	Beattock
15167	Polmadie	15202	Dalry Road	15238	Grangemouth
15168	Dawsholm	15203	Hurlford	15239	Beattock
15169	Manningham	15204	St. Rollox	15240	Dawsholm
15170	Polmadie	15206	Corkerhill	15260	Hurlford
15171	Perth	15207	Polmadie	15261	Carstairs
15172	Forfar	15208	Perth	15262	Ayr
15173	Dundee	15209	Perth	15263	Oban
15174	Dawsholm	15210	Dalry Road	15264	Ayr
15175	Perth	15211	Corkerhill	15265	Polmadie
15176	Perth	15212	Stirling	15266	Corkerhill
15177	Dalry Road	15213	Perth	15267	Polmadie
15178	St. Rollox	15214	Forfar	15268	Polmadie
15179	Polmadie	15215	Oban	15269	Corkerhill
15180	Dundee	15216	Perth		

Class 4P 4-6-2T

15350	Beattock	15354	Beattock	15360	Beattock
15351	Beattock	15355	Greenock	15361	Beattock
15352	Beattock	15356	Beattock		
15353	Beattock	15359	Beattock		

Class 0F 0-4-0ST

16010	Inverness	16026	Dawsholm	16031	Motherwell
16011	Inverness	16027	Shrewsbury	16032	Crewe Works
16020	Burton	16028	Motherwell	16035	Greenock
16025	St. Rollox Works	16029	Motherwell	16038	Dawsholm
		16030	Dawsholm	16039	Dawsholm

Class 2F 0-6-0T

16151	St. Rollox	16159	Polmadie	16167	Polmadie
16152	Grangemouth	16160	Polmadie	16168	Dawsholm
16153	Polmadie	16161	Dawsholm	16169	Dawsholm
16154	Dawsholm	16162	Polmadie	16170	Dawsholm
16155	Motherwell	16163	Greenock	16171	Dawsholm
16156	Greenock	16164	Grangemouth	16172	Polmadie
16157	Greenock	16165	Greenock	16173	Greenock
16158	Dawsholm	16166	Greenock		

Class 3F 0-6-0T

16230	Grangemouth	16240	Aberdeen	16250	Dawsholm
16231	Kingmoor	16241	Motherwell	16251	Aberdeen
16232	Grangemouth	16242	Hamilton	16252	St. Rollox
16233	St. Rollox	16243	Grangemouth	16253	Dalry Road
16234	St. Rollox	16244	Polmadie	16254	Stirling
16235	Kingmoor	16245	Motherwell	16255	Hamilton
16236	Dalry Road	16246	Perth	16256	Hamilton
16237	Hamilton	16247	Motherwell	16257	Ayr
16238	Dawsholm	16248	Kingmoor	16258	Motherwell
16239	Polmadie	16249	Corkerhill	16259	Ardrossan

16260	Polmadie	16299	Inverness	16338	Motherwell	17324	Forfar	17373	St. Rollox	17425	Stirling
16261	Polmadie	16300	Grangemouth	16339	Dawsholm	17325	Motherwell	17375	Stranraer	17426	Dawsholm
16262	Inverness	16301	Forres	16340	Kingmoor	17326	Motherwell	17377	Motherwell	17427	Dawsholm
16263	Polmadie	16302	Dawsholm	16341	Inverness	17327	Motherwell	17378	Dumfries	17429	Dawsholm
16264	Motherwell	16303	Hamilton	16342	Polmadie	17328	Motherwell	17379	Motherwell	17430	Hamilton
16265	Motherwell	16304	Polmadie	16343	Stirling	17329	Dumfries	17380	St. Rollox	17431	Hamilton
16266	Kingmoor	16305	Polmadie	16344	Dawsholm	17330	Polmadie	17381	Polmadie	17432	Polmadie
16267	Grangemouth	16306	Polmadie	16345	Motherwell	17331	Hurlford	17382	Hamilton	17433	Polmadie
16268	Motherwell	16307	Polmadie	16346	Polmadie	17332	St. Rollox	17383	Hurlford	17434	St. Rollox
16269	Motherwell	16308	Polmadie	16347	Perth	17333	St. Rollox	17384	Hamilton	17435	Motherwell
16270	Motherwell	16309	Hamilton	16348	Aberdeen	17334	Grangemouth	17385	Carstairs	17436	Polmadie
16271	Motherwell	16310	Kingmoor	16349	Polmadie	17335	Polmadie	17386	Carstairs	17437	Motherwell
16272	Ayr	16311	Ardrossan	16350	Corkerhill	17336	Dawsholm	17387	Polmadie	17438	Carstairs
16273	Ayr	16312	Dalry Road	16351	Stranraer	17337	Dumfries	17388	Polmadie	17439	Polmadie
16274	Ayr	16313	Dalry Road	16352	Perth	17338	Grangemouth	17389	Polmadie	17440	Stranraer
16275	Grangemouth	16314	Polmadie	16353	Perth	17339	Aberdeen	17390	Ayr	17441	Forfar
16276	Motherwell	16315	Dawsholm	16354	Kingmoor	17340	Carstairs	17391	Dumfries	17442	Grangemouth
16277	Motherwell	16316	Kingmoor	16355	Kingmoor	17341	Dawsholm	17392	Ayr	17443	Polmadie
16278	Aberdeen	16317	Kingmoor	16356	Motherwell	17342	Motherwell	17393	Hamilton	17444	Polmadie
16279	Ardrossan	16318	Polmadie	16357	Motherwell	17343	Dumfries	17394	St. Rollox	17445	Stranraer
16280	Polmadie	16319	Hamilton	16358	Motherwell	17344	Motherwell	17395	Hamilton	17446	Polmadie
16281	Motherwell	16320	Hamilton	16359	Aberdeen	17345	Aberdeen	17396	Oban	17447	Polmadie
16282	Ardrossan	16321	Hamilton	16360	Hamilton	17346	Dawsholm	17397	Perth	17448	Polmadie
16283	Dalry Road	16322	Polmadie	16361	Corkerhill	17347	Polmadie	17398	Hamilton	17449	Perth
16284	Hamilton	16323	Dundee	16362	Hamilton	17348	Ardrossan	17399	Carstairs	17450	Dundee
16285	Motherwell	16324	Polmadie	16363	Ayr	17349	Dumfries	17400	Aberdeen	17451	Carstaris
16286	Hamilton	16325	Dundee	16364	Ardrossan	17350	St. Rollox	17401	Hamilton	17452	Dawsholm
16287	Hamilton	16326	Aberdeen	16365	Stirling	17351	Ayr	17402	Stirling	17453	St. Rollox
16288	Greenock	16327	Kingmoor	16366	Stirling	17352	St. Rollox	17403	Motherwell	17454	St. Rollox
16289	St. Rollox	16328	Perth	16367	Ayr	17353	Hurlford	17404	Motherwell	17455	St. Rollox
16290	Perth	16329	Dalry Road	16368	Hurlford	17354	Ayr	17405	Dumfries	17456	Dawsholm
16291	Inverness	16330	St. Rollox	16369	Corkerhill	17355	Ardrossan	17406	Motherwell	17457	St. Rollox
16292	Polmadie	16331	Perth	16370	St. Rollox	17356	Ardrossan	17407	Hamilton	17458	Stranraer
16293	Inverness	16332	Kingmoor	16371	Hamilton	17357	Ardrossan	17408	Hamilton	17459	Polmadie
16294	Polmadie	16333	Kingmoor	16372	Stranraer	17358	Motherwell	17409	Dumfries	17460	Stirling
16295	Polmadie	16334	Motherwell	16373	Kingmoor	17359	Corkerhill	17410	Hamilton	17461	Motherwell
16296	Hamilton	16335	Motherwell	16374	Kingmoor	17360	Polmadie	17411	Oban	17462	Motherwell
16297	Dawsholm	16336	Grangemouth	16375	Grangemouth	17361	Polmadie	17412	Polmadie	17463	Greenock
16298	Polmadie	16337	Motherwell	16376	Grangemouth	17362	Dumfries	17413	Motherwell	17464	Polmadie
						17363	Motherwell	17414	Motherwell	17465	Polmadie
						17364	Ayr	17415	Motherwell	17466	Stirling
						17365	Polmadie	17416	Motherwell	17467	Polmadie
						17366	Dawsholm	17417	Motherwell	17468	Stirling
						17367	Polmadie	17418	Motherwell	17469	Dawsholm
						17368	Forfar	17419	Motherwell	17470	Dawsholm
						17369	Greenock	17420	Hamilton	17471	Dawsholm
						17370	Polmadie	17421	Stranraer	17472	Dawsholm
						17371	Dawsholm	17422	Stirling	17473	Perth
						17372	Dawsholm	17423	Stirling		
						17373	Grangemouth	17424	Stirling		

Class 2F 0-6-0

17230	Dumfries	17261	Ayr	17292	Polmadie
17231	Motherwell	17262	Ayr	17294	Gramgemouth
17232	Stirling	17263	Ardrossan	17295	Ayr
17233	Stirling	17264	Stirling	17296	Dawsholm
17234	Ayr	17265	Grangemouth	17298	Carstairs
17235	Ayr	17266	Corkerhill	17299	Motherwell
17236	Hurlford	17267	Motherwell	17300	Corkerhill
17237	Hamilton	17268	Polmadie	17301	Motherwell
17238	Dumfries	17269	St. Rollox	17302	Dumfries
17239	Polmadie	17270	Motherwell	17303	Motherwell
17240	St. Rollox	17271	Ayr	17304	Ardrossan
17241	Corkerhill	17272	Motherwell	17305	St. Rollox
17242	Hamilton	17273	Motherwell	17306	Dawsholm
17243	Stirling	17274	Ardrossan	17307	Hamilton
17244	Hamilton	17275	Polmadie	17308	Motherwell
17245	Dawsholm	17276	Ardrossan	17309	Corkerhill
17246	Stirling	17277	Hurlford	17310	Polmadie
17247	Motherwell	17278	Motherwell	17311	St. Rollox
17249	Corkerhill	17279	Ayr	17312	Ayr
17250	Hamilton	17280	Hamilton	17313	Motherwell
17251	St. Rollox	17282	Ardrossan	17314	Dawsholm
17252	Stirling	17283	Aberdeen	17315	Ayr
17253	St. Rollox	17284	Ayr	17316	Polmadie
17254	St. Rollox	17285	Grangemouth	17317	Polmadie
17255	Corkerhill	17286	Dumfries	17318	St. Rollox
17256	Motherwell	17287	Grangemouth	17319	Polmadie
17257	Stirling	17288	Dumfries	17320	Polmadie
17258	Dawsholm	17289	Motherwell	17321	Polmadie
17259	Dawsholm	17290	Motherwell	17322	Dawsholm
17260	Hamilton	17291	Motherwell	17323	Carstairs

Class 3F 0-6-0

17550	Dalry Road	17570	Hurlford	17589	Corkerhill
17551	Greenock	17571	Hurlford	17590	Ardrossan
17552	Greenock	17572	Hurlford	17591	Forres
17553	Dalry Road	17573	Hurlford	17592	Kingmoor
17554	St. Rollox	17574	Hurlford	17593	Motherwell
17555	Polmadie	17575	Corkerhill	17594	Corkerhill
17556	Greenock	17576	Dalry Road	17595	Motherwell
17557	St. Rollox	17577	Ardrossan	17596	Corkerhill
17558	St. Rollox	17578	Dalry Road	17597	Aviemore
17559	Dalry Road	17579	Ardrossan	17599	Motherwell
17560	Corkerhill	17580	Corkerhill	17600	Dumfries
17561	Corkerhill	17581	Polmadie	17601	Dumfries
17562	Corkerhill	17582	Motherwell	17602	Dumfries
17563	Dumfries	17583	Carstairs	17603	Grangemouth
17564	Polmadie	17584	Motherwell	17604	Carstairs
17565	Dalry Road	17585	Inverness	17605	Kingmoor
17566	Corkerhill	17586	Inverness	17606	Motherwell
17568	Dundee	17587	Inverness	17607	Dawsholm
17569	Ayr	17588	Motherwell	17608	Carstairs

189

17609 Hamilton	17632 Polmad	17661 Polmadie
17611 Ayr	17633 Ayr	17663 Hamilton
17612 Dawsolm	17634 Aviemore	17665 Hamilton
17613 Carstairs	17635 Carstairs	17666 Motherwell
17614 Ayr	17636 Dumfries	17667 Grangemouth
17615 Ayr	17637 Dumfies	17668 Motherwell
17616 Ayr	17638 Motherwell	17669 Ardrossan
17617 St. Rollox	17639 Greenock	17670 Carstairs
17618 Carstairs	17640 Ayr	17671 Hurlford
17619 Polmadie	17641 Polmadie	17672 Hurlford
17620 Forres	17642 Forfar	17673 Ardrossan
17621 Dumfries	17643 Hurlford	17674 Dalry Road
17622 Inverness	17644 Ayr	17679 Carstairs
17623 Dumfries	17645 Dalry Road	17681 Motherwell
17624 Corkerhill	17650 Hurlford	17682 Greenock
17625 Inverness	17651 Hurlford	17684 Ayr
17626 Kingmoor	17652 Dawsholm	17686 St. Rollox
17627 Ardrossan	17653 Dundee	17688 Hurlford
17628 Ayr	17654 Dalry Road	17689 Grangemouth
17629 Inverness	17655 Carstairs	17690 Polmadie
17630 Hamilton	17658 Grangemouth	17691 Grangemouth
17631 St. Rollox	17659 Dalry Road	

Highland Railway Locomotives

Loch Class 2P 4-4-0
14379 Loch Insh   Aviemore
14785 Loch Tay   Forres

Small Ben Class 2P 4-4-0

14397 Ben-y-Gloe	Inverness	14404 Ben Clebrig	Inverness
14398 Ben Alder	Aviemore	14409 Ben Alisky	Inverness
14399 Ben Wyvis	Inverness	14410 Ben Dearg	Forres
14401 Ben Vrackie	Inverness	14415 Ben Bhach Ard	Inverness
14403 Ben Attow	Inverness	14416 Ben a'Bhuird	Inverness

Clan Class 4P 4-6-0   *Class 0P 0-4-4T*
14764 Clan Munro   Aviemore   15051 Inverness
14776 Clan Mackinnon Aviemore   15053 Inverness

Class 3F 0-6-0
17693 Corkerhill   17697 Ayr   17702 Corkerhill
17694 Corkerhill   17698 Corkerhill
17695 Corkerhill   17699 Corkerhill

Clan Goods Class 4F 4-6-0
17950 Inverness   17953 Inverness   17955 Inverness
17951 Inverness   17954 Inverness   17956 Inverness

Glasgow & South Western Railway Locomotive

Class 3F 0-6-2T
16905 Kingmoor

Shed Allocations – LNER

Aberdeen Ferryhill
501 502 819 822 824 825 827 851 888 894
919 970 973 3041 3097 3134 4794 4795 4975 9128
9129

Bathgate
2072 2439 2458 2463 2464 4468 4491 4504 4510 4529
4534 5211 5225 5229 5230 5231 5276 5277 5278 5280
5282 5303 5314 5318 5327 5341 5342 5344 9142 9156
9157 9158 9159 9216

Carlisle Canal
68 91 93 95 1217 1219 1222 1851 1854 1858
1882 1898 1936 1937 2059 2060 2730 2731 2732 2734
2735 4478 4499 4511 4526 4875 4877 4880 4884 4888
4892 4895 4899 4912 4930 4932 4946 4948 4963 4964
7481 8499 9139 9155 9174 9185 9197 9215 9218

Dundee
804 838 840 844 920 937 969 971 1101 1102
1263 2409 2410 2412 2418 2434 2438 2485 2713 2718
2728 3071 3077 3123 3142 3194 4482 4485 4493 4506
4512 4523 4530 4537 4548 4575 4587 4593 4615 4619
4620 4627 4631 4634 4786 4790 4792 4822 4950 5319
5328 5330 5333 5614 5622 7461 7471 7483 7484 7486
7489 7490 7491 7498 7499 8100 8107 8108 8110 8114
8123 8446 8452 8455 8466

Dunfermline
2205 2441 2455 2459 4475 4476 4480 4483 4487 4496
4505 4513 4545 4554 4560 4561 4567 4568 4574 4590
4604 4617 4628 4630 5239 5252 5253 5320 5323 5900
5905 5909 5916 5917 5922 5923 5924 5926 5928 5930
5933 5934 7453 7466 7469 7478 7644 7661 8101 8465
8635 9135 9136 9154 9160 9164 9192 9201 9202 9204
9221

Duns
2357

Eastfield
1116 1117 1172 1180 1197 1243 1260 1261 1700 1701
1764 1772 1774 1775 1776 1779 1781 1784 1785 1786
1792 1793 1794 1993 1994 1998 2460 2462 2489 2493
2496 2497 2477 2479 2481 2482 2489 2493 2496 2497
2498 2671 2672 2673 2674 2675 2676 2680 2681 2681
2684 2686 2687 2688 2689 3020 3119 3120 4540 4541
4558 4578 4579 4580 4581 4583 4601 4610 4611 4622
4623 4632 4638 4639 5227 5228 5270 5273
5296 5300 5308 5315 5335 5337 5339 7456 7460 7467
7482 7485 7500 7501 7502 7600 7601 7602 8103 8109
8118 8124 8326 8327 8330 8331 8336 8345 8347 8349
8447 8468 8475 8476 8479 8480 8551 8552 8709 8733
8953 8954 8955 8956 8957 8958 9120 9124 9126 9127
9131 9138 9163 9165 9166 9170 9176 9177 9178 9179
9180 9181 9182 9183 9184 9188 9189 9191 8203 9205
9208 9222 9925 9927

Fort William
1782 1783 1787 1788 1789 1790 1791 1995 1996 2470
2480 5237

Hawick
2208 2417 2422 2423 2425 2428 2432 2440 4463 4494
4509 4539 5232 5242 5259 5279 5317 5340 7457 7459
7465 7472 7473 7477 7480 8138

Haymarket
4 9 11 12 24 27 31 35 37 41
43 57 64 65 66 67 87 94 99 100
101 503 504 505 506 509 510 519 816 834
836 848 882 898 927 931 951 953 955 958
972 980 1007 1072 1076 1081 1178 1221 1244 1245
2214 2403 2413 2437 2677 2678 2679 2683 2685 2690
2691 2692 2693 2694 2705 2706 2709 2711 2712 2719
2721 2733 5204 5243 7610 7615 7620 8328 8339 8457
8460 8473 8478 8481 9169 9220

Keith
1064 1500 1501 1502 1503 2234 2235 2238 2240 2241
2243 2246 2247 2248 2249 2251 2252 2255 2256 2262
2264 2267 7292

Kipps

4460	4470	4472	4473	4498	4507	5210	5215	5226	5236
5238	5245	5247	5249	5255	5256	5260	5264	5266	5285
5287	5289	5325	7475	7627	7660	8094	8106	8112	8116
8117	8120	8461	9141	9196	9206	9207	9503	9508	9509
9511	9518	9553	9563	9596					

Kittybrewster

1067	1132	1133	1134	1146	1147	1148	1242	1504	1505
1507	1508	1511	1513	1521	1524	1526	1528	1529	1532
1536	1539	1543	1552	1526	1563	2062	2064	2065	2066
2225	2227	2265	2268	2269	2270	2271	2272	2273	2274
2275	2276	2277	2278	2279	5294	7151	7164	7287	7327
8190	8191	8192	8193	8700	8710	8717	8719	8749	8750
9125									

Parkhead

1729	4559	4563	4573	4584	4609	4626	5214	5274	5283
5298	5324	7454	7470	7479	7487	7488	7603	7604	7611
7612	7613	7614	7616	7619	7621	7622	7623	7625	7626
7628	7631	7632	7633	7643	7648	7655	7662	7674	7678
8503	8507	9143	9145	9151	9161	9171	9190	9213	9214
9217	9500	9507	9510	9514	9562	9564	9565	9595	

Perth

1002	1061	2215	2426	2427	2457	2466	2714	2725	4536
4588	4591	5213	5297	5309	7455	8469			

Polmont

2411	2476	4484	4490	4502	4528	4531	4551	4570	4571
4589	4613	4621	5220	5222	5233	5241	5244	5246	5257
5268	5275	5290	5306	5313	5329	5338	7463	7464	7468
8104	8113	8324	8350	8354	8471	8524	8533	8544	9137
9162	9200								

Reedsmouth

5101	5331	5343

Rothbury

5083	7296

Stirling

2209	2461	4461	4471	4497	4501	4520	4525	4542	4544
4556	4569	4585	5281	5307	5322	5346	7462	7618	7650
8342	8346	8351							

St Margarets

1823	1855	1857	1876	1879	1885	1900	1909	1911	1916
1924	1931	1933	1955	1968	1983	1988	1990	1991	1992
2400	2402	2404	2405	2451	2453	2454	2471	2483	2484
2487	2488	2490	2494	2495	2702	2715	3038	3063	3089
3090	3115	3126	3147	3148	3172	3175	3180	4462	4479
4486	4489	4492	4515	4517	4518	4547	4552	4555	4557
4562	4566	4572	4576	4577	4582	4586	4592	4594	4595
4599	4603	5292	5305	5310	5311	5316	5334	5617	5623
5625	5906	5912	5914	5915	5918	5920	5927	7497	7605
7606	7607	7608	7609	7617	7624	7629	7630	7649	7659
7666	7670	8092	8093	8115	8119	8122	8320	8325	8334
8338	8340	8470	8472	8474	8477	8492	8505	8511	8525
8562	8568	8623	8952	9130	9133	9134	9140	9144	9146
9147	9148	9149	9152	9167	9168	9172	9173	9175	9186
9187	9219								

Thornton Jct

1103	1118	1262	2401	2406	2419	2429	2430	2431	2436
2442	2447	2467	2468	2475	2478	2492	2704	2708	2716
2717	2729	3004	3017	3019	3049	3058	3143	3151	3168
3177	3610	3806	4464	4466	4474	4477	4488	4495	4500
4514	4516	4521	4522	4546	4549	4550	4553	4564	4565
4596	4597	4598	4600	4602	4612	4616	4618	4629	4635
5218	5291	5345	5901	5902	5903	5904	5907	5908	5910

5911	5913	5921	5925	5931	5932	7452	7476	8321	8322
8323	8332	8333	8335	8337	8341	8353	8451	8453	8456
8458	8459	8467	8504	8535	8550	8555	9132	9150	9153
9211	9223	9224							

Shed Allocations – LMS

Kingmoor 12A

613	615	1129	1139	1140	1141	1142	1143	1146	2742
2743	2744	2745	2746	2748	2749	2751	2752	2780	2802
2803	2830	2831	2832	2833	2834	2835	2836	2837	2875
2876	2877	2878	2880	2881	2882	2883	2884	2905	2906
2907	3868	3902	3922	3973	3996	4001	4008	4009	4016
4181	4183	4189	4199	4315	4324	4326	4795	4877	4878
4879	4882	4883	4884	4994	5005	5006	5009	5013	5014
5015	5017	5022	5023	5081	5082	5083	5084	5096	5100
5118	5119	5126	5127	5151	5152	5169	5241	5266	5363
5364	5429	5432	5443	5454	5455	5482	5564	5577	5579
5580	5581	5582	5713	5714	5715	5716	5727	5728	5729
5730	5731	5732	16231	16235	16248	16266	16310	16316	16317
16327	16332	16333	16340	13654	16355	16373	16374	16905	17592
17605	17626	73798	73799						
Diesels	7111	7112	7113	7114	7115				

Beattock 12F

15164	15181	15232	15237	15239	15350	15351	15352	15353	15354
15356	15359	15360	15361						
SRM	29988								

Dumfries 12G

170	576	577	604	614	902	904	912	1109	1135
1171	1175	1179	2908	2909	2918	2919	6635	6639	17230
17238	17286	17288	17302	17329	17337	17343	17349	17362	17378
17391	17405	17409	17563	17600	17601	17602	17621	17623	17636

Stranraer 12H

600	611	616	623	1092	16351	16372	17375	17421	17440
17445	17458								

Polmadie 27A

916	1131	2200	2201	2202	2203	2204	2205	2206	2207
2208	2211	2213	2214	2215	2216	2238	2239	2240	2241
2242	2243	2244	2245	2246	2247	2274	2688	2689	2690
2691	2692	2693	2694	2695	2696	2698	2699	4234	4281
4793	4794	4978	4979	4980	5309	5484	5485	5486	5487
5583	5584	5691	5692	6102	6104	6105	6107	6143	6220
6221	6222	6223	6224	6230	6231	6232	6242	7331	7332
7536	7537	7540	15116	15123	15127	15141	15167	15170	15179
15183	15197	15201	15207	15221	15224	15228	15265	15267	15268
16153	16159	16160	16162	16167	16172	16239	16244	16260	16261
16263	16280	16292	16294	16295	16298	16304	16305	16306	16307
16308	16314	16318	16322	16324	16342	16346	16349	17239	17268
17275	17292	17310	17316	17317	17319	17320	17321	17330	17335
17347	17360	17361	17365	17367	17370	17379	17443	17444	17446
17447	17448	17459	17464	17465	17467	17555	17564	17581	17619
17632	17641	17661	17690						

Greenock 27B

2400	2415	2416	2417	2418	2419	2420	2421	2422	2423
2697	7167	7168	7169	14440	14443	14444	14445	14457	14468
14479	14492	14497	14508	15355	16035	16156	16157	16163	16165
16166	16173	16288	17369	17463	17551	17556	17639	17682	

Hamilton 27C

150	151	152	153	154	158	2217	2735	2740	2741
6656	14638	14639	14648	15146	16237	16242	16255	16256	16284
16286	16287	16296	16303	16309	16319	16320	16321	16360	16362
16371	17237	17242	17244	17250	17260	17280	17307	17382	17384

17393 17395 17398 17401 17407 17408 17410 17420 17430 17431
17609 17630 17663 17665
Diesel Railcars 29950 29951 29952

Motherwell 28A
159 200 3884 4011 4791 4792 5007 5008 5012 5016
5018 5120 5121 5453 5461 5462 5482 5488 5496 5497
5498 5499 8156 8183 8184 8185 8186 8187 8188 14441
14453 14460 14462 14464 14465 14498 14506 14631 14634 14635
14636 14637 14640 14641 14642 14643 14645 14646 14647 14649
14650 14651 14652 14653 14654 15134 15138 15188 15191 16028
16029 16031 16155 16241 16271 16276 16277 16281 16285 16334
16335 16337 16338 16345 16356 16357 16358 17231 17247 17256
17267 17270 17272 17273 17278 17289 17290 17291 17299 17301
17303 17308 17313 17325 17326 17327 17328 17332 17342 17344
17358 17363 17377 17379 17403 17404 17406 17413 17414 17415
17416 17417 17418 17419 17435 17437 17461 17462 17585 17584
17588 17593 17595 17599 17606 17638 17666 17668 17681

Dalry Road 28B
911 1177 1178 2268 2269 2270 2271 2272 2273 2804
2807 4318 4931 5029 7162 7163 8163 8321 14451 14452
14478 14507 14644 15125 15139 15165 15166 15177 15189 15202
15210 15229 15233 16236 16253 16283 16312 16313 16329 17550
17553 17559 17565 17576 17578 17645 17654 17659 17674

Carstairs 28C
566 592 605 619 666 901 903 907 915 1130
1136 1145 1147 1180 4953 4955 8301 8302 8331 14438
14439 14446 14449 14461 14463 14477 14490 14505 14630 15261
17298 17323 17340 17385 17386 17399 17438 17451 17538 17604
17608 17613 17618 17635 17655 17670 17679

Perth 29A
921 922 923 924 938 939 1099 1125 4193 4196
4251 4258 4314 4322 4328 4768 4769 4770 4796 4797
4885 4924 4925 4958 4959 4960 4961 4972 4973 4974
4975 4976 4977 5010 5011 5036 5085 5086 5087 5125
5161 5162 5163 5164 5165 5166 5167 5170 5171 5172
5173 5174 5175 5213 5357 5365 5366 5389 5452 5456
5457 5458 5459 5460 5463 5464 5465 5466 5467 5469
5470 5472 5473 5474 5475 14447 14448 14458 14459 14467
14469 14476 14489 14499 14500 14501 14502 14503 15144 15171
15175 15176 15208 15209 15213 15216 15218 16246 16290 16328
16331 16347 16352 16353 17397 17449 17473

Aberdeen 29B
1134 1176 1184 15220 15234 16240 16251 16278 16326 16348
16359 17283 17339 17345 17400

Dundee 29C
2154 2155 15173 15180 15186 15196 15217 15223 15226 15231
16323 16325 17450 17568 17653

Forfar 29D
2738 2800 2801 14450 14454 14486 15160 15161 15162 15172
15184 15185 15190 15194 15195 15198 15200 15214 15230 17324
17368 17441 17642

Corkerhill 30A
594 595 596 598 599 602 603 620 621 622
627 636 637 641 642 649 650 651 905 906
909 913 914 919 920 1110 1127 1148 1149 1182
2275 2276 2277 2910 2911 2912 2913 2914 2915 2916
2917 5047 5049 5168 5194 5251 5489 5490 5491 5560
5575 5576 5643 5644 5645 5646 5693 7329 15135 15140
15143 15182 15193 15206 15211 15219 15225 15235 15266 15269
16249 16350 16361 16369 17241 17249 17255 17266 17300 17309
17359 17560 17561 17562 17566 17575 17580 17589 17594 17596
17624 17693 17694 17695 17698 17699 17702

Hurlford 30B
570 571 572 573 593 597 612 617 618 643
644 645 661 662 663 665 686 687 688 689
3899 4159 4198 4312 4319 4323 4325 4329 14456 14504
15203 15236 15260 16368 17236 17277 17331 17353 17383 17570
17571 17572 17573 17574 17637 17643 17650 17651 17671 17672
17688

Ardrossan 30C
578 579 606 607 608 609 624 625 626 667
668 669 2209 2210 2212 16259 16279 16282 16311 16364
17263 17274 17276 17282 17304 17348 17355 17356 17357 17577
17579 17590 17627 17669 17673

Ayr 30D
574 575 590 610 638 640 647 648 664 670
908 1132 1133 1138 1155 1183 2739 2805 2806 2808
2809 2879 2927 7182 15132 15262 15264 16257 16272 16273
16274 16363 16367 17234 17235 17261 17262 17271 17279 17284
17295 17312 17315 17351 17354 17364 17390 17392 17569 17611
17614 17615 17616 17628 17633 17640 17644 17684 17697

St. Rollox 31A
918 1126 1128 3848 3849 4194 4253 4254 4255 4256
4257 4880 4881 4922 4923 4956 4957 4995 4996 5115
5116 5117 5153 5154 5155 5156 5157 5158 5159 5176
5177 5178 5179 5355 5356 5358 5359 5362 5423 5468
5471 5480 5481 14474 14475 14483 14487 14494 15121 15124
15159 15178 15204 16151 16233 16234 16252 16289 16330 16370
17240 17251 17253 17254 17269 17305 17311 17318 17333 17350
17352 17374 17380 17394 17434 17453 17454 17455 17457 17554
17557 17558 17617 17631 17686

Stirling 31B
4283 4330 4331 14455 14466 14485 14491 14496 15117 15122
15126 15212 15222 16254 16343 16365 16366 17232 17233 17243
17246 17252 17257 17264 17402 17422 17423 17424 17425 17460
17466 17468

Oban 31C
15187 15215 15263 17396 17411

Grangemouth 31D
2736 2737 3883 4320 8147 8148 8149 8150 8151 8152
15119 15142 15238 16152 16164 16230 16232 16243 16267 16275
16300 16336 16375 16376 17265 17285 17287 17294 17334 17338
17373 17442 17603 17658 17667 17689 17691

Dawsholm 31E
176 177 185 186 187 188 189 8153 8155 15129
15136 15145 15168 15174 15240 16026 16030 16038 16039 16154
16158 16161 16168 16169 16170 16171 16238 16250 16297 16302
16315 16339 16344 17245 17258 17259 17296 17306 17314 17322
17336 17341 17346 17366 17371 17372 17426 17427 17429 17452
17456 17469 17470 17471 17472 17607 17612 17652

Inverness 32A
4771 4772 4773 4798 4799 4991 4992 5053 5066 5090
5098 5122 5123 5124 5136 5138 5160 5192 5319 5320
5360 5361 5476 5477 5478 5479 7541 14397 14399 14401
14403 14404 14409 14415 14416 14470 14471 14472 14480 14482
14484 14488 14495 15051 15053 15199 16010 16011 16262 16291
16293 16299 16341 17585 17586 17587 17622 17625 17629 17950
17951 17953 17954 17955 17956

Aviemore 32B
14363 14379 14398 14434 14493 14764 14767 15133 17597 17634

Forres 32C
14385 14410 14473 14481 16301 17591 17620

12
CLOSURES AND WITHDRAWALS

WITH its irregular spread of population and many isolated settlements and industries over the mountains and across the sea, Scotland has always been challenging for public transport, but until well after nationalisation of the railways innate common sense with cross-subsidisation and some outright support from south of the border meant that most people were happy. There was great pride in the way that trains, boats and buses worked better together than in England and Wales, and a general belief that things were fair and that value was being given for money. And this despite the fact that the country suffered more than its fair share of early closures, some indeed at the height of the Railway Age.

In 1930, for example, 65 stations were closed to passengers, a figure not surpassed until 1951, and between 1848 when the first closure took place and 1951 almost fifty branch lines totalling 430 route miles were removed from the map. But it was clear to most that at least the majority of these lines should not have been built in the first place – the GNSR closed its Orton–Rothes branch in 1866 after only eight years – and were products of over-optimism or excessive competition between the major companies in Victorian times.

Attitudes began to change at the beginning of the 1950s, 1951 being a particularly difficult year when twenty services were terminated. They

> **Some Entry**
> No route into Scotland can compare with that of the Flying Scotsman: the astonishing beauty of Berwick revealed suddenly as the train comes over the cliffs at Scremerston; the final majestic sweep of the Tweed; the three great bridges, each a masterpiece of its day – and as the train slows and enters upon the loftiest of the three, Robert Stephenson's Royal Border Bridge, the passenger by the Flying Scotsman, surveying this fair scene and watching his motoring friends below...with their eyes more intent on the traffic than the scenery, has, as J.J. Bell once aptly expressed it, 'the advantage of the eagle over the sparrow'. – O.S. Nock, *Scottish Railways*.

Banff, Great North of Scotland Railway on 11 July 1957. An imported locomotive, Caledonian 0–4–4T No 55185 is heading the 5.25pm to Tillynaught. The station which closed to passengers on 6 July 1964 and freight four years later, was tucked away under a cliff, hard by the gas works.

included the Barnton, Polton and Penicuik branches round Edinburgh, the Aberfoyle and Kilsyth lines from Glasgow, the Alyth and Crieff branches in Perthshire, and the Highland's branch to Fortrose. Between nationalisation in 1948 and the end of 1963, the year in which Dr Beeching published his report, the Scottish Region withdrew no less than 59 passenger and 125 freight routes, the latter including some double counting of successive cutbacks of the same route. People were beginning to get worried, yet most of the losses were still marginal. Trams and buses had effectively beaten the suburban railways of Edinburgh, and in the motor age you had to be pretty dedicated to train travel to change at Muir of Ord for Fortrose. More serious perhaps was the closure of some of the smaller stations on the main lines which at least provided sensible journey opportunities, even if they were a nuisance to pathing the accelerated expresses of the day such as the Elizabethan non-stop King's Cross to Edinburgh. 1956 saw the closure en masse of thirty stations between Glasgow, Perth, Dundee and Aberdeen, and four years later a similar process started on the Carlisle via Beattock to Glasgow trunk route – and twenty stations were wiped out on the Far North route from Inverness to Wick.

This was to be a turning point, the Press now ready to campaign against what was seen as unfair treatment of deprived areas. 'Shoddy treatment for the Highlands', and 'Hellish injustice' were the kind of phrases that became all too familiar, along with useless delegations to Westminster and a sense of frustration that BR made up its own mind, whatever was said or done would make no difference and that fairness no longer counted. When the last train left Peebles in February 1962, the council bemoaned the fact that Peeblesshire had become the first county to be trainless, though others were expected to follow soon. And if BR did indeed indulge in running services down before presenting a water-tight closure case, it has to be said that now common sense left the opposition. 'Sheer nonsense,' screamed a member of Dornoch Town Council on hearing that the two daily trains from the Mound, only one with a connection from the South and a badly timed one at that, were to be withdrawn. The trains might be empty but how were the roads to cope with the extra traffic? Hardly any tourists might arrive by train but what a blow to tourism. Yet even where services were useful and used there seemed a remorseless cutting back especially of evening and weekend services timetable by timetable and that destroyed confidence. Railways were on the run.

But it was undoubtedly the publication of the Beeching Report that had people of all political beliefs up in arms. For a start, most regular rail users in Scotland had by now come to believe that the management, though partly local thanks to a Scottish Region, was highly deficient, while the basic dogma that denied that a railway should be judged by its usefulness but rather by its profit-and-loss account was alien to national feeling. There would clearly be no fairness.

Beeching suggested the removal of virtually all branch lines along with many secondary routes including, for example, the isolation of Stranraer, since Ayr was to be the end of the line from Glasgow. The whole Waverley

The Caledonian main line by-passed the town of Moffat, 1 mile 68 chains to the west of Beattock and a short branch was later built to connect it with the outside world. Passenger trains were withdrawn on 6 December 1954 but freight lasted another ten years until 6 April 1964, surprising perhaps if this late 1950s complement of one sheeted and one empty wagon was typical. Caledonian 0–4–4T No 55232 is seen coming off the branch at Beattock.

route was to go, Oban become trainless, and no wheel turn north of Inverness. The end of many important stations like Glasgow St Enoch was inevitable.

Of course it did not all happen. Having gone through the TUCC mill, however unfair many people thought the enquiry rules were (no questions were allowed on BR costs and methods), the Minister reprieved some routes. Other closure plans were not pressed. It was decreed that Wick and Thurso, Fort William and Mallaig, Oban (though reached via the West Highland and not Callander), Stranraer via Ayr should retain passenger trains on social grounds. Replacement bus services seldom lasted long, partly because they lacked publicised connections with main-line trains. Even where a stay of execution was granted – lest for example a new industry should set up – track was soon ripped up.

In what had become open warfare, BR indeed had an incentive to make lines instantly unusable. Thus the Press were invited to see the ritualistic removal of a section of the Waverley route as soon as the last sleeping car train had cleared it on the final Sunday night. What happened to that train perhaps highlights just how strong feelings had become. It was one thing to remove branches which had always had scant and inconvenient services, but the Waverley route between Carlisle and Edinburgh serving a series of important border towns and heavily used by through express freights to relieve pressure on the East Coast main line...that surely was a basic part of the fabric of the nation.

The Waverley had been built largely to get independent access for the North British to the LNWR and thus cock a snook at the obstructive Caledonian, but it was always an albatross round the NB neck. It rose to two summits at 900 and 1,006 feet by long 1 in 70 and 1 in 75 gradients, with abundant curvature, and in its 94 miles served only two sizeable towns, Galashiels and Hawick, which could barely muster 30,000 inhabitants between them. Nevertheless it was a trunk route carrying – in addition to its stopping passenger trains and day and night express to St Pancras – a substantial express fitted freight service linking the east of Scotland with the West Coast main line.

Above, left Renfrew Wharf (Glasgow & South Western) was situated almost on the south bank of the River Clyde and retained its passenger service, no doubt mainly for workmen, until 5 June 1967. LMS class 2P 4–4–0 No 40596 awaits the right-away with the 6.08pm to Glasgow St Enoch on 11 June 1956.

Above, right Heads of Ayr station was on a line which lost its passenger service way back in 1930. The station was opened by the LMS in 1947 specifically for Butlins' Holiday Camp but was also advertised in the public timetable. It closed from 9 September 1968. On 5 July 1958 LMS class 2P 4–4–0 No 40610 (fitted with Stanier chimney) heads the 2.43pm from Ayr and the scene is surveyed by the station master, no doubt a summer only appointment.

Much of Scotland could not generate enough traffic to make lines viable even in the heyday of railways. Crieff in Perthshire appeared to be one of the more prosperous which fell on hard times in BR days. The final rump of the passenger service was from Gleneagles to Crieff and Comrie which closed from 6 July 1964. Latterly the train was a four-wheeled railbus but when this failed a steam engine and two coaches was substituted as on this day in July 1963. LMS class 5 4–6–0 No 45465 had just run round the coaches off the 11.11am ex–Gleneagles and was about to transfer them to the opposite platform ready for the 12.00 noon departure.

In steam days many of its passenger services were in the hands of A3 Pacifics, which shared the freight with V2s and K3s. A curious feature was Riccarton Junction, high in the Cheviots where the Border Counties line to Hexham branched off, a tiny isolated railway community with no road access. A coach attached to freight trains took children to school and housewives to shop. A special Sunday train took churchgoers into Hawick. That the railway would be missed was beyond doubt, and as elsewhere the replacement buses (though they have survived) would not really meet the need.

On the final Saturday the morning train was about to leave Waverley when a bomb was reported to be on board. Nothing was found. An excursion bound for Whitley Bay was halted at Tynehead also with a reported bomb, but again it was a hoax. 'Waverley Line, Born 1849. Killed 1969. Aged 120 years.' was inscribed on a coffin on Hawick station, and local people who had fought and lost the bitter battle to save their railway were intolerant of those who were in lighthearted mood; the trainload of joyriders to Whitley Bay had indeed been jeered on departure, which seemed unfair since they were not responsible for the roundabout route via St Boswells and Tweedmouth.

John Thomas takes up the story: The last train of all was the Night Midland on Sunday 5 January. It was uncommonly well filled. Among its passengers was Mr (now Sir) David Steel, MP for the Waverley route constituency, who had been in the forefront of the campaign to save the line. As the train made its way through Galashiels, Melrose and St Boswells house windows that would normally have been dark were shining oblongs of light. Shadowy figures stood in station entrances watching the train go by.

The people of Hawick who so often had heard the Night Midland and its precessors climbing away into the Border hills heard the familiar sound for the last time. Some of them were on the platform as the train drew in. A lone piper played that most soulful of Scottish laments the 'Flowers of the Forest,' a dirge heard traditionally at the end of lost battles and at the funerals of the great. The coffin of the day before appeared again. It was put in the van, addressed to the Minister of Transport.

The long haul over Whitrope lay ahead. But word came that trouble was brewing over the hills. The Hawick up starter remained red while a light engine was sent out on a path-finding mission. Midnight had struck before news came that it seemed safe to proceed. The piper's lament sounded over the town until the train's tail lamp had disappeared. The Night Midland topped the summit and was sweeping down towards Carlisle when it was brought to a sudden stop. A sagging communication in a toilet told why. The guard ignored the incident and the train proceeded on its way.

At Newcastleton the home signal showed red. Here it was that the fight to save the line had been fiercest. Here it was in the first hour of that Monday morning that the people of Newcastleton made the last stand. The level crossing gates were shut against the express, and behind them were entrenched the minister of the parish and his stubborn flock.

> **Sir Bob**
> Scotland has provided Britain with many key railwaymen... including the present BR chairman Sir Bob Reid who was born the son of a Coupar Angus butcher. It is said that an early accident, when he lost a hand in a mincing machine accident, played a significant part in the shaping of his character and management toughness.

Aberfeldy ex-Highland Railway on a wet 23 July 1954. The locomotive CR 0–4–4T No 55218 on the 1.45pm to Ballinluig unusually comprising two corridor coaches.

The Great North of Scotland suffered badly under the Beeching axe and all that is left is the main line from Aberdeen to Keith as part of the through route to Inverness. Craigellachie was an important junction in the Spey valley where the line to Boat of Garten diverged from one of the two GNSR lines between Cairnie Junction and Elgin. Class B1 4–6–0 No 61400 is heading an Elgin–Aberdeen passenger train in the 'main' platforms at Craigellachie on 2 August 1954. This passenger service was withdrawn from 6 May 1968.

The Speyside line curved away from the 'main' line at Craigellachie and followed the river to Boat of Garten. Class D41 No 62241 stands with a Speyside local in 1951, the locomotive being in early lined black livery and the train made up of an ex-NB corridor composite and an LNER brake third. Passenger services on Speyside were withdrawn from 18 October 1965 after a vain attempt to encourage traffic with four-wheel railbuses and lineside halts. Freight from Dufftown to Aberlour lingered on until 15 November 1971.

The Night Midland stood at the signal for half an hour, its passage blocked by the sullen assembly. At one stage the minister was arrested, but the demonstrators were not intimidated. In the end David Steel emerged from his sleeping car and mediated on the disputed crossing. The outcome was a gentleman's agreement whereby the townsfolk would allow the train to pass provided that their minister was released. The Night Midland resumed its journey piloted as far as the Border... just one of the tales of closure in John Thomas's *Forgotten Railways: Scotland*.

By the end of 1965 virtually every withdrawal proposed by Beeching had gone through the administrative treadmill and been either implemented or refused. LMS and LNER competitive routes in Glasgow and Edinburgh had been rationalised. The parcels and sundries traffic had been largely concentrated, and the first Scottish Freightliner depot opened at Gushetfaulds, Glasgow. Further depots in Edinburgh, Aberdeen and Clydeport Greenock were in the pipeline. Efficient merry-go-round coal working between Monktonhall colliery and Cockenzie power station six miles away, was up and running, and similar services to Longannet power station, then under construction, were agreed.

The Waverley line was the last of the major closures, but the story was not quite over, for in March 1969 a group of London enthusiast businessmen announced they were setting up a company to buy the whole line: not, it was emphasised, as a tourist attraction but to run normal diesel-powered passenger and freight services, topped up with oil-fired steam (*Blue Peter* and *Bittern* were on offer) for tourists. The Border Union Railway Company would need £1.75 million to buy the track, locomotives and rolling stock but would make a profit of £500,000 in its first year. Like many an earlier Scottish railway pipe dream, it came to nothing.

By the time the Waverley route went, another and even faster double main line had been consigned to oblivion, the former Caledonian route taken by Euston and Glasgow expresses from Perth to Aberdeen, 45 miles laid out for fast running between Stanley Junction (where the Highland used to begin north of Perth) and Kinnaber Junction near Montrose (whose signalman determined whether the East or West Coast express got to Aberdeen first in the famous races). With only Forfar as a modest population centre on the route, it was preferable to divert services to cater for Dundee, Arbroath and Montrose. Along with an earlier start on closures, modernisation (especially of freight services) and the abolition of locomotive haulage for local passenger services was the kind of cost-cutting initiative that people came to expect from Scotland...and which no doubt led to so many key positions throughout BR going to those who like Chris Green (now InterCity director) had cut their teeth north of the border.

That of course does not mean that mistakes were not made, and by any objective standards what survives today and what does not is an odd mixture determined by politics and fate. Given that passenger traffic has been so resilient on many routes that did survive, one indeed seriously questions whether the Waverley route should not have been saved, albeit in simplified form like that other extension used by Midland trains, the

The Deeside line in LNER days. Class D41 4–4–0 No 6822 waits at Banchory with an Aberdeen–Ballater train in 1938. This branch was regularly used by the Royal Train en route to the terminus at Ballater which was the nearest station for Balmoral. Prior to closure on 28 February 1966 the service had seen the operation of the Derby built lightweight battery electric twin car set not unlike the diesel sets that operated the last services.

Opposite, below A controversial as well as major closure was that of the former North British Waverley Route from Edinburgh to Carlisle which shut to passengers from 6 January 1969. Freight to Hawick from the north lingered on until 28 April the same year. LNER class K3 2-6-0 No 61876 at Falahill summit on a down fitted freight.

Glasgow & South Western's Carlisle to Glasgow line via Dumfries. The Deeside line to Ballater would probably today be carrying far heavier traffic than uses the Further North route beyond Inverness.

Throughout the nation there are abandoned stations and engineering works testifying to former civilisation, but it is the longer lines such as that between Dumfries and Stranraer, and the secondary systems across Buchan to Fraserburgh and around the coast to Elgin as well as the Waverley route and the abandoned racing ground through Forfar whose ruins especially stir the memory. In a sense Scotland has been lucky to retain such an extensive system as it has, especially in the less populated North, yet nowhere have more main lines and alternative routes (including between Glasgow and Edinburgh) disappeared. Closing a main line used by named expresses is more akin to seeing a young man cut down in his prime; many of the branches had clearly exceeded the years of their usefulness and in their last days carried more enthusiasts than genuine passengers.

One other main line has more recently been removed from the InterCity timetable if not the map: the Caledonian's from Motherwell to Stirling (for Perth). Until relatively recent times, Perth remained an important destination in its own right, served by a series of restaurant car

Above *The Waverley Route again with an up partially fitted freight headed by an LNER class K3 2–6–0 No 61968 of St Margaret's shed at Edinburgh leaving Hawick in the mid 1950s banked by a class J36 0–6–0. The two leading wagons appear to be tanks of Loch Katrine water for either Portal, Dingwall & Norris Ltd, whisky blenders, or Lemon Hart & Son Ltd.*

trains and having its own sleeper. Even until electrification from Carstairs to Edinburgh the Royal Highlander from Euston to Inverness (along with motorail services) went that way. This route has its own culture as much as any other but has been severed without being closed or even mourned and ghosts surely watch the Cumbernauld locals that putter along a few miles on their way from Springburn.

Scotland has always had change, industries rising and falling with uncomfortable rapidity. The coal and steel industries were served by many square miles of railway facilities now abandoned. The 1960s generation of marshalling yards were closed with what seemed indecent haste, certainly before their costs could possibly have been amortised, in the rapid run down of wagon-load freight. Even Beeching's freightliner terminals at favoured locations like Edinburgh and Aberdeen have hit the dust, along with more conventional 'greats' such as Thornton yard and motive power depot which was not so much a world apart but a constellation.

Yet if we were once more to enjoy an abandoned railway installation in its heyday, it would surely be one of those great stations where passengers wore their hearts on their sleeves, hope and fears alternated and not infrequently meetings of a lifetime took place: Glasgow St Enoch and Buchanan Street, one admittedly far grander than the other but each totally different in character from the two termini that remain, and Edinburgh Princes Street of greater decorum than Waverley.

Hawick shed yard as seen from the station in the early 1950s. The two ex-NBR engines with the duty Nos 243 & 244 represent goods and passenger classes of the pre-grouping company whilst the Gresley 4–4–0 in the background is a LNER replacement for the previous generation of small passenger engines. Class D49 No 62719 Peebles-shire, a visitor from Haymarket, was one of the fifteen allocated new to Scotland in 1928 at which time Pacifics were not yet permitted over the Waverley route. The D30 Scott class 4–4–0 Wandering Willie remained in service until 1958 and the 1909 built Class J35 No 64494 lasted until 1961.

Closure Table

Pre Grouping Company and Line	Passenger	Goods
North British		
Greenlaw–Duns		13 Aug 1948
St Boswells–Duns	13 Aug 1948	
Ladybank–Mawcarse	5 Jun 1950	
Banavie Jct–Banavie Pier	4 Sept 1939	6 Aug 1951
Abbeyhill Jct–Leith Central	7 Apr 1952	N/A
Bothwell–Hamilton	15 Sept 1952	see below
Bothwell–Blantyre Jct		15 Sept 1952
Rosyth Naval Base–North Queensferry Goods		4 Oct 1954
Thornton Jct–Methil	10 Jan 1955	
Leuchars Jct–Tayport	9 Jan 1956	9 Jan 1956
Ladybank–Auchtermuchty		29 Jan 1957
Fountainhall–Lauder	12 Sept 1932	1 Oct 1958
Kirkintilloch–Aberfoyle	1 Oct 1951	5 Oct 1959
Bowling New Jct–Dumbarton East Jct	25 Apr 1960	25 Apr 1960
Partick Hill–Hyndland	5 Nov 1960	5 May 1958
Sunnyside–Bothwell	10 Sept 1951	6 Jun 1961
Shettleston–Bothwell	4 Jul 1955	
Mount Vernon N–Bothwell		6 Jun 1961
Burnmouth–Eyemouth	5 Feb 1962	5 Feb 1962
Rosewell & Hawthornden–Galashiels via Peebles	5 Feb 1962	5 Feb 1962
Peacock Cross–Hamilton	15 Sept 1952	
Burnbank–Peacock Cross		11 Feb 1963
Alloa–Alva	1 Nov 1954	
Menstrie–Alva		24 Feb 1964
Bathgate Jct–Airdrie	9 Jan 1956	6 Apr 1964
Kelvin Valley Jct–Kilsyth	6 Aug 1951	4 May 1964
Esk Valley Jct–Polton	10 Sept 1951	18 May 1964
East Fife Central Jct–Lochty		10 Aug 1964
Bathgate–Fauldhouse	1 May 1930	10 Aug 1964
Glenesk Jct–Dalkeith	5 Jan 1942	10 Aug 1964
Roxburgh–Jedburgh	10 Aug 1964	10 Aug 1964
Glenburnie Jct–St Fort	12 Feb 1951	5 Oct 1964
Galashiels–Selkirk	10 Sept 1951	2 Nov 1964
Jordanhill (West) –Whiteinch (Victoria Park)	2 Apr 1951	3 May 1965
Leven–St Andrews	6 Sept 1965	from Crail 6 Sept 1965
Bo'ness Jct H.L.–Bo'ness (preserved)	7 May 1956	8 Nov 1965
Campsie Branch Jct–Kirkintilloch	7 Sept 1964	4 Apr 1966
Broomfield Jct–Inverbervie	1 Oct 1951	23 May 1966
Tayport–Newport on Tay East	22 May 1966	23 May 1966
Leuchars–St Andrews	6 Jan 1969	20 Jun 1966
Morpeth–Reedsmouth	15 Sept 1952	3 Oct 1966
Scotsgap–Rothbury	15 Sept 1952	11 Nov 1963
Reston–Duns	10 Sept 1951	7 Nov 1966
Rosewell & Hawthornden–Penicuik	10 Sept 1951	27 Mar 1967
Riddings–Langholm	15 Jun 1964	18 Sept 1967
Haymarket W. Jct–Corstorphine	1 Jan 1968	5 Feb 1968
Drem–North Berwick	Still open	1 Jan 1968
Longniddry–Haddington	5 Dec 1949	1 Apr 1968
Stirling–Dumfermline Lower	7 Oct 1968	
Edinburgh–Carlisle 'Waverley Route'	6 Jan 1969	
Hawick–Longtown		6 Jan 1969
Lady Victoria Coll–Hawick		28 Apr 1969
Wormit Tay Bridge South–Newport on Tay	5 May 1969	5 May 1969
Thornton Jct–Leven	6 Oct 1969	6 Oct 1969
Cowdenbeath N. Jct–Perth via Glenfarg	5 Jan 1970	5 Jan 1970
Musselburgh branch (trains via Abbeyhill)	7 Sept 1964	6 Sept 1971
Great North of Scotland		
Ellon–Boddam	1 Nov 1932	1 Jan 1949
Fraserburgh–St Combs	3 May 1965	7 Nov 1960
Kintore–Alford	2 Jan 1950	3 Jan 1966
Inverurie–Old Meldrum	2 Nov 1931	3 Jan 1966
Inveramsay–Macduff	1 Oct 1951	
Turriff–Macduff		1 Aug 1961
Inveramsay–Turriff		3 Jan 1966
Elgin–Lossiemouth	6 Apr 1964	28 Mar 1966
Aberdeen–Ballater	28 Feb 1966	
Culter–Ballater		18 Jul 1966
Ferryhill Jct–Culter		2 Jan 1967
Tillynaught–Banff	6 Jul 1964	6 May 1968
Cairnie Jct–Elgin via Buckie	6 May 1968	6 May 1968
Keith Jct–Elgin via Dufftown	6 May 1968	
Dufftown–Craigellachie		15 Nov 1971
Craigellachie–Rothes		4 Nov 1968
Rothes–Elgin		6 May 1968
Keith Jct–Dufftown		1 Oct 1985
(retained for charter passenger traffic)		
Boat of Garten–Craigellachie	18 Oct 1965	
Abelour–Boat of Garten		4 Nov 1968
Craigellachie–Aberlour		15 Nov 1971
Maud Jct–Peterhead	3 May 1965	7 Sept 1970
Dyce–Fraserburgh	4 Oct 1965	8 Oct 1979
Glasgow & South Western		
Cairn Valley Jct–Moniaive	3 May 1943	4 Jul 1949
Holehouse–Belston Jct	3 Apr 1950	
Littlemill Col–Holehouse Jct		3 Apr 1950
Auchinleck–Cronberry	3 Jul 1950	
Annbank Jct–Cronberry	10 Sept 1951	
Heads of Ayr–Girvan		28 Feb 1955
Ayr–Dalmellington	6 Apr 1964	
Kilmarnock–Irvine	6 Apr 1964	6 Jul 1964
Kilmarnock–Darvel	6 Apr 1964	6 Jul 1964
Castle Douglas–Kirkcudbright	3 May 1965	14 Jun 1965
Kilmacolm–Greenock PP	2 Feb 1959	29 Sept 1966
Kilmarnock–Barassie	2 Jan 1967	7 Sept 1964
Hillington West–Renfrew Wharf	5 Jun 1967	c 1958

Ayr–Heads of Ayr (Butlins)		
LMS Station	16 Sept 1968	N/A
Elderslie–Dalry		
via Lochwinnoch	27 Jun 1966	8 Sept 1969
Dalry–Kilmarnock	22 Oct 1973	22 Oct 1973
Mauchline–Ayr	5 May 1975	
Shields Jct–Kilmacolm		
via Paisley Canal	3 Jan 1983	3 Jan 1983
(Goods to Hawkhead never closed)		
Shields Jct–Paisley Canal	reopened passenger 30 July 1990	

Port Patrick & Wigtownshire

Stranraer Town–Portpatrick	6 Feb 1950	
Colfin–Portpatrick		6 Feb 1950
Stranraer Town–Colfin		16 Apr 1959
Newton Stewart–Whithorn		
& Garlieston branch	25 Sept 1950	5 Oct 1964

Caledonian

Lugton East Jct–		
Giffen (local passenger)	4 Jul 1932	31 May 1950
Bothwell Jct–Bothwell	5 Jun 1950	5 Jun 1950
Symington–Peebles	5 Jun 1950	
Peebles–Broughton		7 Jun 1954
Broughton–Symington		4 Apr 1966
Dolphinton Jct–Dolphinton	12 Sept 1932	1 Nov 1950
Morningside Jct–Newmains	1 Dec 1930	5 Feb 1951
Craigleith–Barnton	7 May 1951	
Davidson's Mains–Barnton		7 May 1951
Craigleith–Davidson's Mains		1 Jun 1960
Alyth Jct–Alyth	2 Jul 1951	7 Sept 1964
Auchengray (Wilsontown		
S. Jct)–Wilsontown	10 Sept 1951	4 May 1964
Comrie–Balquhidder	1 Oct 1951	1 Oct 1951
Ferniegair Jct–Brocketsbrae	1 Oct 1951	
Almond Valley Jct–Crieff	1 Oct 1951	11 Sept 1967
Dumfries–Lockerbie	19 May 1952	18 Apr 1966
Bridge of Dun–Brechin	4 Aug 1952	4 May 1981
Brechin–Forfar	4 Aug 1952	7 Sept 1964
Dubton Jct–Broomfield Jct	4 Aug 1952	21 Jun 1963
Kirriemuir Jct–Kirriemuir	4 Aug 1952	21 Jun 1965
Giffen–Ardossan		
Montgomerie Pier		
local passenger trains	4 Jul 1932	30 Mar 1953
High Blantyre–		
Strathaven North	1 Oct 1945	21 Sept 1953
Whiteshawgate Jct–		
Strathaven Cen.	1 Oct 1945	21 Sept 1953
Meikleriggs Jct–		
Meikleriggs Goods		6 Sept 1954
Alton Heights Jct–		
Poneil Jct		13 Sept 1954
Beattock–Moffat	6 Dec 1954	6 Apr 1964
Ninewells Jct–Alyth Jct	10 Jan 1955	
Alyth Jct–Newtyle		7 Sept 1964
Coupar Angus–Blairgowrie	10 Jan 1955	6 Dec 1965
Broughty Jct–Forfar	10 Jan 1955	9 Oct 1967
Kirtlebridge–Annan Shawhill		21 Feb 1955

Shawhill Jct–		
Annan Shawhill		28 Feb 1955
St Vigeans Jct–Guthrie Jct	5 Dec 1955	
St Vigeans–Letham Mill Siding		5 Dec 1955
Stobcross–Maryhill	2 Nov 1959	
Strathaven Jct–High Blantyre	1 Oct 1945	1 Jun 1960
Neilston High–Uplawmoor	2 Apr 1962	2 Apr 1962
Dalry Middle Jct–Leith North	30 Apr 1962	30 Apr 1962
Dalry Middle Jct–		
Haymarket West Jct	2 Mar 1964	2 Mar 1964
Gleneagles–Crieff–Comrie	6 Jul 1964	17 Aug 1964
Brechin–Edzell	27 Sept 1938	7 Sept 1964
Strathord–Bankfoot	13 Apr 1931	7 Sept 1964
Glasgow Central low level lines		
(Coatbridge C & Rutherglen–		
Dumbarton East)		
(and Stobcross–Possil)		
[later reopened]	5 Oct 1964	
Lanark–Muirkirk	5 Oct 1964	5 Oct 1964
Callander–Crianlarich	28 Sept 1965	28 Sept 1965
Killin Jct–Killin	28 Sept 1965	28 Sept 1965
Hamilton–Coalburn	4 Oct 1965	4 Oct 1965
Hamilton–Strathaven	4 Oct 1965	4 Oct 1965
Dunblane–Callander	1 Nov 1965	1 Nov 1965
Connel Ferry–Ballachulish	28 Mar 1966	14 Jun 1965
Stanley Jct–Kinnaber Jct	4 Sept 1967	
Forfar–Bridge of Dun		4 Sept 1967
Stanley Jct–Forfar		5 Jun 1982
Balerno Jct–Balerno	1 Nov 1943	4 Dec 1967
Falkirk (Grahamston)–		
Grangemouth	1 Jan 1968	
Larbert–Alloa	1 Jan 1968	2 Jan 1967
Stevenston No 1–Ardrossan		
Montgomerie Pier	6 May 1968	N/A

Highland

Fodderty Jct–Strathpeffer	23 Feb 1946	26 Mar 1951
Burghead–Hopeman	14 Sept 1931	30 Dec 1957
Gollanfield Jct–Fort George	5 Apr 1943	11 Aug 1958
Muir of Ord–Fortrose	1 Oct 1957	13 Jun 1960
The Mound–Dornoch	13 Jun 1960	13 Jun 1960
Ballinluig–Aberfeldy	3 May 1965	3 May 1965
Aviemore–Forres	18 Oct 1965	5 Jul 1965
Orbliston Jct–		
Fochabers Town	14 Sept 1931	28 Mar 1966

Glasgow Barrhead & Kilmarnock Joint
(Caledonian and Glasgow & South Western)

Barrmill–Beith Town	5 Nov 1962	5 Oct 1964

North British & North Eastern

Tweedmouth–St Boswells	15 Jun 1964	
Tweedmouth–Kelso		29 Mar 1965
St Boswells–Kelso		30 May 1968

Glasgow & South Western/
Port Patrick & Wigtownshire

Dumfries–Stranraer	14 Jun 1965	14 Jun 1965

ACKNOWLEDGEMENTS

Scotland's railways have always been a special favourite of the joint authors whose many visits and journeys set the scene for the content of this book. We have been fortunate to gather together both contributions on broad-based subjects and more technical and specialist aspects of the railway scene.

Patrick Whitehouse again led the consultancy team of John Edgington, David Johnson and John Powell. John Powell's extensive professional railway knowledge of both operational and locomotive matters has been a major source of inspiration and his hand can be found throughout this book. John Edgington's vast resource of numeric and geographical information has enabled a great deal of informative matter to be included and thus add to the reference value of the text. Some line drawings have been reproduced from copies of the *Railway Magazine* and we thank both John Slater and Peter Kelly for their courtesy. Thanks are also due to the staff of Strathkelvin District Council Libraries and Museums, the Mitchell Library, Glasgow and the Springburn Museum Trust. Larry has introduced his own humour to rail travel in Scotland, which we hope you will find apposite. The jacket cover and frontispiece is reproduced from a painting by George Heiron which we feel captures all that makes Scotland's railways attractive to enthusiasts worldwide.

The chapters are based on work by: David St John Thomas (Introduction, The Scottish Country Railway); Patrick Whitehouse (Some Scottish Stations); Dr C.E.J. Fryer (The Port Line); Alan Warren (Four Locomotive Biographies); John Gilks (The Romance of the Callander & Oban); Michael Harris (Very Careful But Not Mean); Robin Barr (Doon the Water); Fred Landery and John Powell (The Caley's Bread and Butter); John Powell (Running the Bon Accord, Ghosts in the Springburn Road, Closures and Withdrawals). 'Fillers' between the chapters were provided by David Stirling (The Monkland Railway); E.D. Bruton (Diary of a Fifties Spotter); M.H. Ellison (Walking Scottish Railways); Peter Hay (Beyond Aberdeen); John Powell (Ore for Ravenscraig, Cock o' The North, Lattice Posts and Tablet Catchers, Watching the LMS at Elderslie, Not Springburn Built); Patrick Whitehouse (Neither LMS nor LNER, Inverness – The Mound, God's Treasure House in Scotland). Alex G. Murdoch supplied some of the material for the snippet on Maud.

The authors gratefully acknowledge illustrations as follows. Black and white photographs: P.M. Alexander/Millbrook House Collection (34 upper); W.J.V. Anderson (27, 89 upper); D.S.M. Barrie Collection (12, 13, 23 upper, 24 lower, 46 upper, 50, 112 upper, 137 both); H. Ballantyne (58, 135); E.D. Bruton (29, 60, 61, 62, 63, 64, 65); W.A. Camwell (166, 171 upper); H.C. Casserley (26, 75 upper, 168 upper); B.K. Cooper (175 lower, 200); D. Cross (78); T.J. Edgington (54, 121 upper left, 147 lower, 151 both, 195 both, 197); R.K. Evans FRPS (30 both, 31, 46 lower, 53, 119, 121 upper right, 145, 146); J.S. Gilks (141); W.L. Good (125); G.F. Heiron (19); Peter Hay (147 upper); D.A. Johnson (37, 55, 80 both, 120, 122, 138, 158, 168 lower, 185, 193); P. Lynch (17, 21, 32 upper, 69, 85, 86, 144); Don Martin (42, 92); M. Mensing (82, 115, 116, 117, 139, 140, 143, 156); Millbrook House Collection (23 lower, 24 upper, 49, 51 upper, 95, 101, 134, 142, 160, 164, 171 lower, 174); Mitchell Library (173, 178, 179, 181 both); National Railway Museum (148 both, 175 upper, 183, – P. Ransome-Wallis collection 126, – A. Cawston collection 129, – R.D. Stephen collection 130); M. Pope (196); Springburn Museum Trust (182); J. Stevenson (72, 77 upper, 77 middle, – collection 71, 76, 77 lower, 159); Strathkelvin D.C., Museum (40); E. Treacy/Millbrook House Collection (9, 16, 32 lower, 34 lower, 35, 36, 38, 48, 51 lower, 56, 57, 59 both, 73, 104, 112 lower, 121 lower, 194, 201 both, 202); C.A. Weston (94); D.C. Williams (97); P.B. Whitehouse ARPS (4, 18, 20, 28, 39, 45, 66, 67 both, 89 lower, 153, 155 both, 169 both, 184, 199 both); Ian Wright collection (75 lower).

Colour photographs: P.M. Alexander/Millbrook House Collection (106 lower); T.J. Edgington (15 upper); J.M. Jarvis (107 both, rear cover); M. Mensing (15 lower, 102 upper); Colour Rail (99 upper, 103 both, – W.J.V. Anderson 102 lower, – D.H Beecroft 98 upper, – D.R. Bissett 106 lower, – D Cross 98 lower).

INDEX

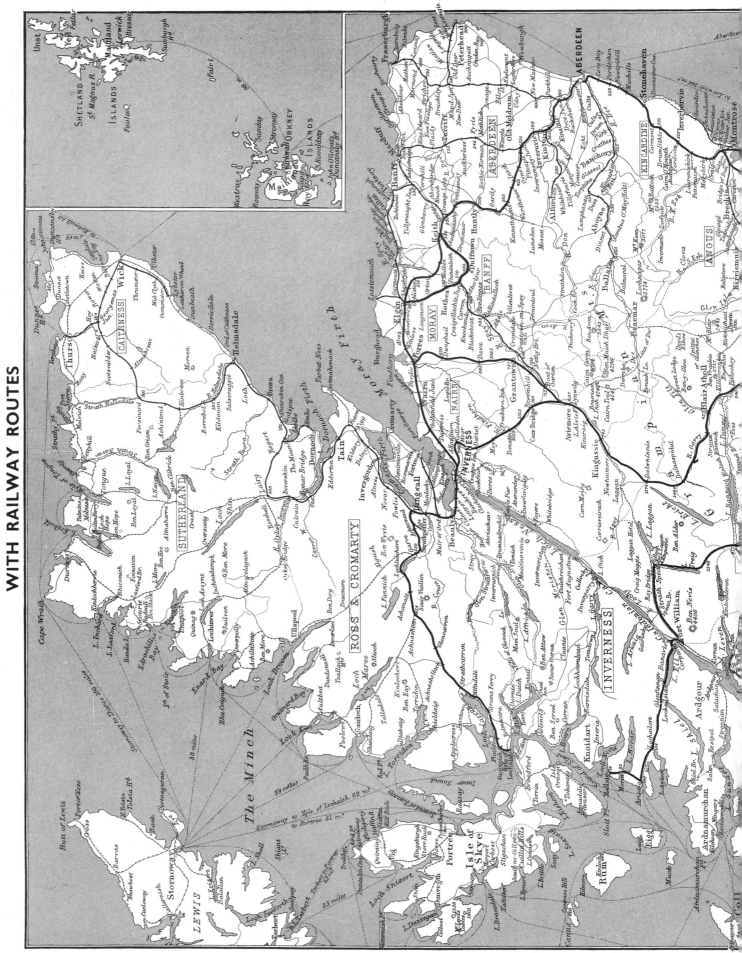

MAP of SCOTLAND
WITH RAILWAY ROUTES